Handbook of Magazine Article Writing

About the Editor

Jean M. Fredette was the acquisitions editor for Writer's Digest Books, the former editor of *Fiction Writer's Market®* for six editions, and she assisted Judson Jerome on the first *Poet's Market®* in 1986. She also edited Writer's Digest Books' *Handbook of Short Story Writing: Volume II*. Jean freelances and has been published in *Writer's Digest, Writer's Yearbook, Cincinnati Magazine, A Beginner's Guide to Getting Published* (edited by Kirk Polking), and local and international publications. She currently works for a small corporate communications company in Cincinnati.

WRITER'S DIGEST

Handbook of
Magazine Article
Writing

Edited by Jean M. Fredette

Writer's
Digest
Books

Cincinnati, Ohio

Writer's Digest Handbook of Magazine Article Writing. Copyright © 1988 by Writer's Digest Books. Printed and bound in the United States of America. All rights reserved. No part of this book may be reproduced in any form or by any electronic or mechanical means including information storage and retrieval systems without permission in writing from the publisher, except by a reviewer, who may quote brief passages in a review. Published by Writer's Digest Books, an imprint of F&W Publications, Inc., 1507 Dana Ave., Cincinnati, Ohio 45207. First edition. First paperback printing 1990.

97 96 95 94   9 8 7 6

Library of Congress Cataloging-in-Publication Data

Writer's Digest handbook of magazine article writing/edited by Jean M. Fredette.

   p. cm.
   ISBN 0-89879-328-9, casebound
   ISBN 0-89879-408-0, paperback
   1. Authorship. I. Fredette, Jean M. II. Writer's Digest (Cincinnati, Ohio)
PN147.W67 1988   88-23680
808'.02 — dc19   CIP

Design by Clare Finney

Contents

Q&A with Bob Greene...1
"Johnny Deadline" discusses his columns and books, getting started writing, and keeping up the pace.

DO YOU HAVE WHAT IT TAKES TO BE A WRITER?
by Art Spikol...10
An editor discusses the all-important characteristics — including talent — a good writer must have.

NOT ONE, NOT TWO, BUT 2,000 SALABLE ARTICLE IDEAS A YEAR
by Michael Bugeja...18
How to seek and find strong feature ideas from common, unexpected, everyday sources.

THE IDEA IDEAL
by Candy Schulman...23
Judith Viorst, Nora Ephron, and Fran Lebowitz on finding and "borrowing" provocative, timely, and salable article ideas.

RESEARCHING FROM MAGAZINES AND REFERENCE BOOKS
by Lois Horowitz...27
Effective, time-saving methods and tips for researching your stories.

A MATTER OF EXPERTISE
by Jay Stuller...34
How to become an expert by writing about what you don't know.

SMALL-TOWN STORIES AND BIG SALES
by Dennis E. Hensley...40
Finding the unusual in the common and most obvious stories — and selling them again and again.

CONFESSIONS OF A CLIPPER
by Stan Bicknell...44
Techniques for clipping and filing printed articles to use for ideas, background material, and ready-made research for your own work.

HOW TO WRITE IRRESISTIBLE QUERY LETTERS
by Lisa Collier Cool...47
How to turn a few well-phrased paragraphs into a profitable article assignment.

THE SECRETS OF SUPERLATIVE SALESMANSHIP
by James Morgan...55
How to sell yourself and your idea to your target editor.

HOW TO LAND INTERVIEWS WITH BUSY AND FAMOUS PEOPLE
by Larry Miller...64
Use your psychology, connections, and stubbornness to talk with busy subjects.

POPPING THE QUESTIONS
by John Brady...69
How to know, arrange, and ask all the right questions to get the best answers in your interview.

DRAW YOUR READERS IN WITH TITLES
by L. Perry Wilbur...85
Title tips to captivate readers and make them buy.

MAKING YOUR ARTICLE LEADS SPARKLE
by Michael J. Bugeja...89
How to make a first and fast pitch to an editor to peddle your prose.

SETTING A GOOD EXAMPLE
by Lorene Hanley Duquin...94
How to make your writing come alive by using samples, examples, analogies, and anecdotes.

GIVE YOUR WRITING THE MIDAS TOUCH
by Barbara Bisantz Raymond...100
Less can be more with strong, clean, and concise "light" writing.

TWELVE WAYS TO END YOUR ARTICLE GRACEFULLY
by Robert L. Baker...109
How to write satisfying closing copy for the most memorable segment of your feature.

REVISION: SEVEN STEPS TO BETTER MANUSCRIPTS
by Marshall Cook...117
A seven-point revision method for stronger and clearer writing.

WRITING THE "ART-OF-LIVING" ARTICLE
by Philip Barry Osborne...125
How to write inspirational essays and self-help articles, the staple of general interest magazines.

WRITING AND SELLING THE LIST ARTICLE
by Charles V. Main...134
How to unify several units of information under a single theme.

HOW TO WRITE PERSONAL EXPERIENCE ARTICLES
by Nancy Kelton...141
Making the reader care about your experience with emotional involvement and your unique point of view.

HOW TO WRITE TRUE-LIFE DRAMAS
by Don McKinney...146
Writing the compelling human interest narrative—the dramatic experiences of real people.

WRITING THE ROUNDUP ARTICLE
by Gary Provost...155
Bringing people together to talk about something, creating a conference on paper.

COOKING UP THE FOOD/RECIPE ARTICLE
by Rona S. Zable...162
The writer's basic recipe for whetting the editor's appetite for food-related articles.

WRITING FOR THE WOMEN'S MAGAZINES
by Elaine Fantle Shimberg...170
How to capitalize on writing about the complicated and many-faceted lives and interests of women today.

WRITING THE "AS-TOLD-TO" ARTICLE
by Lois Duncan...178
How to collaborate with non-writers who have interesting stories to tell and sell.

WHEN THE WRITER TEACHES — WRITING THE HOW-TO ARTICLE
by Helene Schellenberg Barnhart...184
How to write the popular problem-solving, self-improvement, and how-to-make-and -do articles.

SELLING THE SEASONAL ARTICLE IS NO PIECE OF CAKE
by Rebecca Muller...194
Months-ahead writing and marketing strategies for holiday and seasonal articles.

WHAT TO NOTICE FOR YOUR TRAVEL STORIES
by Louise Purwin Zobel...200
Cover the special, the unique, the ordinary angle at home, nearby, or far away.

HOW TO SUPPLEMENT YOUR ARTICLES WITH PHOTOS
by Stuart Cohen...210
Good photos transmit important article information by visual representation alone.

HOW TO TEST YOUR ARTICLES FOR THE 8 ESSENTIALS OF NONFICTION
by Gary Provost...217
A test to gauge the quality of your writing style.

SELLING THE SAME ARTICLE MANY TIMES
by Duane Newcomb...224
How to resell one article to non-competing publications.

MANUSCRIPT MECHANICS: HOW TO SUBMIT YOUR MAGAZINE ARTICLE
by Laurie Henry...235
The final business of properly preparing your work to submit to an editor.

UNDER COVER
by George H. Scithers and Sanford Meschkow...240
Introducing your story with a properly written cover letter to sell your article.

FOREWORD

In the *Writer's Digest Handbook of Magazine Article Writing,* we've presented instruction on the entire magazine article writing process—from getting that first spark of an exciting idea to sending off the professionally-written article to an editor.

Today, because the majority of magazines are specialized in their subjects, formats, and the audiences they serve, we recommend that you abandon the traditional method of writing a complete article first and sending it around—inevitably to receive rejections from several magazines. Today it's the astute freelance writer who will first target a magazine and approach the editor with an idea in a short query letter. This way if the editor decides that such a piece might fit into the lineup, he or she can guide the writer to shape and tailor the outline specifically to the magazine's needs, thus saving precious time and energy for both the freelancer *and* the editor.

Step by step in the order in which you tackle each area, we offer explicit instruction and advice on finding that unique article idea; researching the appropriate magazine markets to pursue; selling your idea and yourself as the writer in a query letter to the editor; interviewing and researching sources for the data to include in the article; developing the best format to present your information; and finally organizing the material, writing the article itself, and sending it off for publication.

With this direct and efficient method, we wish you great success—plus many opportunities in your magazine writing career to refer to Duane Newcomb's article on page 224, when you, too, will be "Selling the Same Article Many Times."

Good luck and good writing.

Jean M. Fredette, editor

INTRODUCTION

Q&A WITH BOB GREENE

If Bob Greene admits to being happiest when he's working, we conclude he's one very contented man. In one way or another, Greene is always working—looking for stories, reporting or interviewing his subjects. As his longtime nickname implies, he *is* Johnny Deadline.

Four times a week with his syndicated newspaper columns and once a month for *Esquire,* Bob Greene entertains his millions of readers. Via his stories he is America's great pal. To maintain such an output is demanding, of course, and the writer's life is frantic. But the end result belies the pace, as Greene's writing style is easy and fluid, straightforward and controlled.

Easily and unobtrusively Greene observes the subjects for his columns and enlists their trust. Whether he's chatting with a bag lady outside his *Chicago Tribune* office, or questioning a disabled Vietnam veteran in a coffee shop, or listening to a lonely senior citizen in a nursing home, the award-winning journalist is uniquely able to find that special human interest angle, to report the personal yet universal in the Little Guy and Everyman, "the real truths" that don't make the six o'clock news or the front page.

Greene's interests also include the Big Stories, and his interviews with "impossible to reach" subjects such as Patricia Hearst, Richard Nixon and Richard Speck made national news. Likewise after John Lennon was shot, his controversial columns on gun control struck a national nerve, as did his satire a few years later on the new Coke formula. Classic Coke lovers, including Greene himself, united, the "revolution" began, and the rest is soft drink history.

Greene is at his best he says in "uncharted territory," the stories never told, like those of the Vietnam vets in his new and moving, *Homecoming.* Even and especially the most common everyday subjects he recounts with warmth and charm—and touching humor such as one finds in his bestselling books, *Good Morning, Merry Sunshine,* the journal of his child's first year, and *Be True to Your School,* his diary of 1964. Readers who don't immediately identify with the highs and lows and fun and woes of seventeen-year-old Bob Greene, have not gone to high school in the U.S.

The writer knows he's very lucky to be able to see and write about the people and parts of life that he chooses—and get paid for it, too. Bob Greene talks about his long, steady and successful writing career with Writer's Digest Books from Florida, where he is vacationing with his family, and where Johnny Deadline is writing his tenth book:

Your entree into magazine and newspaper writing was via journalism school. Do you think that's the best route today?
You have to remember that I started at sixteen when I was in high school. I graduated from Medill [Northwestern's School of Journalism] in '69. I never got a master's degree, as is often required today, and the term "media" hadn't been invented. Then you were a newspaperman; you weren't a "member of the media." So at the time it wasn't a very glamorous profession. And it also wasn't very hard to get into. A newspaperman was simply the sportswriter down the block who walked his dog and mowed his lawn. In recent years, that terrible word "media" has taken over, and journalism has become an allegedly glamorous way to make a living. When I went to school "journalism" was just a fancy way of saying "trade school." I learned my trade: how to report and how to write cleanly. Today I don't know. Editors theoretically say they'd like their writers to have a wide background on various aspects of the world, but I think when it comes down to it, if you can't report, if you can't write, all the sociology or law degrees aren't going to help.

You write regularly for a newspaper, a magazine, and your books. Do these disciplines require a change in your writing style or are they compatible?
They're compatible; they're just different exercises. I do 200 newspaper columns a year, and they appear right away. For *Esquire* I write twelve "American Beat" columns. But it's a little different when you come up to bat twelve times vs. 200 times a year. Also for *Esquire* you have to give yourself three months of lead time—here it is March and I'm late for my July column and starting to write my August column. For the newspaper you write the column for immediate consumption. And "American Beat" is about twice as long. You've got a month to work on it and craft it, while for a newspaper column you do it in one day. In general, magazine writing is physically different—the column appears on very nice glossy stock with a nice photograph, and it has a different feel to it. But what it comes down to for both is reporting an imaginative story idea and doing a nice clean job of writing.

That's how many deadlines for you each week?
I write four newspaper columns a week—three of those go out around the country—plus I'm always working on the next *Esquire* piece, so I'm in contact with *Esquire* just about every day. And I'm always working on a new book so there's never a time when I'm not on deadline.

You've tapped so successfully into the heartbeat of America. How did you find your voice?
Well, it sort of evolved. I think everyone's a derivative in the beginning. I know one advantage I had was growing up in Ohio. I didn't grow up reading *The New York Times, Washington Post* or *Los Angeles Times,* so if I imitated anybody it was our local sportswriters. I didn't have any journalism heroes, but once I got started I must have been emulating something I had read—you don't write in a

vacuum. But I think over the years I found out what my best style is: clean, no-frills, and bare-bones. The basic tenet has always been: Show them, don't tell them. Tell the story and get out. I like to think of myself first as a reporter and whatever comes after that is fine. I figure if the material is compelling enough, then my writing doesn't have to be fancy or rococo to tell the story — for newspaper or magazine stories.

How did you go about starting your newspaper column?
By my byline I guess. I was twenty-two, straight out of college. I had gone to the *Chicago Sun-Times* where I began as a summer intern. From what I'm told people started asking the editors who this kid was; they noticed my byline. I became a fulltime staff member, and they gave me the column the following year, when I was twenty-three. I started it twice a week. And now looking back on it, when people ask me how I got a column so quickly, it does seem amazing to me, but at the time I wondered what took them so long. I felt they were holding me back because I was sure I could do it. So be a reporter first and start getting noticed for your reporting—that's how I think a person should get a column.

Do you think it's easier to get a column today?
Yes, now it seems that newspapers are almost desperate to find columnists. But I don't know if getting a column in your local paper is the honor I thought it was when I started. There also weren't so many columnists back then either. Now I think editors realize that it's the columns that help sell the product—sell the newspapers. And so I think every editor is looking for a good column.

You've written columns for seventeen years. How have you kept up the pace?
I really don't know. At one point I was writing the four columns for the newspaper—for awhile it was five—and I took on the monthly column for *Esquire,* and then on top of that I got the chance to become a correspondent for ABC News *Nightline;* I hadn't done any television work before. I remember thinking to myself, "You can't do all this work." And then it occurred to me that if in five years I look back and say, "Look, you've had a nationally syndicated newspaper column, your own column for *Esquire* and your first TV job on the best news broadcast on television. Sure, you might burn yourself out—but how can you pass up those opportunities?" So I didn't—I did them all. Today though I don't do *Nightline* as often. I prefer to go on live rather than go out and do the field reports. I've also started doing a book a year—after a few years' hiatus. I'm pretty busy.

Do you have suggestions as to how to handle a full writing schedule and still allow quality time for family or a vacation?
I'm afraid if you reach a certain level where you have bosses who regularly expect a column, wherever you go becomes grist for the column. You never say, "Gee, I can't write this because I'm on vacation." You're constantly feeding that machine, the machine being a column. And so I've never been able to say, "OK, this is a week when no matter what happens I'm not going to write it down."

Wherever I am I see stories, and I end up telling those stories. It's just a question of where I tell them.

So wherever you are you're always writing?
Well, I'm always looking for stories. I used to have to actually write them on the road, but today, just because of the mechanics, the logistical transmission which takes so much of the day, I'd rather find the stories on the road and write them later.

Do you keep a file of ideas?
When I get an idea I'll write down a one-word slug, a reminder of what it is. I don't keep a file as such, but if I do have an idea I'll write it down. And if I come upon a day when I don't have anything to say I'll look at that list and I'll remember what it's about.

Your readers sometimes provide ideas. I'm referring to Mike Hayes, and his penny campaign, his request that your readers each send him a penny to assist his folks with his college expenses.
Yeah. There's a pile next to my typewriter, and when Mike Hayes' letter came in I tossed the letter on the pile, and his name went down on the list—I think I wrote "Penny." And then two or three months later, I said I think I'll do this kid. So I dug through the pile, and there was his original letter. I called him, did the interview, and he got his $28,000, the equivalent of 2.8 million pennies. You know it was a clever and funny idea on his part. But there's not a day that goes by that I don't get a letter from someone wanting the same kind of thing. But it wouldn't be funny the second time. Readers wouldn't respond the same way.

How else do you get ideas? Do you find your family a source of inspiration?
No, I've never written a column about my family. I wrote *Good Morning, Merry Sunshine* recording the first year of my daughter's life. But I always hated newspaper columnists who write about what happened at home last night. I've always thought that was too easy. My ideas come from the people I meet and talk to in my travels around the country. I'm on the road at least twice a month for speeches and stories, and I'm always finding things on the road—whether it's at the beach or in the grocery store.

Has there ever been a time when you just didn't know what to write about?
Yes, and those are the columns people talk about the most. It's funny, you can work for weeks getting the reporting done on a column, and write it and hear nothing. But I remember once I was right on deadline. I had nothing, and so I wrote about the fact that I don't drive. I told myself it was a stupid column but at least it would get me through the day. But still today all these years later, I walk down the street and cab drivers yell at me, "Hey, Greene, you still don't drive?" There's a real irony there—the columns you really put effort into, those really good reporting and thoughtful pieces, people maybe nod their heads and like

them. But the ones you think are the last minute throw-away columns are the ones people remember for years.

How do you verify your information? Do you have special research techniques or do you have a staff to help?
I have a secretary. Some columnists use research assistants. But I've never done that. I have to hear the quotes myself. I think the particular kind of writing I do would suffer if there were a third party between the subject and myself. If you're doing a hard news story or if you're an investigative news reporter you'll use a staff. But for the kind of thing I do I have to do the interviewing myself.

You once joined a band and wrote about it from firsthand experience.
Yes, that was my third book. I was writing the newspaper column at the time, and I was only twenty-five or twenty-six. I just thought it would be a good way to report on rock and roll from the inside. I'd just written a book on the Nixon-McGovern Presidential campaign in '72, and it occurred to me that a presidential campaign was very much like a rock tour—with chartered jets crisscrossing the country in search of money and power and fame, and so I decided to report it from the inside. It's the reporter-as-amateur-participant method, basically George Plimpton's idea. His *Paper Lion* was a wonderful book, not so much because it's about him playing quarterback. But once you get inside an organization, be it a football team or a rock band, there are things you see and hear that they won't tell a reporter who just comes in for an "interview." *Billion Dollar Baby* was that book, and I'm very proud of it. I joined the Alice Cooper band as a performing member. Today there's a sort of cult formed around that book—I'd love to see it get back in print in paperback someday. Basically it's a pretty solid piece of reporting about an interesting phenomenon—what it's like to be a member of a multi-million dollar rock band.

Your upcoming book, Homecoming, *is a departure from your other books based on your own personal experiences. Did the idea to interview Vietnam vets on their return from the war evolve from one of your columns?*
Yes, I had heard a rumor for years that returning soldiers had actually been spat upon—in the U.S., after they got home. It was so hard to imagine something that awful had ever happened—American civilians spitting on American soldiers. So out of genuine curiosity I asked that specific question in one of my columns—whether this was rumor or reality. The questions touched a nerve, and I received more than 1,000 letters from veterans all over the country. These men and women poured out their hearts and souls; they took time to put their wrenching, personal thoughts on paper, what really happened when they came home. I did a week's worth of columns based on the responses. But then I began to think that the full story had never been told. It would have been a waste not to have used these letters. I thought the veterans should tell their own stories in their own words. *Homecoming* is a permanent record, an oral history of an experience unique in U.S. history only to the Vietnam War.

How did you personally feel as a result of these interviews?
I was tremendously moved. Each day after I worked with the veterans' letters I'd go home absolutely shaken. I was also terribly shocked. The spitting, the mistreatment of these soldiers took place on American soil—all over the U.S. And these experiences were in their own way as shocking as the horror and violence that came out of the war itself. The veterans are already aware of what happened—my hope is that *Homecoming* will reach people who were never in Vietnam, and need to understand. I should add that not all the stories are sad. Some are inspiring; some veterans were greeted with warmth and even love. But the book is essentially an intimate and untold story—and I hope that readers experience the same set of emotions that I experienced.

Two of your books, Be True to Your School *and* Good Morning, Merry Sunshine, *were based on your journal entries, right?*
Yes, those books were journals. *Good Morning, Merry Sunshine* was the journal I kept the first year I was a father. *Be True to Your School* was based on a diary I actually kept when I was seventeen growing up in Columbus, Ohio, in 1964.

In writing Be True to Your School, *were there many changes to make?*
The basis of the original diary was little snippets, almost in the style of the late Walter Winchell, little bits and pieces of conversations, observations. All the events and people were real, but it wasn't ready for publication. I had to write it as a diary in narrative form and have it seem like the voice of a seventeen-year-old boy and not sound like a forty-year-old man reminiscing. And quite frankly I'm astonished that twenty-three years later, that diary turned out to be a nationally bestselling book. It looks like it will be a movie now, too.

You must put a lot of stock in the journal writing process. Do you still keep a diary?
No, my columns are pretty much my diary. But when high school students ask me for advice I tell them to keep a diary—for two reasons. One, is to give you the discipline to write every day, even when you don't feel like it, which is what a professional journalist needs, and two, it makes you examine the little tiny things in your life that might go unnoticed if you didn't write them down. Journal writing is great training, and it's a wonderful thing to have years later, to look back. Most people bathe their past in the glow of nostalgia, but if you have the journal you can't do that; it's all there, in black and white.

You've known since when that you wanted to be a writer?
In seventh grade we took the Kuder Preference Tests, those little punch out tests that are supposed to tell you what you want to be, and mine said I was supposed to be a journalist or a forest ranger. So I guess I knew from that time. But yet sometimes I think I made the wrong choice . . .

Obviously you didn't. But as far as your having a writing apprenticeship, it's not really typical because you knew exactly what you wanted to do.

No, it wasn't typical, but I'm glad it worked out for me. I never sought out a so-called mentor or anything. I just wrote and I got lucky. I tried to write as well as I could and see if somebody liked the product—and I use the word "product" on purpose. The column is not the person; it's the product of that person. My theory has always been to make that product as well done as I can, rather than to try to get lunch with a famous editor or writer. I never did any of that. I just wrote my stuff and hoped that they would print it.

How long does it take to write your columns, and do you revise much?
No, the writing part, especially if I'm writing the newspaper column on a computer, takes me an hour or less, and the *Esquire* column takes me about two hours. That's just sitting down and writing it, but it may take as many as twenty hours to do the reporting and the research. It's pretty much a given that if you write as much as I do you have to be a facile writer. I write faster than I think.

Do you use a tape recorder?
No, I never use a tape recorder. It gets in the way if the person sees it and is always conscious of it. I always take notes. There've been several occasions when I've used a tape recorder for a souvenir. I taped the interview with Nixon, for two reasons: I wanted every word to be exactly as he said it, and it'll be a nice tape to have someday. But I don't think I've used a tape recorder for a story in five or six years.

You credit your Ohio background for giving you good grounding. What do you think you can bring to your audience that someone from the East or West can't?
Well, when you grow up in the middle of the country as I did, there are no star makers, no agents looking to make you a star. I think you just have to be a little bit better; you really have to stand out. In Washington, New York or Los Angeles, the "news capitals," everybody's chasing after the same story. But when you grow up in the middle of the country, you tend to find your own stories. I still find that on most stories I'm the only one there.

Then you're really not interested in hard news or investigative reporting?
I don't know how you qualify hard news. I consider myself a reporter. Investigative reporting? I've always thought that to be a redundant phrase anyway. But in terms of unearthing political scandals or corruptions, naw. If I had wanted to do that I'd have become a prosecuting attorney. I'm a storyteller. It's as simple as that. If a story interests me viscerally as a person, not as a "journalist," then I'll write about it.

So you have no desire to leave Chicago or go anywhere else?
Actually I *do* go everywhere else. My magazine and TV bosses are in New York and Washington. But I can't see writing my kind of column in New York, and Washington is a nice city, but I just don't like politics. It would be ridiculous to move to Washington and not write about politics. I happen to like Los Angeles

too, but once you get out there, all you think about is movies. So, yeah, I like the idea that I'm here in the middle of the country.

How do you think journalism, in general, has changed since you began?
Today there are probably more magazines but they're more specialized. When I was growing up there were certain magazines, like *The Saturday Evening Post, Esquire, Life,* the superstar magazines you dreamt of writing for. One major change is that the reader's attention span is shorter now. The classic magazine story: "Frank Sinatra Has a Cold," by Gay Talese. Wonderful story. But it's so long that now it would be hard to persuade a magazine editor to run it. The early Tom Wolfe pieces in *Esquire* also. The greatest stuff in the world, but the first thing a magazine editor would say is, "We can't run something that long." That's why for *Esquire* I prefer to write the "American Beat" column instead of longer pieces, because I really think my job is to get the reader to the last period of the last sentence of the last paragraph.

Has TV caused the attention span to shrink?
TV's got a lot to do with it. Even the techniques of television, if you look at the way news features are cut, and MTV videos are cut—you know—Bam, Bam, Bam, Bam, Bam. There's not the sort of relaxed, long, flowing feeling that magazine articles used to have. Except for a very elite audience. I'm happy to have my audience. I just want to reach people, and if to write a little shorter is the way the game has to be played these days, I still hope to bring the same quality of reporting and writing into the "American Beat" column that I would bring into a 10,000 word piece.

What do you think the forecast for the 1990's will be for newspapers and magazines?
That's hard to say. I never think more than about a day in advance. I would guess that newspapers would still be very important and profitable but probably with only one in each city. Really the days of the old competing, brawling journalism have now been replaced by local television, and I think when people pick up their newspapers in the morning, either subconsciously or not, they turn to the columnists. It's pretty much the columnists who sell the papers, because in most cases people have seen the hard news on the evening news the night before. As for magazines, you keep hearing about various problems in the magazine business, and yet at the newsstand there's such a proliferation of specialized magazines there's not enough space for all of them. I just think there will always be room for a storyteller who comes up with ideas that other people don't have.

Do you have tips or advice for beginning writers?
Yeah, try really hard. I know it's a cliché, but it's always worked for me. Try a little harder than you have to; be a little bit better than you have to. Come up with imaginative ideas and then write well. In most magazines it's not that the assignment is not well written; it's that the topic isn't very unusual. And there's a lot of laziness. Most of the stories you see in a national magazine are an attempt to sell a product; a public relations firm calls up a magazine and says their client is doing

a book or a movie or a video or a TV show, so why not do a profile timed with the release of the product. My feeling on that is: Fine. Let them take an ad. Sure, there are occasions when I'll do something like that, especially for the newspaper column. But virtually all my stories come from genuine curiosity. And I think more magazine writers in the future would benefit with a little more imagination when it comes to story selection.

What satisfies you most about your career, about writing, personally?
The nicest thing you can have when you are a storyteller is an audience on the other end. There have been days when I've woken up and had what I consider to be a good column in the paper. And then the *Esquire* came out, and I had a column there I was proud of, and then maybe I made a speech that night, or maybe I'd see someone on the plane reading one of my books. Or later I'd turn on *Nightline* and see my spot, and I'd say, "Boy, I reached a lot of people today." So that's the satisfying part, as a storyteller knowing that you're lucky enough to have that audience out there. And you've reached them, and they maybe say that my writing doesn't sound so much like somebody just sat down at a typewriter, but almost as if I've gotten up and called my best friend and said, "You'll never guess what I saw today. Or you'll never guess who I met today."

You've said you achieved most of your goals by the time you were thirty.
Yes, unfortunately. I really had to kick myself in the pants once I was thirty because I had already met my goals. That's why I took on the *Esquire* column and *Nightline* and started writing books again. Because I didn't want to get lazy. And thirty would have been too young to hang it up.

Have you thought about writing fiction?
Yes, I've considered it. It'd be nice not to have to travel so much. I'm not ruling it out. And I'm really very happy to see Tom Wolfe has done so well with his first novel (*The Bonfire of the Vanities*) because there's a guy who's done nonfiction for so long and wanted to give fiction a try, and all of a sudden his book is number one. That's great. He's one writer I really looked up to when I knew I wanted to be a writer. Yes, it's something I might try someday, but not right away.

If you were starting out today, would you do anything differently?
No, I think I'd still concentrate on making my writing the best I could and letting my stories speak for themselves. I'd still try to let my writing do the job.

What's in the future for Bob Greene?
I really can't say. I think in this business, one of the drawing cards, or draw-backs—take your pick—is that I never get to think more than one or two days in advance. That deadline is always there. It's not like lifting bricks all day. Every time I start to think, gee, I have a tough job, I realize it's not hard manual labor. I get to travel whenever I want and meet interesting people and tell stories that I hope people will enjoy reading. And I hope to keep doing that in one form or another.

BY ART SPIKOL

Do You Have What It Takes to Be a Writer?

In order to answer the question I've just asked in the title, I decided to interview myself. After all, I've made a pretty good living with the written word—and I've helped a lot of other people do the same.

So, I figured, I'll talk to an expert, somebody who's spent a lot of time and money buying the writing of people like you and me. Me.

To get my opinion, I made a list of characteristics—things that I look for in a writer—and gave myself the task of rating them from 1 (most important) to 11 (least important). Before we go further, I'd like to ask you to perform the same exercise. Just number the following characteristics, the definitions of which are subject to your interpretation, in their order of importance as you see them. Put your number in the space to the right of each characteristic.

Don't try to match or second-guess *me*; write down what *you* really believe does—or will—contribute to your success. By the time you're finished reading this article, you'll know something about what the marketplace is looking for, and whether or not you think you can supply it.

And just so this little experiment won't seem too incestuous—after all, I'm only one person—I asked a few dozen editors around the country to join us. You'll get their opinions, too, as we go along, and that's when we'll both find out whether *I'm* in synch with the marketplace (I won't know the results until after I've written my first draft—and made my choices). You could, in fact, disagree with me and end up in the majority. Which would be OK, since I'm not buying much these days anyway.

Here goes:

- Ability to Work With Others
- Appearance
- Integrity
- Love of Writing
- Professionalism
- Quality of Writing
- Self-Assuredness
- Self-Motivation
- Talent
- Writing Style
- Vocabulary, Grammar, etc.

Now, to business.

Anybody who has ever written an article on assignment knows what a "working title" is. It's what you and the editor call the story before you know what you're *really* going to want to call it—before you know how it's going to turn out. Rarely is the working title what finally appears in print.

When I first started this piece, the working title was "Is Talent Necessary?" It soon disappeared, because I realized that I knew people with little "natural" talent for nonfiction who, through the application of sweat, time and good editors, eventually won some of the country's top journalism awards. So, if you figured that the top item on my list would be talent, you were wrong.

INCLINED OF THE MIND

Talent, in my opinion (*most* of this is my opinion), isn't something you struggle to achieve; you can't get it through study or training or osmosis. I figure it's natural, inherent—you're born with it. And if that's the case, talent is no prerequisite to becoming a writer—because I can train anybody with average verbal skills (certainly not what you'd call talent) to write and sell, and people like that are out there selling every day.

Maybe you find that statement troublesome. Frankly, it bothers *me*, too. But it's true. You can *learn* to be a selling writer—although if you lack talent you must work much harder, and differently.

Certainly, talent eliminates a large part of the battle: a talented writer, a *natural* writer, starts out with a certain gut instinct regarding the use of language—a sense of timing, of rhythm, of how words fit together, of when to use a quotation or change a scene and so on—even though it may take a while before all of this comes together. Anybody can learn to play the piano, for instance, but show me somebody who seems to play it instinctively—who can simply think musically and have those thoughts arrive at the keyboard as an original invention—and I'll show you natural talent. The value of that can't be underestimated; my own artistic and writing *talents* are what opened every meaningful door in my life.

But it wasn't automatic; it took constant sharpening and honing. Having talent doesn't mean you can write a great book—not any more than it means that you can become the next Rubinstein. Talent is *potential*. Develop it and you have something; let it atrophy and you squander it. Talent is not ability.

I rated "talent" #6. The largest single voting bloc of editors (25 percent of the respondents) put it at 4, 20.4 percent called it 3, 13.6 percent thought it most important.

(An aside: a few interesting things emerged from this survey. One is that despite individual differences of opinion among editors, the results had a certain weight, a certain direction, with the majority of editors coming down in approximately the same places. At the same time, almost every editor was, on one characteristic or another, in a minority. Further, the "largest bloc" vote as mentioned above won't necessarily agree with the final overall rating by the editors; it simply indicates that the greater force of a vote fell in a certain place.)

Now, suppose you believe that while you're a decent enough writer, talent isn't really your strong point; you can't just sit down and knock out a piece in record time, then sell it on the basis of the writing itself being so good. Then what? Then you have to push harder on the business end: better market research to find your ideal markets, better marketing and merchandising of the product—finding out what people want to buy, and paying more attention to the way you sell it to them.

If you go back and look at the origin of the word *talent,* you'll find that it stems from the Roman words meaning, essentially, "inclination of the mind" as well as from a currency used by many peoples—the Assyrians, Greeks, Babylonians and Romans—a new chariot, for instance, might have cost you sixty silver *talents,* unless you happened to have a cousin Ignatius in the business. Nobody thinks of linking either derivation these days; I personally know people who are talented writers and yet feel no inclination to write—nor to turn the ability into money.

But let's stay with that "inclination of the mind" for a minute. Lots of people *want to be writers;* just about everybody talks about writing a book someday. Most don't know about the typical annual income and the isolation; they know about only the cocktail parties and the bylines. Of those who wouldn't mind being writers, relatively few really *want to write.* It's work.

LOVE OF WRITING

Over the years I've met a lot of writers; most of them thought that making a living at writing was just about the best thing they could ever do. Not all of them were talented, but just about all of them *were* making part or all of their incomes at writing. Let's face it—it's not like being a tennis pro; even the mediocre among us can earn a living.

In fact, that's where talent can be detrimental, if you stop to consider it. Those with writing gifts figure that their ability should somehow make writing easy for them—and when they find out about the frustration, the sometimes plodding writing and research and rewriting and bending to the will of the marketplace that are all part of it, they become disillusioned. Suddenly they realize that something they enjoy as *play* is really going to be *work.*

You can be a writer without talent. But without the desire, every word you write will come hard and leaden. You won't last.

The desire—the need—to write, the love of writing: I think it's an important ingredient. If it's a tossup as to whether you write or sell insurance or stay with the law firm, take my advice: Stay put.

Because I feel that way, I put a 5 beside "Love of Writing," but I was clearly in the minority. Most editors put it way back on the list, and when I Monday-morning-quarterbacked myself, I could see why. I tend to be sort of romantic about writing; most editors tend to be more pragmatic. *And they're right.* Why should anyone care if you like what you're doing? That's *your* problem. In fact, lots of people have jobs they don't love, and most manage to do them well despite that. Our survey reveals that editors couldn't care less about your loving your work: The heaviest concentration rated it 9 and 10 in importance, with virtually every other editor (except me and a couple of other softies) seeing it as 8 or 11.

Held in almost as low esteem was "Self-Assuredness." I don't know if you've ever noticed, but people who are good on paper often aren't good in person, and vice versa. Show me somebody who's good at selling real estate and I'll show you somebody who probably can't write. Show me a great writer and I'll show you someone who's rarely the life of the party. (Yes, there are exceptions; don't throw William Buckley at me.)

In fact, I believe that early-life social ineptitude and shyness are probably major reasons why writers start writing in the first place. Writers are rarely the big people on campus, the sought-after dates, the sports heroes. If I say "bookish," you think of prim, quiet, nerdy, thick glasses, ordinary looks. It's pointless to discuss whether or not this is fair; all stereotypes are based on *something*—and if you go to a writers workshop, it's not going to be populated by tall, well-tailored, neatly trimmed corporate sales types.

Instead, you'll find people who are rarely seen in a public forum, and usually for good reason.

Time can change this. Success breeds confidence; confidence makes one more secure; eventually successful writers may become pretty good speakers. But having heard the best of them, I'd rather they wrote.

So while self-assuredness is a tremendous tool in most arenas—the kind of trait that's valuable for job interviews or most selling situations—it's not that meaningful to me as a barometer of writing ability, even if it comes packaged with a terrific vocabulary. But I do like it in someone who will be meeting the public, doing in-person interviews, possibly someday having to get up in a courtroom.

NONFICTION POWER

When you come right down to it, self-assuredness—as well as other qualities we're going to discuss here—is subject to the interpretation of the viewer. I can't determine that you're a self-assured writer; I can determine only that you *seem* to be. And there's no question that people who are self-assured inspire confidence, which is something you can't give a numerical rating. Perception is everything, and if I see you as someone who will do a good job, *then you get the job*. I can be fooled.

Still, I rated "Self-Assuredness" 9, which put me squarely in the mainstream—most of the editors rated it 8 and 9 (32 percent each), with 10 getting 25 percent of the vote. No surprises here.

But remember: A good front can be very convincing, and the editors themselves are probably poor judges as to how effective self-assuredness can be when it's turned on them. And if that's the case, why can't you sway an editor simply by looking and sounding better than you write?

That's where "Quality of Writing" comes in, and certainly most of the editors saw it that way; *no* editor in our survey rated it out of the top 5. In fact, 56 percent of them called it #1. I, along with another 27 percent, called it #2. All of which means that it's what most editors look for first.

Recognizing this, you should realize that if your work's good, I'll know it. That's how editors get to be editors. If you show me a published sample that's uneven, I'll suspect that the best of it is due to a good editor, and the worst of it is what you'll deliver if I assign you. Show me one piece that's mediocre and I'll automatically adjust downward the best of everything else you show me. That tip alone, if you take it seriously, should be worth plenty to you over the years. And one other: If an editor decides not to buy your work, don't try to figure out what's wrong with the editor. Ninety-nine times out of a hundred, the problem is your writing, and only by facing that will you get it to the point where it sells.

I think it's appropriate to talk about another kind of quality next, something that's just about even with #2 on my list. While "Quality of Writing" is what the public will see of you, the "Quality of You" is what's underneath everything you have to give. It's on the list; it's called "Integrity."

If we were talking about fiction, I wouldn't care about integrity. Some pretty awful people have written some pretty good novels.

But if you write nonfiction, you have a lot of power—power you get without deserving it. You write about real people, which means that your flesh-and-blood subjects can be hurt. You're a critic-at-large; because you're a good writer, people may assume that you have taste, or that you're smart, or that you're otherwise worthy of your access to the press. It's easy to confuse *ability* with *quality*, and that's what gives voice to columnists whose own bitterness and hostility cause them to strike out at easy targets; to editors who invoke the First Amendment so they can talk about themselves as its champion; to writers whose personality problems are so enormous that they literally can't keep these problems from coloring their work—or from affecting their dealings with fellow workers. I know people like these, and they are rarely prevented from affecting public opinion—a right they inherit simply because they're good writers.

APPROPRIATE DRESS

So when I hire writers, the *kind of people* I hire is tremendously important—because I value journalistic fair play above almost anything else. I want responsible people who are mature enough to keep their private wars and hidden agendas where they can't compromise that spirit of fair play. I don't want people who are knee-jerk anything—liberal or conservative, pro-art or anti-business. I want somebody who never forgets that freedom of the press is not free—that it comes with enormous responsibilities. And I don't want to have to be a watchdog. If it ever comes time to put a writer on the witness stand in a libel trial—and it will, considering how litigious society is these days—I want to know exactly what kind of person will be up there.

I put a 3 next to "Integrity." The largest single body of editors—25 percent of the respondents—put a 5 there, although (good news, as I see it) most of the remaining votes—about 60 percent—resided between 1 and 4.

To digress for a moment, there are eleven items on this list. I thought hard before I selected them, and simply because something is relegated to 10 or 11 doesn't mean I think it's totally unimportant. If I did, I wouldn't have put it on the list at all.

Take "Appearance." It's last on my list, number 11—and it's last on the respondent list, too, with about 66 percent thinking it least important and 22.7 percent putting it in 10th place—but it is on the list. Had I created this list back in the early '70s, it probably wouldn't have occurred to me; I'd often show up at work in a T-shirt. What difference did it make? Wasn't I getting paid for the quality of my writing and editing? I wanted to be judged for performance, not for appearance. In fact, I still feel that way, and when I deal with people who know me, it's jeans all the way.

But like it or not, people will make certain assumptions about you based on what you give them to work with. If I wear a particular kind of white jacket, people will figure I'm a dentist or a doctor or a pharmacist. If I dress in a shirt and tie and jacket, they will assume that I am conducting some kind of intercourse that will bring me into relatively structured contact with others. If I dye my hair purple or wear a swastika, those messages will take precedence over all others. All of these things are manifestations of style—the way we tell people how we feel about ourselves or about our function. Let one of these visual stimuli, or any of a thousand others, come down the street toward us, and we will base our first opinion on *what we see*. I don't care how open-minded you are—it's unavoidable.

So when I give a writer an assignment that will mean personal contact with the public, I expect the writer to dress for the engagement. That doesn't necessarily mean a suit or a dress or a shirt and tie—it means being appropriate. And to those who don't know what that means to the extent that they'd be *in*appropriate, I'd have to say, "Come back when you do." Again, I think appearance is one of those things that editors don't care much about on a conscious level—it certainly wouldn't be very fashionable to care—but that can have an impact.

Of course, this article is really devoted to freelance writers. But in most cases, I'd look for these same qualities if I were building a staff.

One area in which that's not always so is "Ability to Work With Others"; it's obviously more important if you spend all your time in a heavily populated editorial department than if you spend it all in a closet. And so it's less important for a freelance writer than for a staffer. Nevertheless, I consider it a fairly reliable personality benchmark—if I'm going to use you, I want you to be someone who can be persuasive without being abrasive, who can work with art directors and copy editors, etc., as part of a team, who can see both sides of a story, who can compromise when necessary, who can respect people who are lower on the totem pole. These are all components of getting along with others—and are all important characteristics for a writer. People who don't have these traits are people I choose not to employ—good writers, perhaps, but bad people. I've never regretted getting rid of them when I had to.

SELF-STARTERS

I'll rate "Ability to Work With Others" 8. The largest vote bloc—25 percent—put it at 7.

I was just about as mainstream when it came to "Writing Style."

Style gets a lot of lip service; when beginning writers talk about it, it's apparent that they view it as something as unique as a fingerprint, a way of writing that will put their own inimitable stamp upon their product.

That's not it, really. Style is simply how you string your words together. It doesn't have to be unique; in fact, when it is it can get in the way: Unique gets tiresome.

Style's important enough for me to have rated it #4, and for the other editors to have rated it predominantly between 2 and 4, but I don't think it's anything you can intentionally develop—not any more than you can wish wrinkles on yourself. Nor is it important that your body of work be encompassed by any such personalizing description. Write long enough and you may develop something that people think of as uniquely you—or not. It doesn't matter much. What does matter is writing with a form and logic and flow that propels the reader along and makes the reading just about irresistible. The more you do it, the more natural it'll become. And when it reaches the point when the paper you've just typed on tells *you* what's needed instead of the other way around, you'll have developed style.

Nothing to it.

As for "Vocabulary, Grammar, etc.," I am clearly out of synch. My colleagues voted this most heavily around 5 to 6; I put it at 10. Again, that doesn't mean I don't think it's important; it's just that I'm one of those editors who puts other things first—and who doesn't believe that knowing the rules and a plethora of words is anything like a necessity. I think good writing usually communicates directly, and in words that most people understand, and I'm not too concerned if I have to go through a piece and make a few corrections here and there.

But don't get me wrong—there's a difference between not having a huge vocabulary and having one that's so small that the writer is hampered when trying to say what needs to be said, and there's a difference between an occasional error in grammar and the kind of obvious lack of sophistication in the use of the language that casts doubt on the writer's credibility. What it really comes down to here is a trade-off—if I'm going to give up something, I'm going to have to be compensated.

If I could change our profession, I'd make it like Hollywood used to see it back in the '40s. I love those movies about the cub reporter who wants to achieve some recognition, be a star—and who sees something suspicious, decides to do a little digging, then goes after a tough-to-get story despite little encouragement from the disbelieving, hard-boiled city editor.

I know it sounds corny, but I *like* that world. And I also think that self-starters are worth their weight in gold. Give me people who figure things out instead of asking me a lot of questions: who don't bitch about having to type their own copy or transcribe their own tapes; who pick up the phone or wear out the shoe leather tracking down the facts; who are relentless in their pursuit of accuracy; and who would be writing even if there was no such thing as a magazine or paper to publish them—and I'll show you writers.

THE PROFESSIONAL

What I'm talking about is enthusiasm mixed with a desire to achieve: "Self-Motivation." And while we all gave it the #7 spot here, I think that's not a bad showing. Self-motivation is one of the key characteristics that, all things considered, could make me choose one writer over another. You may think that kind of enthusiasm is merely naiveté in disguise, but I wouldn't mind having some more of it myself.

I've left the best for last, and it won't take me long to explain it. It's what lets me feel certain that I'm going to get a good piece of writing when I assign a particular writer to a story. It's knowing that I'll get that piece on time. It's knowing that it will come in at the appropriate length, with the facts checked and the tapes and notes and research kept in good shape in case they should ever be needed. It's knowing that any feedback I get about the performance of the writer will be positive, even if grudgingly so—because the writer is worthy of representing my magazine or newspaper in an interview with a celebrity or a giant of industry. It's knowing that the writer will be fair—forget objectivity, it's not possible; but I do expect fairness. It's knowing that the piece is going to be one hell of a good "read." It's knowing that there won't be any unpleasant surprises—that I'll get what I assigned or know why not well in advance. It's what makes a writer get the goods, hang in when the going gets tough, be there at the final curtain.

The largest group of editors put it at 3, but it's #1 in my book. That's "Professionalism."

Those are my opinions, and those of many of my colleagues: the people who buy your work. And now you know what we're looking for. If you're not delivering the most important parts of it, you're probably not selling.

BY MICHAEL J. BUGEJA

Not One, Not Two, But 2,000 Salable Article Ideas a Year

In one day, any writer can find enough ideas for feature stories to stay busy for months of research and writing.

I guarantee it.

As a university writing coach, I propose more than 2,000 feature story ideas to students *every year*. The number always staggers me. But my sources for feature ideas—and they can be your sources, too—are so rich and renewable that I generate enough ideas to satisfy both my students and my own freelance writing.

Where can you find all these ideas? Follow me.

THE FACTS OF YOUR LIFE

"Write about what you know" is advice that every novice writer hears. And we know many things. But because our knowledge is rooted in personal experiences, we dismiss it as a source of ideas for feature stories—even though we own the psychological copyrights to those stories. The trick is to take a broad, objective look at what you know.

Jot down the "facts" of your life—the highs, lows and turning points—the elements that distinguish your life from someone else's. Here are a few items from my list:

I'm a first-generation American; I'm the oldest child; I married as a teenager; I am divorced; my father died of cancer; I remarried; my first baby was stillborn; I adopted an infant; I adapted as a father.

Each of these facts or events can yield at least ten feature ideas. When I wrote for United Press International, I drew on parts of this list for articles accepted for the national wire (the moral equivalent of a magazine sale). Based on my list, I could write articles about:

• First-generation Americans of today, no longer European, but from such locales as Asia and the Middle East: "The Changing Faces of America's New First Generation."
• The responsibility and stress of the first-born in family matters: "From Executor to Executive: Assuming the Family Business."
• Advice for teenage marriage success: "How Parents Can Help Their Children Make a Go of It."
• Offbeat divorce settlements: "If We Part, Who Gets the Football Tickets?"
• The last chance for terminal cancer victims: "Remission: A Time to Make Up for Lost Time."

• The effect of stillborns on marriage: "Couples Most Likely to Divorce: How to Beat the Odds."
• Failed parenthood: "Adoptive Parents Who Return Their Children."

Some of these stories have been done before. Cancer is a topic that, sadly, appears on many writers' lists. But don't eliminate topics because you've read—or even written—about them before. Your feature will be unique because it comes from a different locale and perspective and is intended for a different readership. Two of my students put together an award-winning newspaper series about cancer that included a feature about a journalism department academic adviser who courageously confronted and overcame the disease.

SENSORY PERCEPTION

I don't find all my feature ideas in my background. I find many in the world around me. I've trained myself to consider everything I hear, see, smell, taste or touch as a potential feature article. Take last week, for instance.

• *Listen.* On my way to the campus library, I overheard a man tell his friend, "Tomorrow at the checkpoints, you'll see deer obviously dead for two days." I checked the date and learned the next day was the opening of deer-hunting season. The men were talking about hunters who stash their too-early kills until the season opens. Feature: "Hunters Who Jump the Gun."
• *Look.* In a campus elevator I saw a poster that bore a swastika and anti-black sentiments. I questioned whether it was the start of an American Nazi Party recruitment drive on campus. Feature: "The Nazis in Our Midst."
• *Smell.* Visiting a friend's home, I could smell a factory and garbage dump. Residents hate the stench and have tried to do something about it. Feature: "The Zoning War."
• *Taste.* In the grocery store, I sampled some exotic fruits, among them breadfruit. I wondered who buys these delicacies and where they find recipes. Feature: "Fruit From Paradise."
• *Touch.* In the school cafeteria, I shook hands with a new music professor. His hands were long and elegant. I asked if physical traits of musicians (not just pianists) dictate success or failure with a particular instrument. Feature: "Maestros Who Measure Up."

These story ideas would have escaped me had I not been alert for them. Ideas occur at any moment.

More difficult is the "sixth sense" that the most successful feature writers develop: foreseeing fads and trends.

Although features about both are salable, those that identify trends are the most valuable. Trends endure and influence society more than short-lived fads. Many articles were written about the Pac-Man fad, but only the most astute writers recognized that fad as part of a trend toward computers.

Developing this sixth sense means, again, being perceptive about your surroundings.

● As I write this, bright-colored plastic shoes are the campus rage. By the time you read this, the shoes will have been replaced by some other fad, but both are part of the trend I wrote about when I first spotted the shoes. Feature: "Anything to Be Stylish."

If you want to try your hand at a fad-feature, but you have no ideas, scan your environment.

● My wife rummaged in her mother's basement to find our daughter a Shirley Temple doll . . . worth at least $1,000 from a collector. The collecting part is more trend than fad, and the bids on these dolls have become so outrageous that I know a collector somewhere has hocked a wedding ring to buy one. Feature: "Dolls We'd Give Anything to Keep From Our Kids."

● In spring my neighbors plant vegetable gardens, part of the trend toward healthier living. But do they exercise—another part of the trend—by digging their plots by hand? No, they buy tillers. Feature: "Only a Little Health, Please."

● That home computer my colleagues acquired not only helps them prepare tax returns, but also serves as a deduction. Feature: "If My Computer Lives With Me, Can I List It as a Dependent?"

Procrastinators have no business writing the fad-feature. But the good news for such writers is that the death of a fad or trend can be as intriguing as its birth and usually contains more human interest. For instance, a local company thrived when the craze for citizen's band radios was at its peak. When the CB fad died, my story focused on the consequences of the company's collapse to the fired workers as well as the manufacturer.

REFERENTIAL TREATMENT

Some of the best feature ideas—especially for fad- and trend-spotting features—hide in bland places. Trade, technical, scientific, government and corporate publications and directories contain a wealth of ideas for the writer able to look through dry prose and see a fresh idea hiding inside.

Some of these sources are written for a national audience. You can often make a sale to a local or regional publication by narrowing the subject's focus to produce a new article on the subject's effect in your community or region.

Here are some examples of unusual sources and salable story ideas I brought home from a reading session at my local library:

● From a trade journal for retailers: Shoplifting is down. An article notes that US stores annually lose $24 billion in shoplifting, one third of that between Thanksgiving and Christmas. A feature could focus on whether shoplifting in your city follows the national trend and the steps local merchants take to prevent it.

● From a librarians' newsletter: A dozen communities received federal grants to renovate their libraries. That's good for twelve features, easily sold to weekly newspapers in those communities. And don't dismiss a more in-depth piece without checking. Maybe one of these libraries intends to restore (or tear down) a structure listed on The National Register of Historic Places.

• From a statistical abstract: Marriages once outnumbered divorces five to one in one particular state; now that figure is two to one. By interviewing judges, couples, clergy and counselors, you can write a feature that explains the statistic and the reasons behind it.

• From a corporate annual report: A large manufacturer showed a financial loss for the most recent corporate year. But the company is predicting it will recover the loss by introducing new products. These plans could be the basis for a feature on how the communities around the plant are depending on its recovery.

Common reference books take on new value when seen as story starters. I find about one feature possibility for every five pages of the telephone directory. Look under the letter *A*:

• *Abortion Information & Services*. Interview counselors at the centers and at centers that offer alternatives. Feature: "What Do You Tell a Pregnant Teen-ager?"

• *Antiques—Dealers*. What's the current collecting fad? What basement/attic dweller is now a hot seller? Feature: "Depression Glass, Modern Gold."

• *Art Galleries—Dealers*. Is there any unusual material or high-ticket art work currently in vogue? Feature: "Surreal Art at Unreal Prices."

Directories of names or dates are inexhaustible sources for profiles and follow-up features. Let's say you look up someone interesting—someone who *used* to be famous. Capitalize by writing what's called the follow-up feature. You can follow up on people, events, predictions, and so on. The back issue file of any daily newspaper will provide you with a directory of stories listed by name or topic. Check for annual, fifth, tenth, twentieth, and twenty-fifth anniversaries of news events. What begins as a simple follow-up may turn into a major feature, especially if new developments have gone unreported.

   This happened with a follow-up feature I did on a black National Guardsman who was the victim of a mock hanging in the South. The man was distraught and eventually shot himself playing Russian roulette. The shooting incident was big news, but a year later nobody remembered the man, who was still recovering from his wound at the time my feature was published. The story stirred up interest with new details and reports of government red tape in investigating the mock hanging.

   (Many newspaper libraries—or "morgues"—are not open to the public. If your local paper's is among those, write the publisher for permission to use it. Assure the publisher that you will not sell your features to competitors and that you will use the morgue at its least busy hours. For a morning newspaper, that will be about 8-10 a.m.; for an afternoon newspaper, about 3-5 p.m.)

The classified ad section of your newspaper is another directory for features. Ideas often can be found in several categories:

● Lost and found notices. At my university, students return thousands of dollars in jewelry, cameras and the like. A student writer detailed the efforts of Lost and Found personnel to locate a person whose expensive watch was recovered.
● Personal ads. This is a great source since typical entries contain notices for runaways to return home, offers of romance and adventure, and public warnings to estranged lovers. One student wrote about couples who advertise nationwide wanting to adopt unwed mothers' babies.
● Help wanted ads. A help wanted ad once led me to a feature about the expansion of a local factory. The plant manager told me over the phone that his facility was beginning production of new products. I set up an interview and toured the plant. My resulting feature was distributed nationwide.

An idea is only the start of the feature story process—a process that ends with publication. Along the way, expect to revise your idea many times. Sometimes your published article will bear little resemblance to the idea that sparked it. But successful writers realize that they must mold their ideas to fit a particular publication, a particular audience. And as they shape their ideas for publication, they often discover new angles that are more exciting than their original idea.

Test the salability of each topic that excites you. Write a few paragraphs about your initial idea. Describe what your feature concerns, who you'll need to talk to, and what other research you'll want to do to make it complete. This alone may modify your idea.

Then study the market. Which publications might have an interest in your feature? When you have identified several potential buyers, consult back issues of those publications to familiarize yourself with their content and overall tone.

Now rewrite your idea. As you do, address these questions:

● How will my feature appeal to readers of this publication?
● How can I learn more about the topic to attract these readers?
● What insight can I add to make my feature special?
● Have I left out anything that can strengthen my idea?
● How can I tailor my writing to the market?

When you're satisfied that your rewritten idea is as strong as it can be, take it to market, either in a query (the form most editors prefer) or as a complete manuscript. Either way, be ready to change it again. Even if an editor likes the heart of your idea, he or she may ask for another focus or a different slant to meet the publication's current needs. And while each change that the editor suggests takes you one step further away from your original idea, it brings you one step closer to publication.

Editors won't turn bad ideas into good ones, however. You must develop those on your own. Learn to view the world creatively, alert for the sparks that fire ideas, and you, too, can guarantee yourself enough ideas to keep you—and your editors—busy for months.

BY CANDY SCHULMAN

The Idea Ideal

Wouldn't the writing life be simple if a light bulb illuminated above our heads every time a new idea materialized? We could even deduct our rise in electricity bills as business expenses. A nice fantasy, perhaps, but ideas do not appear supernaturally.

Beginning and experienced writers alike are constantly searching for fresh, provocative, timely, salable ideas. That search needn't be an awesome task—as we find out when we listen to what some veteran writers have to say about their ideas . . . and yours.

JUDITH VIORST: EAVESDROPPING ON IDEAS

"Most of the ideas I get come from my own conversations, curiosities, interests and personal explorations," says Judith Viorst. "My article ideas come out of the life I live, think about, eavesdrop on, and am involved in."

Contributing editor and monthly columnist for *Redbook,* Viorst speaks in a clear, organized manner that gives one the impression she might never have to revise written first drafts. The author of five books of poems and eight children's books lives in Washington, D.C., with her husband, Milton, and her three sons (when they are home)—whom she often writes about. Her book *My Mama Says There Aren't Any Zombies, Ghosts, Vampires, Creatures, Demons, Monsters, Fiends, Goblins, or Things* was written when her son, Nick, was frightened of monsters. Ideas are often very close to home.

"I'm having a conversation with somebody, or I'm telling somebody a story, or I go to a baby shower where everyone's talking about getting pregnant, and I'm enjoying myself. Something clicks somewhere in me when I come home, or maybe even at the time: 'That would really make a good article.' That seems to happen all the time.

"Sometimes I'm on the telephone having a social conversation. We're tugging back and forth on some issue we're both concerned with, and if *we're* concerned about it, then it has some kind of universal application: lots of other people might be concerned, interested, amused by it, or have something to say about it."

In her search for ideas, Viorst often asks herself, "What are the things that really interest me that are generalizable? I'm not interested in writing about quirky, limited things that only 12½ people understand. The best letter I ever got was from a lady who said, 'I'm a short, plump, blonde Methodist from Iowa, and I think you're a tall, thin, Jewish person from the East Coast—and we live the same lives.' "

The subjects that interest Viorst concern "family life, growth and development of being a woman, the aging process. Even my public concerns seem to coincide with readers' interests. After Three Mile Island, we sat around talking about it in a lot of living rooms. I'd talk to people I liked and respected—had been on peace marches with—and they were in favor of nuclear power plants. Were they right? Wrong? Let's find out."

Viorst researched the subject and wrote a column about it for *Redbook*. "You must have a passion for the subject in order to write about the idea."

Once she has an idea, Viorst mentions it over the telephone to editors at *Redbook* "to make sure others aren't working on the idea and that it's in the ballpark of ideas they're interested in.

"After *Redbook* says 'Yes,' I write a couple of paragraphs, often including my lead. I indicate the scope and convey the tone I'm going to take. In writing these paragraphs, I clarify to myself that this is an idea with enough body and material to write 2,000 words on. It sets my own limits and inclusions.

"*Redbook* will say, 'Yes, go ahead with that idea, but weed out that part because it takes us too far afield, or why don't you add something, or be sure to mention so-and-so.' This way there's an objective document that I and the editors can look at which says, 'This is what she's going to write about.' "

Viorst advises other writers to enclose an accompanying letter with their queries using "whatever credit you can mobilize to help you sound professional." She thinks queries are "seductive. They're an effort to say 'I've got a good idea; it's going to be executed in a pleasing way; it's going to cover a lot of interesting ground.' I think you can get that into a few paragraphs."

NORA EPHRON: BENEVOLENT THEFT

"I'm a great believer of 'stealing' ideas," says Nora Ephron, who has not yet been arrested for grand larceny. *Crazy Salad* and *Scribble Scribble* are two of her article collections, and *Heartburn* was her very successful first novel.

"For example, the lady who cuts my hair knows everything that is happening in New York City two months before everyone else. She was the first person I knew with roller skates; the first person in a pyramid scheme. There are lots of people who will give you ideas if you listen to them. I don't mean truly *stealing* ideas, but a lot of your friends will be useful."

Articles based on Ephron's ideas have appeared in publications such as *The New York Times, Rolling Stone, Cosmopolitan* and *Esquire*, where she wrote a monthly column from 1972 to 1977. Was she ever stuck with no idea and a fast-approaching deadline?

"I was trained as a newspaper reporter, so there's no such thing as writer's block. You get fired for having writer's block.

"You can't sit there and wait for ideas to smash into you. It's not a passive process. So much of being a nonfiction writer is forcing yourself to find things to write about. It's an active process of looking at something in the newspaper, or some *thing* that's going around, and thinking: 'How do I feel about this? . . . Can I get anything out of this? . . . Can I push myself a little further on this topic?' "

Ephron has experienced both sides of the mailbox: She has been a freelance journalist and has held editorial positions at *New York* magazine and *Esquire*. "A lot of people starting out will send in a suggestion saying, 'I want to do a piece on Burt Reynolds.' They're not well-known, and the editor writes back and says, 'No thank you.' Six months later, that writer sees a piece on Burt Reynolds and thinks, 'That magazine stole my idea!' Well, interviewing a movie star isn't an *idea*. "The idea is your point of view. You must come up with some little thing that *you* know about that others don't. A good journalist figures that out. It means reading everything possible to keep up with what's going on. You can't merely find a subject that may interest a magazine editor. Find a subject on which you have something interesting, surprising or perverse to say.

"When I started out as a magazine writer, I'd get an appointment with a magazine editor and go in with five *great* ideas, and I couldn't get an assignment because I wasn't an established writer. You have to start in small places, which pay less money and are open to new writers, before you can trade up, little by little."

FRAN LEBOWITZ: ONE SENTENCE AT A TIME

"More often than not, I sit down at the desk with *no* ideas," complains Fran Lebowitz. Anyone familiar with Lebowitz's acerbic wit knows that this alleged curmudgeon complains about a lot of things in her two bestselling books, *Metropolitan Life* and *Social Studies*.

"The advantage of being overly opinionated is that you have an opinion on *every* subject," she says before recalling how some of her ideas first arose.

How to Be a Directory Assistance Operator: A Manual "comes from my unpleasant associations several thousand times every month of my life with information operators, because I never use a phone book."

Pointers for Pets was written because "I knew it would be funny since I didn't like them. Pets are like people; they sense your dislike and come over to lick your hand."

The Modern-Day Lives of the Saints originated because "I had a friend who became immersed in Catholicism. I was sitting around her house one day reading hagiographies when I came up with the idea."

Lebowitz even wrote about houseplants when "they become so prevalent. One day I walked into a restaurant that had previously been a normal restaurant, and suddenly discovered myself in the middle of a South African jungle."

Not every idea works, however. "You don't know until you sit down to write. In humor, the form is as important as the idea. You have to find a way to break the idea into smaller pieces—even if it's an infinitesimal idea."

Lebowitz throws nothing away. Many of her ideas that didn't work are now being incorporated into a novel. "I've written sentences that I *love* as sentences, but don't work in the piece. Of course, I save them in a sentence box. You never know when you can use an extra sentence."

Lebowitz's past professions in New York include driving a taxi, cleaning apartments, bulk mailing, and writing columns for *Mademoiselle* and Andy Warhol's *Interview*. "When I was writing two columns a month, sometimes it was difficult to come up with ideas. I had certain friends that I have a humorous rapport with, and I'd talk to them on the phone until something came up. I made no bones about it. 'Hello, I have to write a column,' I'd say, and start talking. It was a way to hear my own voice back. I often found it useful in a pinch. Certain people inspired me or provoked something in me.

"Concentration is important in coming up with ideas. Your mind is arranged to think for ideas, and instead of letting something go by in conversation, you *stop* it and use it.

"Grown-up writers who get up every day and write from 9 to 12 and then chop down trees have to think like that all the time. Direct your thinking and concentration toward idea sources—although I find it very easy to lapse into the world of game shows and soap operas, and not pay attention."

ANDY ROONEY: IDEAS WON'T SAVE YOU

"These things I do, are they really *ideas*? I mean, is a paper clip really an idea? I don't know if it is," ponders Andy Rooney from his office in CBS Television Studios, New York City.

The wry *60 Minutes* commentator finds ideas in everything from soap to bathtubs, telephones to eyeglasses, and instructions on how to read *The New York Times*—never seriously, of course. All you ever wanted to know about glue, neat people, fences, and even dirty words can be found in his bestselling *And More by Andy Rooney*. Rooney's witty essays come from what might appear to be mundane ideas.

"The notion that an idea will save a writer is probably wrong," he says. Rooney believes that good writing is essentially more important than the idea itself.

"My advice is not to wait to be struck by an idea. If you're a writer, you sit down and damn well decide to *have* an idea. That's the way to get an idea."

Our "few minutes with Andy Rooney" are up. He has a deadline and a column to write. And, you can be sure, a new idea.

BY LOIS HOROWITZ

Researching from Magazines and Reference Books

The world is flooded with magazines—several times more than the 200 or so that you see on newsstands and in chain stores. This is an advantage for writers. There are a number of ways to use magazines, some you haven't tried before.

Magazines with circulations from under 1,000 to over 6 million are written for different audiences. Some magazines are sold only in specialty shops—railroading magazines in model train shops, for example. Others are sold by subscription only to teachers, plumbers, lawyers, and others in trades and professions—one reason we don't see *Journal of the American Bar Association, Kidney,* and *Footwear Focus* on newsstands.

More magazines are generated by banks, membership department stores, airlines, and associations. This helps boost the number of magazines published in this country into the tens of thousands.

Though there are many "invisible" magazines, most are potentially useful in research, and many are paying markets for writers.

WHERE CAN I FIND MAGAZINES?

Freelancers find many magazine markets by accident—on a friend's coffee table, in a doctor's office, or at a book sale.

Libraries are sources of varied magazines, too. Small libraries subscribe to perhaps one or two hundred mass-appeal newsstand magazines. Large libraries carry much more—hundreds, even thousands of special-interest, technical, and popular magazines published in this country and abroad.

Finding magazines is just half the battle, however. You must also be able to locate specific articles within them.

THE KEY TO FINDING ARTICLES

The fastest way to find articles in magazines is to use a periodical index. There are *more than 100* from which to choose.

Reader's Guide to Periodical Literature (RG) is the index familiar to most of us. We started using it in high school and continue using it as writers to check the competition for an article idea and to do actual research.

RG is severely limited, however. Of the thousands of magazines in print, it covers fewer than 200. (*Writer's Market* lists more than 4,000 magazines.) You wouldn't use *RG* to find an article in a specialty medical magazine or for the latest research on the psychological basis of shyness because it doesn't cover the right magazines for those purposes.

With magazines published in all subjects from art to zoology, you must choose the right index covering the right magazines. In most instances, the index you use won't be *RG*.

USING MAGAZINES IN MARKET RESEARCH

Article writers check *RG* to see what has run in other magazines on their subject. There are other indexes you'll want to consider, too. For example, if you want to query *Backpacker Magazine,* you'd check an index called *Access.* You might also try *Physical Education Index (PEI)* which covers sports and athletics magazines. Not only does *PEI* cover *Backpacker* (remember, several indexes cover the same magazines simultaneously) but it shows you what other, similar magazines have printed about backpacking.

USING ARTICLES IN RESEARCH

Market research is only one reason you'll need articles. You'll also use articles in researching your actual writing assignments. Be aware, however, that articles from newsstand magazines are not valid for all kinds of projects. In one article I wrote giving tips to graduating high school seniors on how to live on their own, I gathered all my information from interviews and newsstand magazines. Had I needed information on the latest cancer treatments for an article intended for a top women's magazine, I would not have researched the topic from the newsstand magazines except for background information.

Top magazine markets require that their article contain the latest developments, not warmed-over, secondhand news. If I used studies reported in other national women's magazines, the information would probably be too stale to be sold back to the same market. To get inside information on new research and trends, check scholarly and professional magazines that document original research, studies, and surveys conducted and written by specialists.

A final word on magazine articles. You can also use them as self-help in your writing. There may not always be someone handy to ask about syndicating columns, copyright, or agents when you need help. Even if you've read articles on these topics, you might not be able to find them again.

To get information on these topics, follow the steps described above—check indexes for articles in magazines. The following extract shows some of the relevant articles I found through *Magazine Index.*

LITERARY AGENTS
   How to get a literary agent. Writer *v97 - June '84 - p21 (4)*
COPYRIGHT—LAW AND LEGISLATION
   Does copyright really protect nonfiction? Occasionally yes, but mostly no; here's why. Publishers Weekly. *v224 - Dec 9 '83 - p28 (2)*

SYNDICATES (JOURNALISM)
> *Syndicates: how they work, and how they can work for you (newspaper syndicates) il* Writer's Digest *v64 - Feb '84 - p31 (3)*

The value of a periodical index is that it tells you exactly where to find an article *on any subject* when you need it.

FINDING INDEXES

The list of indexes in this chapter is not comprehensive, but it covers most subjects. I've omitted many highly technical indexes such as *Nuclear Science Abstracts*. Most magazines are covered by more than one index (*Journal of Urban Studies,* for example, is covered by five indexes), so you'll find most of the information you need anyway. If you want to check technical indexes, you'll find them in science libraries.

Choosing the Right Index

Indexes, like books, cover more subjects than their titles imply. You'll use some "obvious" indexes for your particular project and some apparently unrelated indexes, too.

The "think in categories" rule applies here. For example, to research religious music, think "religion" and "music." This will lead you to *Music Index* and also to *Religion Index,* where the topic is covered as well.

For a project on juvenile delinquency, you can search several indexes, such as *Education Index, Criminology and Penology Abstracts, Psychological Abstracts, Social Sciences Index,* and *Index to Legal Periodicals,* depending on the focus you want to take.

When you must make a decision about the "right" index based on its title, remember that indexes are broad. *Art Index* covers archaeology, city planning, antiques, interior design, and film as well as crafts and fine arts. *Writings on American History (WAH)* covers theater, politics, business, literature, science—*everything* of interest in past people's lives. Note below the scope of the articles from *WAH.*

> *IVAN F. DUFF. Medical aspects of submarine warfare: the human factor as reflected in war patrol reports (1941-45)* Arch. internal med., *84:246-60 (Aug. 1949). [AMA Archives of Internal Medicine], vol. 84, pages 246-60.*
>
> *ZEVI H. HARRIS. The growth of Jewish education for girls in New York City [1905-56].* Jew. educ., *29 (1):32-8 (fall) [Jewish Education, vol. 29, no. 1, pages 32-38, fall issue.]*
>
> *CHARLEY McDONALD HEARD. Hollywood gunmen.* Gun Digest, *13:186-94.*

Guides to Indexes

The directories below identify many of the scholarly indexes and abstracts in print. They're both arranged by broad topic (biological sciences, for example). A list of indexes by title appears in each directory's index.

1. Abstracts and Indexes in Science and Technology *by Dolores B. Owen 2d ed. Scarecrow Press. 1985.*

2. Periodical Indexes in the Social Sciences and Humanities: A Subject Guide *by Lois Harzfeld. Scarecrow Press. 1978.*

Look for the most recent edition of any guide you use, though older guides mention standard indexes and they are still useful.

TIPS ON USING INDEXES

The following tips will help you use indexes effectively.

Abstracts vs. Indexes

Abstracts and indexes both locate articles in magazines but abstracts include a summary of articles they refer to; indexes do not. Indexes are arranged alphabetically by subject. Abstracts print their subject index in the back or front of a volume and refer you to article abstracts within the publication by a number.

Although abstracts are extremely useful for their article summaries, their subject indexes are often too broad to be helpful. An article I once found in *Sage Urban Studies Abstracts* on municipal car-pooling programs appeared under TRANSPORTATION, not CAR-POOLING. (The latter heading wasn't even used.) I found the article only by accident.

What periodicals does the index or abstract cover? Periodicals listed in an index are usually listed in the front or back of a volume (though not necessarily every volume). For magazines listed by abbreviations, you can find the full title of the magazine in the key.

Does the index or abstract cover articles alone? Many indexes and abstracts cover books, chapters in books, conference proceedings, select newspapers like the *Wall Street Journal,* and government documents as well as periodical articles. The coverage is usually mentioned in the volume's introduction.

Does the index or abstract include an author approach? If you want to check an article by an author's name, you must first determine if the index you're using is cross-referenced according to author. Choose an article and check its author in the index to find out. Abstracts do include separate author indexes, usually at the back of a volume.

Look for cumulations. Most indexes come out from four to twelve times a year. After a year, the library usually receives a hardcover volume integrating all the data from the past year's loose volumes and discards the paper issues.

Searching annual indexes is tedious, especially when you must check five or ten volumes at one time. Look for cumulations that include several years of the index filed in one alphabet. They're faster to search than yearly volumes.

FINDING THE MAGAZINE OR PERIODICAL ON LIBRARY SHELVES

Once you've identified a periodical through an index, you must know how to look it up in a library catalog. It sounds simple, but often it's not.

Many scholarly periodicals are not listed under the titles on their covers. If the magazine's title names the issuing association or organization, whether it's a bank, a social club, or a university, you must look for the publication under the organization's name. *Journal of the American Bar Association* is filed under *A,* not *J.* This kind of arrangement keeps all the organization's publications together in a list or catalog.

American Bar Association. Bulletin.
American Bar Association. Journal.
American Bar Association. Papers.

In other cases, periodicals are filed as they are worded. *Journal of British Law* is found under *J.*

Periodical Title Abbreviations (Gale Research Co.) will help you transcribe periodical title abbreviations you've forgotten to check in an index key.

WHO INDEXES WHAT

Suppose you want to know who indexes a particular magazine—say *Scholastic Update* (formerly *Senior Scholastic*). *Ulrich's International Periodicals Directory* (R. R. Bowker Co., annual) will tell you.

The information appears abbreviated at the bottom of the magazine's entry in *Ulrich's. Scholastic Update* is indexed by *Reader's Guide, Abridged Reader's Guide, Abstrax, Index to Children's Magazines, Magazine Index,* and *Popular Magazine Review.*

Ulrich's is not comprehensive. Two other guides are also useful if you keep their date limitations in mind.

1. *Chicorel Index to Abstracting and Indexing Services.* Chicorel Publishing Corp. Alphabetizes some 50,000 popular and scholarly magazines followed by a list of the indexes covering each.

2. *Magazines for Libraries.* Bowker Co. Describes approximately 6,500 magazines recommended for small and medium sized libraries. Each magazine entry includes the index or indexes that cover it.

Magazines themselves may offer clues as to where they're indexed. Look for the indexing information in the masthead, the section listing the magazine's staff, near the table of contents.

Also check a magazine's December or January issue. Many magazines include an annual index to their articles.

Some magazines also publish a cumulated index covering years or decades of issues in a separate volume or set. *Scientific American* and *National Geographic* are two magazines that do this.

MAGAZINE RESEARCH BY COMPUTER

Thanks to new technology, most of the indexes mentioned in this chapter can be searched by computer.

Databases that store magazine indexes are called bibliographic databases. They give you a bibliographic citation or reference, not the article itself.

Computerized search services are offered by commercial firms and some large libraries for a fee. Corporations are the major users of computerized literature searching, since the cost is high, presently ranging from $10 to more than $300 an hour per database. A single search, however, can average $30 or less, and at times you might want to consider having a computer search.

Let's say you want information from periodicals on learning disabilities among children of migrant workers.

You might start your search by checking *Education Index, Social Sciences Index,* and other pertinent indexes under LEARNING DISABILITIES. There's only one problem. The topic is too broad, and you must scan every article under the term to see which ones specifically tie in learning disabilities with children of migrant workers. The terms CHILDREN and MIGRANT WORKERS present the same problems. They're too general.

This topic is a perfect candidate for a computer search. When you want two or more distinct subjects to cross, the computer will do it in a way that you cannot quickly accomplish with the printed indexes. The computer scans keywords from the articles themselves or their abstracts and finds the articles for you.

Your computer search starts with a presearch appointment. You'll select the indexes you want to search and choose primary and alternate terms from the index's thesaurus that describe your topic. (The computer recognizes only acceptable terms.) This process helps reduce wasted time once you're on-line and time is ticking away at one dollar per minute.

After your presearch interview, the searcher goes on-line, that is, he or she calls the database the search service subscribes to. The computer connected to the database then begins the search.

The index and time period you designated are selected. Then your preselected words or terms are fed in.

We'll assume that LEARNING DISABILITIES is an acceptable term to search through the index you've selected. The computer may then scan, say, five years of the index and count the number of articles during that period with LEARNING DISABILITIES in the titles or abstracts. Perhaps it will be 273.

The searcher may then key in the word CHILDREN to see how many articles include that word in their titles or abstracts. That would probably elicit many citations, say, 1,500. The term MIGRANT WORKERS (or MIGRANT WORKER) may elicit fifty citations. The searcher feeds in as many related terms as you have preselected.

When this process is over, the searcher combines the words or terms. For example, the computer may be asked to count articles with LEARNING DIS-ABILITIES *and* CHILDREN *and* MIGRANT WORKERS in their titles or abstracts. The result of this search might then be two articles.

Finally, the searcher will print out the two article citations. You must get the articles from the library on your own. Though many articles can be printed out on demand, most often you'll get just the citation. On-demand printing is still quite expensive.

A computer search is thorough and fast. If you're researching a dissertation, book or other long project, a computer search may be worthwhile.

Some academic libraries offer computerized search services, though they may be limited only to their students and faculty. Commercial brokers are appearing in large cities nationwide. Check the Yellow Pages of the phone book under LIBRARY RESEARCH, INFORMATION BROKERS, or similar terms. The library may also be able to recommend commercial brokers.

MAGAZINES ON MICROFILM

Libraries are replacing many of their print runs of magazines with microfilm copies. In time, *all* magazines and newsletters will likely be on microfilm, though large libraries will continue to carry recent copies in the print version. Special photocopy machines can make paper copies from microfilm for about fifteen to twenty-five cents per page.

Micropublishers are also filming many century-old and subject-specialized magazines that are deteriorating and getting lost. Microform's compactness and low cost have made it possible for large libraries to buy old magazines they never owned before.

Check large public and academic libraries for a large selection of magazines in print and in microform.

THE OLD REGULARS: ENCYCLOPEDIAS, ALMANACS, DICTIONARIES, CHRONOLOGIES, AND YEARBOOKS

Encyclopedias are one of the most obvious research tools published. That's why high school teachers prefer that their students use them as little as possible. Writers do more original and creative research than students. Still, encyclopedias play an important role.

Almanacs, chronologies, yearbooks, and special dictionaries are effective resources, too. But we use them far *less* than we should. With directories, these tools are the backbone of a library's reference collection. Each has special talents you may not have tapped.

BY JAY STULLER

A Matter of Expertise

There are months when I feel like The Great Imposter. A copy of *The American Legion* arrives bearing my story on the People's Republic of China; it identifies me as a writer who "frequently covers international politics." A few days later, *The Physician & Sportsmedicine* shows up, containing my analysis of custom-made knee braces. Then comes an inflight, with my essay on ethics and business, and later *Inside Sports* with an article of mine on National Football League passing attacks, replete with esoteric X's and O's.

What qualifies me to write such things? I'm certainly not a licensed Sinologist, and I wouldn't dare attempt a piece on China for *Foreign Affairs*. Yet *American Legion* accepted my interpretation of China's future course because it was *based* on the advice of serious, practicing scholars. Similarly, if I took charge of an NFL offense, the team would likely go 0 and 16. But with guidance from five coaches, the article accurately reflected pro football trends.

An initial lack of expertise should not deter any writer from taking on a topic of interest. In fact, there are relatively few subjects and magazines outside the range of a competent writer who can develop a good idea for a specific market, and who knows how to research and present the material.

Nevertheless, taking on a complex subject about which you know relatively little is one of the largest psychological hurdles—as well as a practical problem—for beginning writers. You might recognize the seed of a good article and a magazine where it might fit, but how do you convince the editor that you're capable of pulling it off? How do you develop that "instant expertise"? Worse, how can you discuss the matter with knowledgeable sources, without sounding foolish, benumbed by the righteous fear of falling in over your head?

"I've often felt like I'm in over my head," says California writer Glen Martin. "But I've learned that you don't have to be an expert to cover a topic. You simply have to *consult* experts. The greatest talent a writer can develop is learning who to talk to, or perhaps better, learning *how* to find who to talk to."

For instance, Martin once received an assignment from *Cuisine* for a 2,000-word piece on horseradishes. Up to that point, he knew only that the stuff can make your eyes water and that it's grown in California's Tule Lake region.

"I figured there had to be some kind of horseradish or growers association up there," he explains. "I called Information and found a growers group that also represented a horseradish processing firm. From there I also got the names of some farmers. I researched some history on the horseradish and learned considerably more about it than I ever wanted to know; certainly enough for a solid article."

GETTING SMART

Convincing an editor that you can research a solid article is, obviously, your first step. An editor may be willing to take a chance on a good idea concerning nuclear power, even if the writer proposing it isn't a nuclear physicist. However, you must prove that you know something about the topic; enough, at least, to articulate the idea and show how you'll go about developing it.

"A writer who is new to us just can't pitch an idea without some supporting material, or at least giving an idea of a modus operandi," says former *Ford Times* editor Arnold Hirsch. When making an assignment, or even asking to see a piece on spec, Hirsch wants some assurance that the writer can "absorb information from many sources, filter out what's necessary and translate it into a specific viewpoint.

"You don't have to be an expert in a certain field to get an assignment on that topic," says Hirsch. "But you do have to be smart."

It's easy for the smart *writer* to develop sufficient knowledge to write about most subjects. Perhaps the most time-efficient first stop when dealing with a new topic is the public library, where you may find a little background material, or unexpectedly, an awful lot.

Frequently, says *Audubon* managing editor Roxanna Sayre, "writers will think of an idea that seems fresh and interesting, only to later learn it's been covered extensively." Finding that others beat you to the punch can be daunting. On the other hand, the germ of a new angle of the story may rest in that extensive coverage. Better still, it means there's a wealth of research available.

To find such material for a query or assignment, I begin with the *Reader's Guide to Periodical Literature*. A two- or three-year survey of the specific subject's magazine coverage, and any side elements that seem promising, is my research foundation. Then, I check the card catalog for any books that touch on the area, or browse through a bookstore for new releases. Computerized data bases, such as those that tap *The New York Times* or the *Wall Street Journal*, also are windows to information.

While clips and books can provide background research, they also can lead to live interview sources. An expert given one line in *Time* clearly has more to tell. An author of a book often will have fresh information that came as a response to the published work; he or she will be glad to talk, since mention in a magazine piece is a good sales plug.

Furthermore, there are associations for virtually every product, social group, political viewpoint, trade class and professional organization in existence. These groups are eager for publicity, and can be a tremendous asset for a freelancer. You'll find some 20,000 of them listed in the multiple-volume *Encyclopedia of Associations* (Gale Research), a marvelous reference source. In it are addresses and phone numbers for such disparate groups as the American Bladesmiths Society, the International Polka Association, the Django Reinhardt Appreciation Society, the Renaissance English Text Society and the American Turpentine Farmers Association Cooperative.

I also rely heavily on universities, institutions and government agencies. College professors—from biology to medicine and forestry—are a tremendous resource. Research organizations, like the Rand Corp., the Brookings Institution, SRI International and the American Enterprise Institute, have studies relating to social issues, economics, and public and foreign policies. Many such groups publish catalogs, a source for ideas and research, and either sell books and papers for a nominal fee or give them away to writers.

Likewise, the United States Geological Survey, NASA and branches of the military all have public information offices. The National Institutes of Health are a fantastic source for medical information. The American Cancer Society, American Heart Association and similar groups—found in the *Encyclopedia of Associations* or even the Yellow Pages—also are sources for background information.

EXPERT COMMENTARY

Next comes phone calls, and perhaps later visits, to the real experts. Be honest with these folks: Make it clear whether you've got a hard assignment, are doing the story on spec, or are just exploring the feasibility of an idea. I don't want to waste their time or mine, especially if I'm just making preliminary investigations. Many experts are willing to talk about their field to anyone, at any time, and for any length of time; others won't unless the piece is likely to hit print.

I'm also up front on whether I know much about their area of expertise. It certainly helps to have read a few articles or a book on the subject; such research enables you to develop questions and make the interview more of a conversation than a one-way lecture. This also can loosen up the person being interviewed.

On the other hand, if I admit to starting from scratch—and that's sometimes the case when little printed research material can be uncovered—I've found that most, if not all sources, are exceptionally kind, going slowly over the basics until I develop an understanding of the topic.

"Never be ashamed to ask an authority to render something in simpler terms until you understand it," says Glen Martin. "And if you're still having trouble, keep asking for simpler and simpler renditions. If you don't understand it, your readers never will. But almost anything can be simplified, once you've tossed out all the jargon and patois of a given field."

One of the most delightful interviews I've ever conducted was with California Institute of Technology astronomer Maarten Schmidt, for a profile in the Dutch edition of *Reader's Digest.* A pioneer in the study of quasars, Schmidt could tell I had little background in this highly technical area. But before we even started the interview, I explained that the magazine was looking for a personality piece, rich on details of his childhood in The Netherlands, how he grew interested in astronomy, and *simple* explanations of his work.

Given this outline, Schmidt unveiled his story in a basic-but-elegant form. (Later, as I started writing, I found the notes in near-perfect sequential order for the story; it reminded me that if I articulate what I'm trying to accomplish, my subjects can make my job that much easier.) Only rarely did I have to ask for technical clarifications—I'd done enough advance reading on quasars to at least converse on these astronomical oddities.

Yet Schmidt mercifully kept it simple. When I explained that *Reader's Digest* would need some thoughts that could viscerally connect astronomy to its average reader, Schmidt offered the idea that if the universe were born during the Big Bang, out of one exploding atom, we humans, plants, animals and every bit of matter in the heavens are related. The wondrous notion that we are all "stardust" gave the complexities of quasar and other astronomical research a *raison d'être*, a kicker that made the article sing. Nothing could be more simple and less technical, and say so much.

CLEAN SLATES

So why don't editors simply commission experts to write the articles? While there are editors who insist contributors have certain credentials to match the story, other editors believe a general interest writer holds an advantage over a so-called expert. "Experts," says *Audubon*'s Sayre, "sometimes don't look beyond the immediate subject to the greater meaning of a story." For example, someone specializing in the technical aspects of astronomy might have ignored Schmidt's stardust comment, or failed even to steer the conversation in that direction.

Experts bring a wealth of knowledge to a story, while the novice brings a blank slate. The latter can be an advantage, because what impresses and interests the novice also is likely to interest the story's audience, who are, after all, reading the piece to learn something new.

"We put more value on a freelance writer's ability to gather information, quotations from expert sources and subject matter through research and investigation than we do on someone who is part of a specialized field," says *Kiwanis* executive editor Chuck Jonak. And though he admits that it may sound odd, Jonak feels that a piece written by an expert lacks a certain "authoritative edge."

Jonak prefers an objective viewpoint in his articles. "Experts often toot their own horn or put too much weight on one side of a question. We also don't use author biographies or put IDs at the end of stories, which you'd almost have to do in such cases. So, we generally tend to stay away from expert-authored articles."

Jonak does believe, however, that some expertise in a given field is useful to a writer. "For example, we'll use a specific writer for small-business articles, because we know he's got the background for the subject." And yet, at the bottom line, he adds, "an experienced freelance writer will know how to research any subject, whether it's new to him or her or not."

Indeed, I do far more research on topics new to me than for ones I've previously covered. Moreover, rarely do I go with only one or two sources for any story; three or four opinions on a topic, even if they're not all quoted or included, are important if one is to understand the nuances of a story.

For instance, *Audubon* recently assigned me to write about the Velella, a small jellyfish also known as the "By-the-wind Sailor." I knew little about them, only that they sometimes littered California beaches in the spring.

One marine biologist told me they could sting. However, I later learned from several other biologists — and books on marine life — that Velella had stinging cells, but few humans could feel their sting. They are perfectly safe to handle. Similarly, a park ranger told me that Velella off the Asian coast have their little sails set exactly opposite from those off North America. But a professor with the Scripps Institute of Oceanography delightfully recounted how that particular myth had come about and debunked it.

Had I not made extra phone calls, had I merely accepted what I had initially heard, the story would have contained errors. The extra digging led to an accurate and much more interesting piece.

GOING THE EXTRA DRINK

There's no hard and fast rule governing when you've compiled enough "instant expertise." Good journalists probably use less than half of their research in writing the final draft. Knowing when and where to draw the line on research—getting too much is time-consuming and can complicate thinking by making it hard to sort out the essentials—is a skill that comes with the experience of preparing dozens of articles.

To be safe, when you think you have more than enough for the piece, seek out one more interview and find one more related clip for insurance. Even experienced writers sometimes fail to cover all the bases and angles.

For example, *Reader's Digest* senior editor Clell Bryant asked me to write for the magazine's French edition a piece on the invasion of French winemakers into California's Napa Valley. I told Bryant that I really didn't like wine. But I agreed to look into the idea, and assured him that the story would at least have that fresh slant.

During preliminary research for a proposal, I found that winemakers and corporations from Japan, Germany, Switzerland and several other countries also were expanding into California vineyards. The *Digest* assigned me to write one piece for the French, along with a second version that could be tailored for some of its other editions.

Completing the research, I put together two comprehensive articles covering the business and social reasons for foreign winemakers' move into California.

Bryant, who is quick and effusive with praise and equally quick and blunt when things go wrong, phoned me the day the article arrived. "You covered everything," he said, "but the stories sound as if they were written by someone who doesn't like wine."

"But I told you I didn't like wine."

"I know," he said, "but the articles can't *sound* that way. Go buy a few bottles of the wine you're writing about and drink them," counseled Bryant. "Put a little bouquet, romance and *joie de vivre* into the story. Remember, a lot of the people who will read this *like* wine, even if you don't."

The *Digest*'s accountants had a minor seizure at the $150 tab for four bottles, but Bryant convinced them it was a small expense for the impact. Thanks to his suggestion and my line-of-duty drinking, I was able to put the requisite pizazz into the articles, which were then useful for a half-dozen or more foreign *Digest* editions.

Although it may not always allow you to be so self-indulgent, you should be willing to go the extra mile to properly research a story. If you're writing a medical piece on open heart surgery, get into an operating room and watch, listen, smell and *feel* the experience. (I've done this, and neither fainted nor was grossed out; the color and action from the surgeries made the article many times better than a simple dry report.) If you're covering a new roller coaster, ride it. (I won't write about roller coasters.) If you're writing about wine, drink it.

Research, and then still more research, usually ensures that you won't go wrong on an article. The vast majority of magazines are speaking to audiences who don't know much about the topics therein. Therefore, your research qualifies you as an expert.

It doesn't take long to develop relative expertise in any subject. In fact, your own personal experiences can, if you learn to recognize it, provide a large research base.

For example, until a few years ago I knew nothing about bad knees, other than the hope I'd never hurt one of mine. But I did, seriously, in a basketball game. Determined to learn more about my injury, and perhaps to turn a buck out of a bad situation, I began researching the subject.

In the midst of rehabilitation I convinced *Inside Sports* to commission a piece on how pro athletes recover from knee injuries, from nuts-and-bolts therapy to the psychological trauma of trying to return to a sport. From there I learned about knee braces, which led to a *Physician & Sportsmedicine* article. Following a later reinjury of my knee, I needed surgery.

Reader's Digest, obviously impressed with such dedication to research, assigned me to write an "all-about" knee article, which heavily focused on arthroscopies. I now know as much about bad knees as any layman, and though I'm a bit weary of the topic, I can use the background to my advantage by doing updates and reworking the angles. (In fact, my surgery led to a *Digest* assignment on anesthesia, for which I was again starting from scratch, interviewing anesthesiologists, reading textbooks and observing an operation.)

Expertise is, to be sure, valuable. But I wouldn't want to be pegged into any limiting slot; I'd rather be known as a writer who can handle any topic, whether I've got a background in it or not.

My credo is to write about what I *want* to know. Taking on new and unfamiliar subjects is one of the most enjoyable facets of freelance writing. For the curious, it's a license to explore almost any idea, location or subject in the world; getting paid for it makes writing about what you learn the next best thing to independent wealth.

BY DENNIS E. HENSLEY

Small-Town Stories and Big Sales

Small towns are no less busy than big towns for the freelancer who knows how to dig out and market article ideas. A few years ago I learned that I could train my ears and eyes to detect article ideas everywhere I went locally. What's more, by applying a few professional modifications, I found I could resell one original small-town news item to several statewide newspapers and national magazines. You can do the same thing by following a few basic steps.

START WITH THE OBVIOUS

Holmes once told Watson that the first error in investigative work is that the obvious is always overlooked. He was right. Before you travel to the far corners of the globe seeking news or interviews, give a professional look to your friends and relatives. Do any have fascinating hobbies? Are any involved in unusual occupations? Have any survived a trying ordeal worth retelling?

Make a list of whatever comes to mind about your cousin or school roommate or your lodge or bridge club members. Then press for details. Don't pass up the opportunity to land a great interview, as I once did.

When I began working as a freelance writer ten years ago, a man suggested I do a feature on him and the research he was doing in the field of artificial eyes. I declined, saying it was too technical (and too morbid for that matter) to interest general readers. The fellow (an oculist he's called) nagged me until I decided I'd write an article just to prove my point to him. I went to his laboratory and observed his work.

But it wasn't morbid at all; it was fascinating. People entering the lab with distorted faces left with perfectly natural appearances. I was amazed. I further was amazed to learn that Morris Udall, Peter Falk, Rex Harrison, Sammy Davis, Jr. and many other well-known persons wore artificial eyes. I left the lab that day with a handful of story ideas in mind. Within eight months I had sold articles on artificial eyes to 15 different periodicals.

That excellent local feature story had been right in front of my *own* eyes for years and I had ignored it. It was one of those cases of being too close to the story to see the royalty check. Or checks, I should say, since I pocketed over $500 by the time I exhausted that story's resales. Oh, by the way, the oculist I referred to was L. Edward Hensley, my father.

I now keep close tabs on all my relatives. I also know a lot about the people I live near or associate with. And it pays off. One of my neighbors told me that she had three sons, each born in different years on May 16. I gained four sales from that article. A retired gentleman who attends my church told me he had the world's largest collection of company seal imprint makers. Six editors bought that feature as a filler item. Keep in mind that "famous" people and events have something unique unto themselves for which they draw attention. Maybe the fact won't impress the Guinness Book or Ripley's people, but often it *will* impress a Sunday magazine editor who needs filler or local material.

BE BOLD WITH STRANGERS

It's really not all that hard to find big news items in small towns. A little mingling with strangers can sometimes bring out incredible scoops worthy of numerous sales.

Take, for example, the night my wife dragged me to her ladies' club potluck dinner. I was introduced to an elderly gentleman, a physician, across the table from me who seemed as bored as I. After five minutes of conversation the man laughed and said, "For a stranger, you sure ask a lot of questions."

"Sorry. It's my nature," I said. "I'm a freelance writer and I have this theory that there is at least one major story in everyone. I try to find it. Ever had anything unusual happen to you?"

"Well, one thing," he said modestly, "but I don't know how important it is. It may be nothing, but back in 1970 I was Health Services Director at Kent State University. When the National Guard shot the nine students on May 4, I was the first doctor to examine the victims."

I bolted upright. "You what!?"

Pulling my always-ready dime notebook from my sportcoat pocket, I hurried to the other side of the table and began to jot down the full eye-witness account of what Dr. Ralph Honzik had seen and heard—and done professionally—on that eventful day. My notes led to a large feature article the following Sunday morning in the *Muncie Star*, my hometown daily.

LEARN TO LISTEN

Begin your search by learning to listen. When you are at a PTA meeting, a church social, a garage sale or at work, close your mouth and absorb what people around you are saying. If someone is talking and others are listening, there must be something interesting being told . . . perhaps something that can be developed into a written article; so, pay attention!

Listen also to TV and radio newscasts. Find a national news item that you can investigate locally. If the anniversary of Elvis' death is being commemorated big in Memphis, see how well his records and souvenirs are selling in your area. Very often national events and anniversaries lend themselves to an original local angle.

Be sure to ask *enough* questions when you go out on an interview. Just because a person in your town is known for one major accomplishment, it does not mean he or she might not have done other things also worthy of writing about.

This was the case when I interviewed Ben Timmons, a champion high-school wrestler who overcame a handicap of deafness to earn his place on the varsity team. After we had discussed his wrestling trophies for an hour, I asked Ben some unrelated questions about his home, parents and future plans. He told me that he had just finished an apprenticeship as a blacksmith and that he was taking over a retiring man's livery stable. When I asked him how he hoped to make a living in the twentieth century with a nineteenth-century skill, his answer intrigued me.

Ben explained that he had mounted an anvil, bellows, coal bed and forge onto the back of a flatbed truck and had placed a fiberglass cab over the top. He then threw in supplies of nails, horseshoes, rasps and hammers, and there he had it— a stable on wheels!

The upshot was that I wrote and sold seven articles on Ben Timmons the mobile blacksmith and nothing on Ben Timmons the deaf wrestler. As you see, finding one story can lead you to another.

I was once talking to a local man I knew through my work. He mentioned that his sixty-five-year-old brother, Walter O. Miles, a former resident of our town, ran a printing shop in California and that for extra money he did walk-ons and bit parts in TV shows and movies. He was coming home to visit his brother; so, I set up an interview appointment.

Admittedly, Walt Miles turned out to be small pickings in the Hollywood scene, but he had been connected in minor ways to several smash movies, including a three-minute scene in *MacArthur* and a non-speaking role in *Close Encounters of the Third Kind*.

I could have wasted my time writing articles like, "Another Extra Tells His Story," but there would have been nothing eye-catching about such features and they would not have sold. However, I bypassed the obvious story—the tie to Hollywood—and instead focused upon the fact that when most men were getting ready to retire, Walt Miles was beginning a new and quite glamorous career.

That news peg worked very well. I sold "He Didn't Retire: He Became A Star!" to *New England Senior Citizen*; I sold "Close Encounters of the Late in Life Kind" to *The Indianapolis Star Magazine*; I sold "Late Blooming Hoosier Actor Faces Busy Season" to *Michiana*; I sold "Actor Walt Miles Won't Retire" to the *Muncie Star*; I sold "Senior Citizen Has Unique Pastime" to *Grit*; and I sold "No Rocking Chair For Actor Walt Miles" to the *Camden Chronicle*.

Being a Hollywood extra was somewhat unusual, but being a post-retirement Hollywood extra was downright unique. And, as I said before, it is being unique that makes your characters or local events "famous."

MULTIPLE SALES

When selling one article idea to multiple markets, I use a marketing approach geared to ever-enlarging circles. I sell first to the city paper ($8-$15), then to the large statewide papers ($50-$60 for magazine supplements), then to the regional periodicals ($50-$75), then to the national outlets ($75 & up), and, whenever possible, to international publications ($50 & up).

Each time I resell the article idea, I try to make the new version different in at least three ways: (1) I provide photos of the person or event which have not appeared in other publications; (2) I insert one or two new facts about the incident which were not emphasized in a previous article; and (3) I attempt to write the article as stylistically close to the established format of the receiving publication as possible, while also trying to gear the event to its geographical locale.

For example, an area man named Pete Schlatter invented a workable two-wheel automobile last year and I played that story for all it was worth. My first article appeared in the *Muncie Star*, a city paper, with a local-boy-makes-good angle. It mentioned area people who had influenced Schlatter and gave a short history of his years in town. My next article appeared in *The Muncie Weekly News*, a countywide paper, with an area-resident-is-inventor angle. I next sold the article to the magazine sections of *The Indianapolis Star* and *The South Bend Tribune*, two statewide papers, with a Hoosier-man-is-unique-mechanic angle. The article covered statewide auto shows at which the car had been displayed. Afterward, I submitted the article to *Hot Rod* for national publication, focusing strictly on the auto itself, and it eventually went international when I sold it to the *Christian Science Monitor* for its overseas and Canadian editions. Milking an article is a trick of the trade for a small town writer who enjoys a worldwide audience.

TIPS ON SUBMISSIONS

Once your article is written, remember to accompany it with good photos and to send it off at an advantageous time.

Good photos enhance any article, particularly when it is a personality piece. Walt Miles' agent provided me with photos of Walt and Gregory Peck in a scene from *MacArthur*. For the birthday story, I had all three brothers put their faces behind one cake which had "May 16th" written on it. For the artificial eye articles, I had photos of the oculist holding a prosthetic eye near one of his own real eyes to show the similarity.

Good timing can also generate sales. I sold the article on the three May 16th birthdays in May. Had I tried to sell it in August, I probably would have failed. I sold follow-up features on Dr. Honzik near the May 4th anniversary date of the Kent State shootings. Editors love timely material, so pace your submissions.

More important, get out there and dig up information *for* those submissions. So often budding writers will lament, "I'd love to do an interview with someone famous, but here in Villeville, U.S.A., I never come in contact with anyone." Whenever I hear that line, I wince and warn, "Don't overlook your dad."

BY STAN BICKNELL

Confessions of a Clipper

For nearly 15 years hardly a day has passed that I haven't taken up shears and cut out one or more news and feature stories from the daily papers. Magazines that come into the house throughout the month receive exactly the same treatment. This chore takes only a few odd minutes at a time, but, aside from writing itself, I consider it the most important thing I do.

These clippings don't so much spark ideas for articles—maybe one in fifty does that; rather, they provide background and ready-made research that would take hours, even days to dig out of the public library.

Years ago, I worked on the evening shift of a daily newspaper and one of the first things I noticed was the way many reporters and feature writers tore odds and ends out of every edition that came up to the city room. The three constant sounds of an evening were raised voices, typewriters and the *riiiip* of a clipping being born. This was, I realized, one way a good newsman generated his own story ideas on a slow news day when the editor in his doldrums would gaze out across the city room and wonder if such a large staff was really all that necessary.

TIME AND MONEY SAVED

Over the years I've developed some forty subject categories with as many as three file folders each ranging from Religion, Medicine and Energy to Crime, Work and Dance. You might think that storing this much paper would take up the space of a small warehouse, yet I've managed to keep it in a dozen plastic milk cases, all tidy and tucked away in a closet.

When I say "clippings," I'm really using a shorthand for anything in print that can easily be contained in a file folder. Newspaper and magazine articles make up the bulk of what I save for the thirty-five to fifty features I do in a year, but I also squirrel away handbills, advertising flyers and scholarly monographs with equal fervor. Thanks to photocopiers and lowcost offset printing, the world is being flooded with printed paper. Not so long ago I saw a handbill at the local adult education center advertising a course in teacher re-training. What an odd thing! Why would teachers need to be re-trained—and for what? By going through my Education folder, I learned that teachers were leaving the school systems in droves around Boston because they were either "burned out" or being "riffed"—jargon for "reduction in force." In other words, they were fired. My clippings told me about the declining school age population, vandalism, violence, and the cutbacks in funding that were contributing to these two sad events. The handbill was the "hook" and the clippings formed background for a query and story I sold to the *Boston Herald Magazine*.

I don't save stories on politics, defense, foreign affairs and the like. They are too vast and open-ended for me to deal with. Some issues or societal stories, however, have a scale that I feel comfortable with. And these I keep. A few years ago, for instance, Congress enacted legislation prohibiting foreign fishing fleets from competing with our own commercial fishermen within 200 miles of our shores. I saved these stories and put them in my New England folder with nothing specific in mind.

About a year later, during a conversation with the editor of *Yankee*, we danced lightly over the subject of commercial fishing. *Yankee*, it seems, had planned a historical article on fishing and was toying with the idea of pairing it with a contemporary account of the industry. Did I know anything about commercial fishing? Not really, I replied, although I did have a lot of material on the 200-mile legislation and its effects. Once again, my files gave me what I needed—the pros and cons of the issue together with the names of New England fishermen, industry spokesmen and government people who could give the story real dimension. The rest was relatively easy after that. But if I had had to start from scratch and go through back issues of the papers, I could not have done it profitably. The time spent would have made it prohibitive.

CLIP TIPS

I read the Boston papers, *The New York Times* and the *Wall Street Journal* in the morning and clip them in the afternoon when the day's business is finished. I go through them page by page, glancing at *everything*—news stories, ads, letters to the editors, even fillers at the bottom of a column. (A two-sentence filler on ice in a Hawaiian volcano once prompted an article on permafrost for *Science Digest*.)

The only thing I consciously look for is stories on subjects on which I've written in the past. These items become the best reference, updates on my own knowledge. If I come across an article—even if the dateline is Paraguay—on teacher re-training or commercial fishing, for example, I clip it out without mercy or hesitation. Having once written about a topic, I'm halfway into the next article.

Each clipping gets date stamped. I use rubber cement to glue stories that jump to another page. If something below the lead is of special interest, I underline it, using a red felt-tip pen. I also glue 3x5 notepaper to a clipping if it's small enough to get lost or if I want to make a note then and there.

A file folder fits perfectly into a plastic milk case. These colorful receptacles can be found behind most groceries or can be bought inexpensively in specialty stores. A filing cabinet just for clippings seems too expensive, and, besides, the cases are easy to handle and store. Adding a case at a time as the files expand is ultimately more efficient.

I do the filing every couple of weeks, depending on how much paper I've collected in the basket. One thing I don't do is get bogged down with filing, debating with myself whether a clipping on the common cold should be filed under Medicine or Health. If it's research, then Medicine; if prevention, Health. But it really doesn't matter. If I write a piece on sniffles this winter, I'll go through both as a matter of course.

This is an active system meant to serve my needs. I'm not a curator filing away news clippings for future generations. Insofar as indexing goes, I will, if I collect a great many clippings on one subject, jot a word or two on the folder—"Alcoholism" under Health or "Wood Stoves" under Energy. Still, I don't put too fine a point on it. Ultimately, the best index any of us can devise is an orderly mind. There is but one danger in having this information at your finger tips: It can make you lazy.

CORRECT THE RECORD

Clippings should never be a substitute for original research. Why bother to write at all if you can't add information or insight to a subject? Total reliance on clippings is "cut and paste" journalism and that leads only to shallow hackwork. There may be occasions when, because of a short deadline or a low rate of pay, you can't spend too much time on a piece. I've used clippings and not talked to anyone or asked a question, but I've always felt a little ashamed afterwards. Bear in mind, too, that it's risky to assume that a news story contains the whole truth. This doesn't mean a story is false or distorted, but a writer may have gotten his facts wrong, inadvertently used quotes out of context, misplaced the emphasis because he didn't really understand what he was writing about, or unknowingly let his bias creep in.

Consequently, I try to be scrupulous when using the facts in my clipping as the basis for research, especially when interviewing someone, so that I don't perpetuate errors. Is the man I'm talking to really forty-eight as it says in the article I have in my file? Did he get a B.A. from Stanford? Or was it his master's? Does he have two boys and a girl or is it two girls and a boy? I ask fairly standard questions at the start of an interview such as "Are you aware of the stories published in _____?" and "Are they complete and factually correct?" If there's time, I let him go through my sheaf of clippings. An OK means you're past the preliminaries and you can talk on the subject at hand. If they are incorrect, here's a chance to correct the record, and that's part of the story, too.

I couldn't begin to estimate how many hours of mind-numbing drudge work my clippings have saved me. Nor could I guess what I might have missed—the new facts, perspectives and appreciations they have brought to the topics that interest me.

Once in a while I even discover a fellow spirit in the audience Out There. One time, for instance, I spoke with a young lady who had read one of my articles and was deeply moved by the experience. "It told me a lot I never knew," she said. "In fact, I liked it so much I clipped it and saved it."

BY LISA COLLIER COOL

How to Write Irresistible Query Letters

How would you like to turn a few paragraphs into a profitable article assignment? A query letter, brief and to the point, can be your shortcut to sales. Not just for the experienced pro, queries can work for any writer. As a literary agent and writing teacher, I've seen queries produce writers' very first sales.

Making queries work for you is a matter of mastering two skills: presentation of an idea and presentation of a writer—you. Here's how:

With a query that began with those two paragraphs, I received the assignment to write this article. While many writers would write the complete article first, then try to sell it, selling first—through a query—*then* writing, is a more profitable and efficient approach.

A combination summary and sales pitch, a query describes your idea in a page or two. Querying allows you to get timely ideas out more quickly. It allows you to submit more article ideas, to receive faster answers, and to reduce research and writing time spent on potentially unsalable material.

Most magazine editors prefer queries over complete manuscripts, too. Queries are easier and faster to read than manuscripts, and they allow editorial input *before* the article is written. Often an editor will hesitate to ask a writer to revise an already-completed piece, but feels no such reluctance about suggesting a new slant for a query. My query proposing an article on consumer advocacy, for example, produced an assignment from *Harper's* to write about deceptive food packaging, an angle I'd never considered.

Queries can be used to propose almost any kind of article, though for humor pieces, editorials, newspaper pieces, and general articles shorter than 1,000 words, it's best to submit a completed article. Also, a few magazines insist that only completed manuscripts be submitted. To learn specific preferences, check *Writer's Market* or ask the magazine for writer's guidelines.

TESTING YOUR IDEA

To lead to a sale, your query must convince the editor that you have a clear idea of what you plan to cover in the article and what approach you intend to take. So *before* you begin writing your query letter, think your article idea through carefully. Imagine you are describing the article to a friend. Could you get the point across in just a few words? In his book *Adventures in the Screen Trade* screenwriter William Goldman describes how he found a handle on the 650-page bestseller *A Bridge Too Far*: to him, it was "a cavalry-to-the-rescue story—one in which the cavalry fails to arrive, ending, sadly, one mile too short." Once he had found this main idea, the rest was simple: "That was my spine, and everything that wouldn't cling to it I couldn't use."

Finding your angle is often a matter of narrowing your topic. A topic like "Sports" is far too general to produce an assignment. Narrowing it to, say, "Table Tennis" helps, but not enough. Often, reducing the story to a single dimension—focusing on a key person, place or event—gives you a salable angle. With further funneling of my "Table Tennis" idea, I found my slant: "Confessions of a Table Tennis Hustler," which I sold to *Gallery*.

When your subject is popular, you must present the editor with a fresh approach. One way to do this is to take an idea like "Overcoming Failure" and give it a 180-degree twist into "Failure Can Be Good For You." To use this approach, pick a topic like "In-Laws," and imagine a typical reader's first reaction: "Ugh!" Now, figure out how to reverse this reaction. Using the title "Enjoying Your In-Laws," I sold the piece to *Modern Bride*.

Another way to find a slant for your topic is to juxtapose two apparently unrelated concepts to create a fresh approach: In a recent article on "Revamping Your Office Image," I showed the reader how to use sophisticated marketing techniques to enhance office image.

Letting the *reader* suggest an angle is a third approach. Ask yourself, for example, what the Cosmo girl or the Penthouse male would like to learn about banking and finance. The answer is your slant.

Your angle need not be exotic in order to sell. A commonly used but effective approach might be summarized as "new and improved." This approach spices up an average idea by adding new ingredients—such as the latest research, hot trends, juicy gossip—and adds a dash of originality with unusual viewpoints, provocative questions or surprising solutions. A while ago the managing editor of *American Baby* bought two queries of this type: "Infant Psychiatry" and a piece on the controversy about plastic surgery for victims of Down's Syndrome.

If little or nothing has previously been written on your topic, you don't need much of an angle to sell. When I decided to write a query on "Pheromones," most editors had never heard of these natural chemicals that attract the sexes to one another. Though I had no special angle, I sold the piece on the first submission. With an original or offbeat idea, seduce the editor with your facts, not your slant.

A FEW WORDS ON SEDUCTION

While many queries can be written entirely from your own knowledge, a little research can pay big dividends in your query. Facts help sell editors on an idea. At *Omni*, senior editor Patrice Adcroft looks for queries with many specifics: "Don't just tell me that 'Last year millions of people suffered from yeast infections.' I want to know how many millions and why."

In doing your research, investigate both the topic *and* the markets you are aiming it at. According to senior editor Louise Tutelian of *Savvy*, a common reason for rejection is inadequate knowledge of the magazine. "*Savvy* differs from other women's magazines because it has a strong business focus. Reading the last six or eight issues will help you to understand us and our needs, as well as prevent duplication of recently published material."

SHAPING YOUR RAW MATERIAL

After you have the basic ingredients—the idea, the slant, the facts and the market—you're ready to write your query.

According to one editor I know, the best way to get an editor's attention is to "punch him in the nose and keep fighting until you hear the bell." He means that a good query starts strong, and never lets up until the editor is sold. In composing your query, keep in mind two newspaper dictums. The first, the five W's (who, what, where, when, why), reminds you to explain the story immediately. The second, the inverted triangle, emphasizes the importance of putting the most interesting information *first*. Don't save the best for last, or you'll have lost the editor's interest by the time it appears.

Your query should include three main sections: the lead paragraph, the summary and the author's bio. Each section has a specific purpose; as articles editor Julia Kagan of *Working Woman* says, "First, tell me what the story is, then why we should buy it, and finally who is going to write it."

HOOKING THE EDITOR

Your lead paragraph should have solid impact. This is your chance to audition before the editor, to give him or her a taste of your writing. A good lead not only helps sell the editor on the idea, but also can be used in the actual article. While many writers like to open with an anecdote, other effective approaches include: provocative quotes, surprising facts or statistics, references to celebrities or news events, wittiness or exaggeration, references to dramatic events or common situations with a new twist, vivid descriptions, thought-provoking questions, commands to the reader, unusual definitions, and surprising comparisons or contrasts. Here's how I've used some of these techniques in the first paragraphs of queries:

> *Though he may not be able to leap tall buildings in a single bound, 16-year-old Philip Marshall Hecht is considered a Superman of the comic book world. In just three years of buying and selling old comic books, the teenaged tycoon has turned $60 into $60,000.*

> *It's all very well for Melville's character to say "Call me Ishmael," but what's Mrs. Ishmael to do if, like so many of us, she uses her married name at home, and her maiden name at work?*

> *When asked just how you get rich playing table tennis, hustler extraordinaire*

Marty Reisman smiles and says, "First, you need a good racquet, then you need a lot of balls." Reisman has plenty of both.

While a magazine lead can—and should—be more creative than a newspaper's five W's lead, it must let the reader know exactly what to expect from the article that will follow. And, whatever lead you choose, remember that it must convey the tone—as well as the topic—of your proposed article to the editor. You're courting rejection if your lead promises a lively anecdotal piece, when you really intend to write a straightforward how-to article.

THE HEART OF THE MATTER

Once you've aroused the editor's attention with your lead, move directly to a summary of the article. This section of your query should convince the editor that you know where you want to go with the article; it should outline the points you plan to cover, or provide important factual information about your topic. As Louise Tutelian of *Savvy* puts it: "Show us you've already gone halfway down the road. Give enough facts, figures and details to prove that your story is real." In a recent query on genetic counseling, I handled the details this way:

Genetic disorders affect about 15 million people in the US, with 4 to 5 percent of babies born each year showing a detectable genetic disease. More than 3,000 such disorders have been identified, ranging from color blindness or a tendency to nosebleeds to such serious conditions as Tay-Sachs disease and hemophilia. Until recently, conception was a form of genetic roulette, but today medical genetics can . . .

Your summary should be succinct and clear. Here are two methods of presentation I've used successfully. For a simple idea, the flat summary will work:

My idea is "I Do, I Do!," a guide to double weddings: the etiquette, the logistics, from showers to ceremony, with a few interesting anecdotes (like the most double wedding ever, when twin sisters married twin brothers, with thirty-eight pairs of twins participating in the festivities) and quotes from ministers and other authorities.

For a more complex idea, the "bullet formation" might be preferable. In a query titled "Creative Failure," which I sold to *Glamour*, I described the main idea (that failure can be good for you), then listed some key points in this format:

● *Guilt-free Failure:* The importance of understanding that failure is normal and often necessary.
● *The Failure Fallacy:* How to steer clear of the debilitating belief that one failure will inevitably lead to another.
● *Creative Failure:* A program for analyzing your failures and using them as tools for future success.

• *Running the Marathon:* Why making the effort is often more important than coming out #1.

• *The Risk for Success Equation:* By increasing the possibility of failing, you can actually increase your potential for success.

Next, mention your sources. "Tell us who you'll be talking to," says Patrice Adcroft of *Omni.* "Are your experts just the guys who've been around forever, or are they on the cutting edge of today's technology?" Add any relevant sales points: news pegs, similarity to previous articles in the publication, points of particular appeal to the magazine's readers, significant dates that the article might tie into, and any other strong reasons to buy now. Then list any important nuts-and-bolts information the editor should have, such as projected word length, availability of photos or illustrations, and the amount of time needed to complete the piece.

Finally, always present in the summary a working title for your proposed article, but don't worry if you can't think of a brilliant headline. If your title makes the topic clear, like "Gardening Tips," it's good enough. From talking to editors, I have found that your own titles can be helpful (unless it is something ludicrous, like "The World's Greatest Article"), but the working title is often changed before publication.

SELLING YOURSELF

After you've sold the editor on the idea, start selling yourself as a writer. Many writers are overcome by modesty at this point, but there's no reason to be bashful. Editors expect a bit of sell in the bio—within reason. There's nothing wrong with saying, "I am highly qualified to write this article because . . ." if a convincing reason follows.

Start your bio with your publishing credits, if you have any. If the list is extensive, select the magazines most similar to the one you are submitting to, and any others that are particularly impressive. If you only have a few credits, list them all, regardless of how obscure the magazine, whether or not it's currently being published, or how long ago the article appeared. If you have only one credit, say, "My work has been published in *XYZ* magazine." And if you have previously published any similar articles, send tearsheets or photocopies as samples of your writing.

If you are unpublished, don't worry. You can emphasize other qualifications. For example, for *American Baby* magazine, having children might be your best qualification. "We often buy articles by parents," says editor Phyllis Evans. "Writing credentials are not important if you understand our reader."

Students in my writing class, most of whom are unpublished, are often unsure what qualifications to include when writing a first query. "I don't think I have any," one complained. After reviewing her professional and personal background, I pointed out that she had on-the-job writing experience as an advertising copywriter, that she was a former teacher (her topic was choosing your child's first school), and that she had three children in school. Unqualified? Hardly.

The ideal author's bio is short, but convincing. To compose it, look for relevant material from:

Your job: Does it involve any sort of writing or publishing? Or does it relate to your topic? What about former jobs? If your work experience is relevant, briefly describe it, mentioning your title (if reasonably impressive) and the name of your company.

Your hobbies: A passionate interest in your subject can be an excellent qualification. If your subject is "Profiting From Collectibles," and you've attended every stamp, coin and miniature show in the state for the past five years while building a library of 200 back issues of various collector's magazines, say so. If you can truthfully add that your personal collection, put together at a cost of $1,500, was recently appraised at $25,000, you've probably made the sale.

Your family: When appropriate, mention family members: "As the wife of an executive in a multi-national corporation, I have moved 17 times in the past five years, so I feel uniquely qualified to write 'Avoiding the Moving Day Blues.' "

Your personal life: If you have had personal experience with the subject, explain the connection: "After recently ending a live-in relationship, I have many insights on 'Surviving the Break-up.' "

Your education: If you hold an advanced degree (beyond a bachelor's) or have attended a particularly prestigious college, mention these facts in your bio. Also, mention any specialized training or courses taken in the topic you propose to write about.

If you have been the topic of an article or book that deals with your query subject, either send copies of the material, or name the publications you were mentioned in. Editors may also be interested in lectures or courses you've given, radio and television appearances, awards you've received, and other significant achievements. Throughout the query, avoid negative remarks like "I'm an unpublished author, but . . ."

After the bio, close with a sentence asking for the sale: "What do you think?" or "I'll be looking forward to hearing from you." Be sure your close is upbeat.

My query for *this* article closed with a simple, confident "I look forward to your reaction."

Obviously, the reaction was positive.

TO THE LETTER

Two formats are commonly used for queries. The letter query takes the form of a business letter addressed to a specific editor at the magazine. Or you can compose a brief cover letter to the editor, attaching your query material as a separate document. Each format has advantages.

The traditional method—the business letter query—seems more personal, since each query is a personal letter to the editor.

The two-document approach is better suited to multiple submissions (which many editors grudgingly accept these days), since you can photocopy the actual query material, and type a short, individual cover letter to accompany each copy.

If you are submitting the query to more than one magazine, be sure to inform the editor of that fact in your cover letter, and briefly explain how you would tailor the piece to the needs of that particular magazine.

When typing a query letter, either use your letterhead stationery, or type your name, address and phone numbers (home and office) at the top of the page. Single-space your query, following the standard layout of a business letter. If you choose to send your query material as a separate document, make sure your name, address and phone numbers appear on both your cover letter and your query. Your letter should be single-spaced, while the query material should be double-spaced.

Keep queries short and precise. While some editors recommend limiting the traditional letter query to one page, most are willing to consider two-page queries "if the topic warrants it." It's better to err on the side of being too short, though, as an interested editor often will ask for more material if necessary.

If you are submitting more than one idea to the magazine, write a separate query for each one: Different editors at the magazine might want to consider the different ideas.

Include a stamped self-addressed envelope (SASE); with rising costs, most magazines will not return material without SASE.

Two final notes:

Consider getting an answering machine if you are out a lot. If the editor can't reach you, you may lose the assignment.

Give the editor a reasonable period of time, about six weeks, before calling or writing about your query. If the idea is of interest, it may have to be reviewed by several editors, which takes time.

(A successful sample query to *Writer's Digest* appears on the following page.)

Mr. William Brohaugh
Writer's Digest

Dear Bill:

I'd like to write a piece on "How to Write a Selling Query and Author's Bio—Even If You Have No Credits at All." Here's how I'd handle it:

> How would you like to turn a few paragraphs into a profitable article assignment? A query letter, brief and to the point, can be your shortcut to sales. Not just for the experienced pro, queries can work for any writer. As a literary agent and writing teacher, I've seen queries produce writers' very first sales.
> Making queries work for you is a matter of mastering two skills: presentation of an idea and presentation of a writer—you. Here's how:

The article would then go on to cover, step-by-step, how to write your query and author's bio. Some main points:

● Grab the editor's attention. Tips on writing the lead paragraph, the 5 W's, the inverted triangle (say the most interesting thing first), other leads and examples.

● Give your slant. Examples of how to narrow the focus and make the idea specific.

● Outline the piece. The eye-catching "bullet formation" and other ways to make your description dramatic.

● Give a sales pitch. Ways to identify the best marketing points and use them.

● The nuts and bolts: include length, time needed to complete, availability of photos (optional).

● The author's bio. How you, too, can be an expert. Ways to toot your own horn, even if you think there is nothing to toot about.

● Formats for your query. Precise how-tos of the letter query and the cover letter plus separate query.

● How and where to submit your query.

Naturally, all this would be developed with much more detail, with examples from successful queries and bios, for both new and experienced writers.

As a writing teacher (I am a faculty member at Parsons School of Design, teaching "Magazine Writing") and a literary agent of more than ten years' experience, I have noticed that many people actually have significant qualifications (like the high school teacher writing on "when your child is having trouble in school") and never think to mention them. I will show how professional, personal, social, romantic, academic and other experience can be translated in the author's bio into "expertise." Also, I will try to convince readers to overcome their modesty and toot their horns loudly—it really works.

In addition to my publishing and teaching background, I have sold my own writing to many magazines and newspapers, including Harper's, Family Circle, Cosmopolitan, Glamour, Penthouse and maybe 20 others. If you wish, I could send clips of some of my published pieces, several of which deal with various kinds of writing.

I look forward to your reaction.

Sincerely yours,

BY JAMES MORGAN

The Secrets of Superlative Salesmanship

You're a salesperson with a hot idea to peddle. You know you're up against stiff competition, so you wrestle with the question every salesperson faces: When you call on the customer, what stance do you take? Do you come on with gimmicks and geegaws, or is your best shot the low-key, modest and dignified pitch? Do you give it the street-smart tough talk, or the eloquent, highbrow air?

Obviously, we're talking about writers trying to sell to editors, a case in which the query letter is usually the *only* pitch. As with any sales job, the object is to be in the right place at the right time with the right product. And the right presentation.

You may not always be able to control those first three "rights," but the fourth is entirely up to you. Some freelancers don't seem to understand that with every query letter they're trying to make a "double sale"; they're trying to sell *two* things—themselves and the idea. It's hard to say which is more important, but I can tell you that a lot of pretty good ideas get spiked because something in the presentation makes the editor think the writer just wouldn't be able to do the job.

With that in mind, here's a quick course in query-letter salesmanship. The first part focuses on selling yourself; once you have that down, you can move on to the business of selling your idea. As a wise editor I know says, "This ain't no science"; but if you take these suggestions to heart, I'm confident you'll up your chances of making that double sale the next time you write a letter to your target editor.

PART I: SELLING YOURSELF

If there's a theme to this first section, it's "Be yourself." A lot of freelancers don't seem to understand that.

Never Forget: Gimmicks Don't Work

Some writers decide they have to come on like the proverbial gangbusters, but from my side of the desk, they come *across* as kamikazes. One recently sent me a query letter that looked just like a summons. You can bet that it got my attention, but when I realized what it was—sort of the query-letter equivalent of pulling down your pants for attention—I wasn't even interested in reading what idea the writer was trying to sell. Once my heart stopped pounding, I suggested he take his appeal to a different court.

Another freelancer used to attach some personal item to his letter—an old college ID card, maybe, or a ticket stub from a recent rock concert. I recall even getting one of his expired passports. It worked against him: the stuff he attached was always more interesting than the ideas he suggested.

Remember that your query letter represents *you* to the editor; usually it's all he knows about you. If you're the kind of person who pulls down his pants to get attention in person, a gimmick isn't really a gimmick to you: It's your personality, and that's your problem. But too often a writer—sitting in the loneliness of his room with a terrific idea and a horrific sense of the competition—decides he has to give his letter that something extra so he'll stand out from the crowd. Most of the time it's not as overtly obnoxious as the mock summons or the passport attachments; it may take the form of a studied braggadocio, or perhaps a hohum, take-it-or-leave-it jadedness. Whatever it is, forget it. Quit posing and just be yourself.

Never Forget: Neatness Counts

Seasoned salespeople know that the first few seconds of a sales call are the most important. You should remember that, too. Anything you can do to project the total impression of taste, intelligence and personality will always work to your advantage. Unfortunately, the inverse is also true. Some of what follows may seem basic, or harsh, or even haughty, but the point is this: It's hard enough to sell an unsolicited idea to a busy editor; the last thing you need is for your own letter to join the opposition.

Type your queries. Editors believe that the only people who send handwritten query letters are convicts and amateurs, and if you're not in prison you have no excuse.

Keep your typewriter keys clean, don't send a letter with a bunch of erasures in it, and try not to get coffee cup rings all over the paper.

Speaking of paper, let me give you a big hint: Don't have reams of stationery printed up with your name in 14-point type, or in script, or with your name and the word *Journalist* coming out of a little picture of a typewriter. Remember what I said about gimmicks? For that matter, I'd leave off all those lines of affiliation—the ones that say you belong to various writing groups. I can't explain why, nor can I back it up with proof, but I've always felt that what those lines were *really* saying was, "Member of the Hack Writers of America."

Anybody who gets anything printed anywhere can join a writers' group, and such groups are useful for exchanging ideas, market tips or the latest Insensitive Editor story. But you're not likely to get an assignment because you belong to a writers' group; you'll get an assignment if all the stars are aligned right (more about that later), and if you sell yourself and your idea.

So, back to stationery—the simpler, the better; the simpler, the more professional. And if you're going to personalize your paper, the most professional personalization of all is simply your name—maybe not even your address—engraved very small in the top center of the page. You can type an inside address, and you can tell the editor how to phone you when you're signing off. It's a clean look; it says you're comfortable with who you are.

And why shouldn't you be? You're *obviously* someone of quality and good taste.

Be Conversational

I don't see much point in reading past an opening sentence that begins, "Enclosed please find," because even if the idea is good, I don't have any faith in the writer's ability to write it.

Think of your query letter as a letter to a friend, not one to your banker. Use contractions—say *I'll* instead of *I shall*. Let your sense of humor come out. It's the old "be yourself" theme again. This indicates that you're loose, that you're at ease sitting at the typewriter.

One of the most enjoyable correspondences I had at *Playboy* was with a guy who wrote me a letter that began:

Dear Mr. Morgan,

We are a nation preoccupied with looking good, and our list of bestsellers proves it: Linda Evans, Jane Fonda, Wendy Stehling, Covert Bailey, Charles Hix and Audrey Eyton this week ask us fit or fat?, tell us about beauty and exercise, warn us about flabby thighs, explain about diet, so we jog, run, fast, we play racquetball and handball and we dance aerobic, we sweat, starve, and pump dumbbells, we worry and woe over our girth. But none of it's free—there is a trade for looking good, and there is a trend that concerns me.

He was proposing a piece called "How to Look Smart," and his entire letter—slightly askew style and all—came across as a bright, witty conversation with somebody who was just being himself.

I'll discuss the use of big words and selected foreign phrases. . . . I'll list the facial gestures that smart people use. . . .

I *knew* I liked him when he typed his letter almost to the bottom of the first page, and when I turned to page 2, I found this:

. . . I'll discuss how much of a margin to leave at the first page of a query letter.

Did I give him the assignment? Well, no, and that's one of freelancing's hardest lessons (see "Timing Is Everything," to follow): We already had something similar in the works. I've no doubt that his piece would have been smarter and funnier than what we eventually ran, but I was already committed.

Still, his was an excellent query letter on many counts. He came across as a thoughtful person with a sense of humor, someone you like to get letters from. I can't emphasize it enough—the query is all the editor knows of you. As with the salesperson on his initial call, if you're witty and conversational, not stiff and uncomfortable, the editor/prospect is going to listen a lot more attentively.

Be Sure You Want the Assignment

Sound crazy? Maybe so, but I'm convinced that there are writers whose métier is the query letter: They'll blitz you with proposals, and when you finally give them assignments, you never hear from them again.

I think I understand what's going on with these people, because I was probably one of them myself—except for one crucial difference. Years ago when I was blitzing magazines like *Playboy* and *Esquire* with proposals for some very ambitious projects, I lived in fear that I would actually get an assignment. The problem was, I had a full-time job and a family that had dibs on my vacation time. There was no way I was going to be able to spend six weeks or two months doing a freelance piece—unless I stretched it out over two years, and what kind of editor is going to let that happen? I think I just figured I'd deal with the problem when it presented itself. And that leads us to the crucial difference I mentioned earlier—*I never got an assignment.* Just lucky, I guess.

Of course, there are some writers who don't deliver because they get themselves overbooked, or because they never learned to honor commitments. Others get writer's block whenever it's time to deliver the goods.

But mostly, I think the problem is with ambitious, well-intentioned people who work day jobs and freelance on the side. Some of them probably haven't come to terms with their situation—with the fact that they can't take six weeks to retrace Lewis and Clark's steps for *American Heritage* and still keep their company dental plan intact.

If you're one of those people, you should be straight with yourself, and with your editors. Before you send off a query, ask yourself two questions: *Do I really want to do this? If assigned, can I handle the assignment?* If the answer to both questions is an honest *no*, you'd better come up with a new article idea.

Or you can send the query and tell the editor you have an idea for a piece you don't want to write yourself. If the idea is unique enough (no, "a profile of Clint Eastwood" doesn't count), most major magazines will pay you an "idea fee," and assign the article to another writer. You may not get a byline, but at least you're being honest with yourself; and when the story that you *do* want to handle comes along, the editor—who by now has some respect for your judgment—will be much more inclined to give you a shot.

Include Your Credentials

While at *Playboy*, I once got a letter that began, "I am a correspondent in the Washington bureau of *The New York Times*. . . . Among my duties at the *Times*, I am in charge of covering drug enforcement and international drug trafficking. In the last year, I have written more than three dozen articles on the subject. . . ."

When he then said he wanted to interest me in a freelance piece on the subject of drug enforcement, I was already interested. This guy knew what he was talking about.

Part of getting an assignment is convincing the editor that you're the right person to handle it, and credentials pertinent to your particular article will help. These don't necessarily have to be "professional" credentials, such as the *Times* writer had; if you're suggesting an article on the Congressional aides of Capitol Hill, say, and you were once an aide, by all means say so. That could give you a unique perspective on the piece, one most writers wouldn't have. You're trying to create a situation in which, all other things being equal, the job will go to you.

But if you don't have an inside track on the piece you're proposing, you should still go ahead and list your general publishing credentials.

To the editor receiving your query, you're just a name with an idea—until he finds out that you've been published in other magazines. Send along a couple of copies of the published pieces you like best, or that you think are most like the style of the magazine you're pitching. But don't overdo it by sending the editor a copy of every piece you've ever written. Editors have lots of paper on their desks, and you want them to view your query as a nice, easy-to-read *letter*, not a daunting *package*.

In your query, jot a brief paragraph saying, "Incidentally, I've been published in _____, _____, and _____. I've included a couple of samples of pieces I'm particularly proud of. Be glad to send other tearsheets if you'd like to see them."

That does it—suddenly you're not merely a name with an idea anymore: you're a writer *other editors* have trusted, and apparently have been satisfied with. Of course, this isn't to say that you'll be ignored if you have neither credentials for your proposed piece *nor* prior publishing credits; the point is simply the one Joe Namath used to make—if you got 'em, flaunt 'em.

One postscript to this section: If you *don't* got 'em, don't propose high-blown essays on cosmic subjects. Every day I get a letter from some ordinary person like you and me, who may be a part-time freelancer, who wants to write an essay for *Playboy* on "How to Avoid World War III" or "What to Do About the Economy." *Playboy* is not a town meeting; when we—or any other major magazine, for that matter—want a piece on public policy, we go to someone who is *perceived* as having the credentials to comment on it.

You may be smarter on the subject than the person we hire, but those are the breaks—*he* has the credentials.

PART II: SELLING THE IDEA

OK, you've done your best to sell yourself, but that's only half the job—what about that hot article idea?

The successful freelancer thinks like an editor. He tries to figure out not just what the editor would say about a given idea, but *why* he would say it. And that means understanding what problems and pressures the editor faces. Bear that in mind as you read these next few sections.

Study the Whole Field

You often hear editors and journalism teachers telling you to read the magazine you're trying to sell to, and there's nothing wrong with that advice—as far as it goes.

But just as you're competing with lots of writers to sell an idea to an editor, that editor is competing with editors of other magazines in his field to come up with articles that appeal to the readers they share. You may not read the competing magazines, but you can bet an editor does, and if you send him an idea similar to something recently published in another publication, he's probably going to turn it down.

Playboy is such a wide-ranging magazine that there are lots of publications whose ideas we don't want to duplicate. I once rejected a proposal for a piece on Jerry Lee Lewis primarily because *Rolling Stone* had published an excellent article on Lewis a year and a half earlier. And a few years ago I rejected a profile on Carl Lewis (in the business, we call this tendency The Lewis Syndrome. Just kidding) because *Esquire* had run a cover piece on him just prior to the 1984 Olympics.

But those are negative examples of why you should read an editor's competition. One writer noticed how seriously other magazines were writing about a decidedly non-serious topic: The Power Lunch. He suggested we put things in perspective with a piece called "Beyond the Power Lunch," which includes such nonsense as power bath robes, power memo pads, and, for the power luncher who works in his yard on weekends, power tools. It's a contrarian point of view, and it sets us apart from that earnest herd of magazines that regards the power lunch as anything other than an opportunity for humor.

Read the editor's competition—and then tell him how to look smarter than the other guys.

Tell the Editor Why He Needs Your Article

A while back I got a letter from a writer proposing a piece on "The Fine Art of Cocksurety."

"Few things in life are more beautiful" he began, "than when some cocky SOB points his finger at the TV camera, jabs it at the viewer a few times to make sure we know who he's talking to, then declares in no uncertain terms, 'I am the greatest!' *And then goes out and proves it.*"

So far, I wasn't buying. It was an interesting enough notion, but I had plenty of interesting notions lying around. In what way was this one different?

"Americans," the writer went on to say, "have forgotten not only how to be cocksure, but why." This was post-Iran-hostage America, of course, and as the writer started making his case about a country *founded* on cocksurety and now not feeling it at all, I began to see the piece as more than just a light little bit of entertainment. It was that—it was *mostly* that—but the underlying subject was one that might touch a nerve. We ran the piece and got great response.

That writer was thinking like an editor. In his query letter he developed a rationale for me to buy his idea. He essentially told me that it was not only a timely idea but also a piece that readers *needed*. In these days of heavy hype, how many articles can you say that about?

Magazine editors want to reach their readers. If you can convince an editor that the subject you're proposing is one his readers are *going to want to know about,* you'll have a much better chance of making the sale.

Most of the time this rationale will revolve around timeliness and topicality. Don't suggest a piece on an obscure actor, for example, because *you* think he's terrific; give evidence that others are beginning to think so, too (editors all too often follow the herd instinct—e.g., the Power Lunch); quote various columnists, maybe, and include some information about projects this actor will be working on in the future.

That way, you're building your case—it's not just that you like this actor, it's that he's *going to be hot.* Translated, that means that the editor's readers are going to want to read about this actor.

If you want to explore the ramifications of some Congressional bill, you must show the editor that those ramifications will touch his readers' lives. You have to make a case for your article's *relevance.* Of course, the editor must decide whether your story is more relevant than another he's considering, and you may not win out. But at least you'll be in the running.

Pitch an Angle . . .

What's your angle? . . . besides selling your story, that is. A lot of writers (and—keep this quiet—editors, too) have a tough time distinguishing between a subject and an angle. The angle is what gives a piece its uniqueness, its edge.

Capital punishment is a subject; a look at capital punishment through the eyes of the executioners is an angle. The "war between the sexes" is a subject; a look at the burgeoning debate among psychologists over whether males or females are "more moral" is an angle. Business takeovers is a subject; a diary of a takeover by a participant is an angle.

Not long ago I received a letter from a man wanting to do a piece on child support. But this wasn't just any old piece on that subject (in fact, we already *had* a general article on child support sitting in inventory). This man was a writer only part of the time; during the days, he worked for a state child support enforcement unit collecting overdue child support payments.

But it was the way he viewed the job that jarred me. Here's how he started the letter: "Think of me as a hired gun, a hit man with a government salary. I don't do kneecaps, though, or litter the landscape with bodies. I don't take the lives of my victims, just their paychecks and bank accounts." Now *here* was an angle.

In the wrong hands, of course, this stance could have come across as one of those gimmicky ones I warned you against earlier. Here, though, it seemed to add a dimension to the piece—probably because this hired gun could also control his writing.

But it wasn't necessary for the writer and the child support collector to be the same person; any freelancer could have looked at the subject of child support—a subject of real interest to millions of people these days—and figured out that writing *about* the guy who collects child support would be a fresh angle.

Sometimes you can't find the angle to a piece until you've done some digging, but when trying to sell an editor, it behooves you to do that digging. Besides, the more you explore a subject, the more angles you may find—which means you may be able to get more than one piece out of a subject, tailoring different angles to different magazines.

Be Aware That Timing Is Everything

Ah, timing. Remember what I said about all the stars being lined up right?

Actually, there are two kinds of timing that will affect you when you try to sell a piece. The first you can do something about; the second you can't.

Selling a "seasonal" piece to a magazine editor is a little like shooting skeet—you've got to aim ahead of where the target is at the moment. If you have a boffo story about pro football, don't wait until kickoff to send your query. By the time the first regular-season game gets underway each fall, most magazine editors are already working on the next spring's issues. When a national election is a year or so away, start thinking political stories—because that's when the magazine staff is ready to consider them. We observe Christmas in July and Father's Day in January. It's a strange way to live.

But understanding a magazine's lead time is basic; the impact of timing on a magazine's story selection can be much more subtle. A magazine reflects the culture in which it operates, and that means that editors want to publish articles about subjects that will *interest* the readers *at the time they come out in print.* For that reason, books, movies and television are more than just entertainments for yourself; they are *events*, pegs for stories. Is it any wonder that I was barraged with MIA queries just when the *Rambo* movies and their clones invaded the theaters? Do you think it's coincidence that John DeLorean got grilled in *Playboy* at the time there were books coming out about him?

What does this mean—that you should subscribe to *Variety, Billboard* and *Publishers Weekly* (not to mention other publications that tell you what's going to happen)? All I can say is, many editors do. Think of it as investing in your own kind of commodities market: articles futures. Nothing makes an editor look more brilliant than being right on top of a trend; if you can convince him of the coming trend early enough, you'll look brilliant, too.

That's as good a spot as any for me to segue to my last point about timing. Some freelancers will undoubtedly think that if they send me a query with everything done just as I've suggested here, I'll automatically make them an assignment. Not so. Remember, you're a salesperson, and this is a market you're dealing in. And as with any market, there are variables you can't control.

Such as the editor already having a similar piece inhouse. Or the fact that he hates country music just when you've discovered The Judds. Or—and this is *really* inside stuff—that your query letter lands on his desk just when he's fighting a heavy deadline, or a hangover, and the last thing he wants is another decision with implications. A *no* is easy; a *yes* is asking for problems.

But that's not your fault. If you've done your sales job the best way you know how—and the tips I've outlined here won't hurt a bit—that's all you can do. If you get a rejection, don't take it personally. Remember, every salesperson will have his day.

Be Concise

I think it's past time for me to take my own advice here, but let me leave you with this: a one-page query letter is plenty. Instead of telling every bit of the story in the letter, choose those parts of it ("Tell the Editor Why He Needs Your Article") that will make him see the potential; tell him a little about how you intend to treat the subject ("Pitch an Angle").

And then offer to give him a longer outline if he needs it. Take it from someone on *this* side of the sales pitch—the query letter is sort of like those other pages in *Playboy*—less is often much, much more.

BY LARRY MILLER

How to Land Interviews with Busy and Famous People

I called Diane Sawyer twenty-seven times.

I was writing a piece for *Cosmopolitan* on how to get a job in television, and I needed to talk not only to Diane Sawyer but also to a lot of other famous and busy people. Not the kind who pick up the phone and say "hi," but the kind that have squadrons of secretaries and assistants to screen calls and keep them from being bothered by the public—and writers.

Getting through to these people to interview them often seems impossible, but it can be done. On the twenty-seventh time, Diane Sawyer came to the phone and I conducted a twenty-minute interview.

But why, you ask, *do I want to go to all this trouble? I can write a perfectly fine article without interviewing any famous people.* Believe me, all the hassle *is* worth it; quotes from celebrities and noted authorities give your pieces impact and authenticity. They help your articles *sell.* Readers love to hear from household names, and editors love to see these names in copy. And you'll sharply increase your chances of getting more assignments; editors are impressed by writers who can come up with material from celebrities. What's more, these writers are in a good position to bargain for more money for future articles.

THE STUBBORNNESS FACTOR

One technique for landing interviews with busy and famous people, as you can guess from the Diane Sawyer case, is using sheer, dogged persistence. But always remain polite, and make sure your tone is one of an appeal for help rather than one of exasperation or impatience. If you call enough times, one of two things will almost always happen. Either the VIP will say, "Oh, him again, let me talk to him and get it over with so he'll stop calling," or the secretary will say, "The poor guy's called twenty times, and he seems so eager—why don't you just talk to him?"

At the time, Diane Sawyer was co-anchor of *The CBS Morning News,* and her workday started at around 3 a.m. I knew that the closer she got to airtime, the busier she would get, so I set my alarm for 3:15. At that ungodly hour, I got out of bed, gave myself a few minutes to wake up, and dialed the newsroom.

"Diane Sawyer, please."

"She's busy right now," a woman, probably a news assistant, would say. "Who's calling?"

"Larry Miller."

Never identify yourself further at this point; just give your name in a confident, positive tone, as if you expect it to be recognized.

"From where?"

This is a standard question and a dangerous point. Don't reply "I'm not really from anywhere" or "I'm not with any company," and *never, ever* say you're a freelance writer. This implies that you have no assignment, no connections and no importance, that you are a dissolute and irresponsible soul (very far from the truth, I know, but unfortunately the phrase "freelance writer" still conjures up these impressions in most people's minds).

"I'm writing an article for *Cosmopolitan* that I need to talk to her about."

Note that I didn't specify the subject of the article. Never tell the person who answers the phone what you're writing about; this almost always elicits the response that someone else would be better suited to talk about the topic or that Ms. X doesn't want to discuss it. Sticking to just "an article" will pique curiosity, which is precisely what you want. If you're pressed, say the subject is complex and technical and you really need to talk to Ms. X about it.

The phrase "for *Cosmopolitan*" is also crucial; it is not inaccurate in the slightest, but it implies that you're on the staff of the magazine. If people want to draw erroneous conclusions when you've told them the truth, it isn't your fault. But don't give them too much time to think about it. Follow up immediately with "What would be the most convenient time for her?"

"Well, there's no really good time, but she's usually less busy right around now."

"OK, I'll try again tomorrow, if that's all right. I don't really mind getting up this early."

The assistant laughs; now she is suddenly on my side. Interrupted sleep is something everyone can identify and sympathize with. "OK, if you want to try. Bye."

During the next few days I got up at the same wee hour and tried again. But Diane Sawyer was always "busy." Finally the news assistant took pity on me and told me that Sawyer sometimes hung around after the show until 10:30 or 11 and that I might try then.

I did call at around 10:30 for two solid weeks, sometimes twice a day when I was told that Sawyer was still in the studio, but she was never available. But of course I got to know the dayside news assistant, and finally, on the 27th call, the assistant told me: "She is around somewhere. Let me try to get her on the phone—you've been so persistent you deserve to talk to her."

Success! Diane Sawyer came on the line and said, "Hello, Mr. Miller." She had heard my name so many times by now that she felt as if she almost knew me. She was helpful and patient, and I got good quotes. *Cosmo* ran her picture with the article, and all the effort turned out to be worth it.

CONNECTIONS

It's not always necessary to go to such lengths. Another effective technique, though sometimes almost as time-consuming, is to use all your friends, acquaintances and other connections until you finally hit someone who knows someone who knows your target. I used this approach on the same article to get to Carol Jenkins, the NBC reporter. A friend knew somebody who knew somebody who worked at NBC, and by invoking the name of the friend of this employee I was able to get Carol Jenkins' home telephone number.

Getting a home number gives you a tremendous advantage, because you don't have to work your way through the protective guard of assistants. And since most celebrities have unlisted numbers that are given out to very few people, they don't hesitate to pick up the phone themselves. Many have answering machines, but you can usually avoid these by calling when you think the person is likely to be home, such as early in the evening. If you get a machine, leave only your name and number; don't say what you want. And keep calling back until you get a response.

Publicity and public relations agents will usually help you get home numbers, especially if you can cite an assignment from a national magazine or major newspaper. Appeal to the desire for exposure; fame gives a celebrity power and profit, and fame is like money—there's no such thing as having too much. If your subject has written a book, you'll find that publicity directors at publishing companies are especially helpful at putting you in touch.

This preliminary research will also point you to the celebrities you want to interview. Information sources to begin tracking down famous folks include *Reader's Guide to Periodical Literature*, the subject volumes of *Books in Print*, and, perhaps most crucial of all, *Who's Who in America*, which lists home and business addresses for just about every noted person. Trade and professional organizations and talent agents are also good sources.

And occasionally finding a phone number can be surprisingly easy: I wanted to interview Gay Talese for another *Cosmopolitan* piece. When I called his publisher for his home number, I was told, "Look in the phone book." And there it was: Talese, Gay. A man's voice answered and I asked if Mr. Talese was there; he said, "This is Gay Talese" and proceeded to spend almost an hour with me. Make the phone directory your first stop.

BASE OF OPERATIONS

Although as a freelancer you have little power, using the power of your publication can be enormously effective. When I worked for *The New York Times*, I would call for interviews and be told that Mr. X was in conference and asked who was calling. I would reply, "Larry Miller from *The New York Times*," and the response would be instantaneous: "Oh, just a moment, please, Mr. Miller, and Mr. X will be right with you." Even though you many not be on a publication's staff, say, "I'm doing an article for *Boys' Life*"—or *Parade* or *Sport* or whatever the magazine or newspaper is. Ask your editor if you can identify yourself as a contributor or regular contributor; this sounds impressive and to most people implies that you're on staff. And stress the fact that the article has been definitely assigned, that you are not merely prospecting. When I called Dr. Joyce Brothers for an interview, her response was frank: "Is this an *assignment* from the magazine? It is? OK, I'll talk to you."

Of course, you can use these techniques only if you *do* have an assignment. Don't say, "I'm writing an article for *The Monthly Megabook*" if you only plan to send the article to that publication when it's finished. If the celebrity calls the magazine's editor and asks, "Is Mr. X working for you? He called me today" and the editor has never heard of you, your career with that publication is over before it has even started. As a general rule, never work on speculation, because that's not the way to become a successful freelancer. But if you insist on writing without assignments, you obviously can't use assignments as a wedge to get celebrity interviews.

Remember that the phrases "he's in conference" or "he's in a meeting" are almost always automatic responses and almost always untrue. Ask when he will be free or where you can reach him; being persistent in a very courteous way gets across the impression that your call is important and that you really need to talk to him. (I don't recommend saying "I'm returning his call"; it's sometimes effective in getting your subject on the line but can backfire if he's certain that he didn't call you.) But if you're told, "He's on another line," you've hit the jackpot; ask or even beg, if necessary, to hold on, and wait as long as it takes.

MESSAGE CENTER

If you've ever worked in an office, you know what happens to telephone messages for a busy person; they pile up quickly. Often a VIP never even looks at all the messages, or they're divided by a secretary into two batches—those from people the VIP knows and may call back and those from unknowns who don't have a chance in the world. There are only three ways to get around this: using the technique of persistence and winning the secretary's sympathy that we've already discussed, leaving a message that will pique the VIP's curiosity, or getting yourself into the "known" stack.

A message that will arouse your subject's curiosity will depend, of course, on his interests, which will either be obvious or become clear in your preliminary research. Either forge a link between these interests and your topic or lead into your topic after the conversation is going well.

Getting yourself into the "known" stack is often surprisingly easy if you use what I think of as the "familiar approach." You call the celebrity's office and say, "This is James Smith calling for Ed," in a tone and manner that indicate you've known Edward G. Notable for years.

When the secretary says Mr. Ed Notable is not available, you come right back with, "Could you ask him to call me, please?"—*without* giving your number, to leave the impression that Mr. Notable knows it or at least has it in his Rolodex. And almost always the secretary will say, like the conscientious person he is, wanting to save his boss the small trouble of looking it up, "Could you give me your number again, please, just to make sure."

When you use this "familiar approach," you are not deceiving anyone—you never actually say that you even know Mr. Notable. You do not say anything untrue. This approach carries a great potential for misuse; to keep it within the bounds of standard and accepted procedures, you must scrupulously refrain from pushing it too far or actually saying that you know Mr. Notable.

But I've found that this approach, used as described, works nine times out of ten. The famous meet so many people that they can't possibly remember them all. Occasionally, however, when Mr. Notable does call you back he will say, "Do I know you?" Don't try to apologize or explain; simply say, "No, sir, but I was very interested in getting your views on" whatever your subject is.

Never say that you're "doing an article on such-and-such"; come at the subject indirectly in a way that will interest the interviewee without turning him off. Later, after the conversation is well launched, you can ease into your specific questions.

And what if none of this works? There is a last resort—write a letter. Mark it "Personal and Confidential," send it by Express Mail, and appeal to two things: the desire to help another human being and the desire for more exposure. Composing such a letter is a good way to test and strengthen your writing ability. Don't enclose a self-addressed envelope, but do include your phone number.

And tell yourself that if you become famous, you'll go out of your way to help other writers.

BY JOHN BRADY

Popping the Questions

> *REPORTER*
> *Glad to be back, Mr. Kane?*
> *KANE*
> *I'm always glad to get back, young man.*
> *I'm an American. (Sharply) Anything else?*
> *Come young man—when I was a reporter*
> *we asked them faster than that.*
> > *—Citizen Kane shooting script*
> > *Orson Welles,*
> > *Herman J. Mankiewicz*

Interviewing is the modest, immediate science of gaining trust, then gaining information. Both ends must be balanced if the interview is to be balanced and incisive. Yet they are often fumbled in the anxious heat of an interview. The interviewer will either yearn too desperately for his subject's trust, and evoke flatulence, or he will restrain his sympathies, demand data—and get like in return.

Much depends on popping the right questions. It is the only way to persuade the specialist (your subject) to accept and feed the ignoramus (you).

"It is impractical to know something about everything," says Robert Wells of the *Milwaukee Journal*, "although that would be the ideal preparation for your career. But if you know enough to ask the right questions about as many topics as possible, you're doing pretty well."

"Mr. Wells puts it mildly," retorts Neale Copple in *Depth Reporting*. "If the reporter knows the right questions to ask, he has an unbeatable edge on the competition."

When he asks the *wrong* questions—the snide, the vacuous, the tasteless—he is in for an edgy interview. Take those hungry television newsmen, who seem compelled to match the stomach-churning impact of a Minicam shot with a stomach-churning quote. Nora Ephron tells of working side by side with TV reporters, and watching "in dismay as the cameras moved in and the television reporter cornered the politician ('How do you feel about the vote, Senator?') or cornered the man on the stretcher being carried out of the burning building ('How do you feel about the fact that your legs were just blown off, sir?'). . . ."

HOW DO YOU FEEL?

In his fine collection of TV writings, *Living-Room War*, Michael J. Arlen elaborates on the proliferation and uselessness of the "how do you feel" school of broadcast interviewing:

I mean, the 'how-do-you-feel' stuff would be okay if it led anywhere, if it were something people could respond to . . . but in a professional interview what it really amounts to is a sort of marking time while the reporter thinks up some real questions, or maybe while he hopes that this one time the Personage will actually include a bit of genuine information in his inevitably mechanical reply, which the reporter can then happily pursue.

Arlen maintains, and rightly I think, that "How do you feel?" is either ridiculous—"Well, Archduke, how does it *feel* to have been shot three times in the thigh and shoulder?"—or unanswerable except for occasional mumbles and vapidity:

Or, to put it another way, if time is running short, and you have cornered the man who has just thrown the convention over to Oscar W. Underwood as a result of having brought up 117 votes from the State of New Jersey during tea- time, "How do you feel?" or "What's your reaction?" might be fairly far down toward the bottom of a list of the thirty-seven most useful questions you might ask him at that point. In these circumstances what in hell is anybody going to say except "Well, Buzz, I feel real good."

Arlen envisions the ultimate in "how do you feel" journalism:

Sometimes . . . I have this picture of the last great interview: The polar icecaps are melting. The San Andreas Fault has swallowed up half of California . . . The cities of the plain are leveled. We switch from Walter Cronkite in End-of- the-World Central to Buzz Joplin, who is standing on a piece of rock south of the Galápagos with the last man on earth, the water rising now just above their chins. Joplin strains himself up on tiptoe, lifts his microphone out of the water, and, with a last desperate gallant effort—the culmination of all his years as a TV newsman—places it in front of the survivor's mouth. "How do you feel, sir?" he asks. "I mean, being the last man on earth and so forth. Would you give us your personal reaction?" The last survivor adopts that helpless vacant look, the water already beginning to trickle into his mouth. "Well, Buzz," he says, gazing wildly into the middle distance, "I feel real good."

WELL, I FEEL PUT UPON

Often the thin question is the offspring of thin research. "I don't mind doing *in- terviews*," rock star Ian Anderson told Colman Andrews. "But I don't like answering questions such as 'How'd you get the name Jethro Tull?' or 'How many of you are there in the group, and which one of you plays the flute?' In a country like Japan or New Zealand or Australia, where we've just been on tour, people ask these questions because they're genuinely curious, and they don't have access to a tremendous amount of information. But I shouldn't have to answer those questions here. Jethro Tull has been around a bunch of years. We answered those questions the first, second and third time we toured here. All the facts about us are available in this country, because there are lots of press hand-outs here—which were done at *my* request to make life easier for me. So I shouldn't have to waste time answering those kinds of questions."

Worst of all, the careless interviewer may draw the weary, all-too-obliging subject. "Some of the media ask questions that are not really questions," says baseball superstealer Lou Brock. "They're requests for confirmation of opinions they have going in. They've already written the answers in their minds and what they want from me is reassurance. I'll give it to them to keep everybody happy, if it doesn't go against my conscience."

KNOW WHAT YOU WANT TO KNOW

The thoughtful interviewer works in an open, critical spirit. He does not judge his subject; he waits for his subject to judge himself. An interview often depends less on questions than on one's spirit of questioning. Fragmentary research and clumsy, sore-eyed questioning will convince the subject that his interviewer is uninterested. And he'll clam up. The good interviewer is deeply interested, of course—but he is also disinterested. He is a conduit for his readers.

And he fashions the interview in the interests of his readers. If he is writing for the *Cincinnati Post,* he may ask his subject about the future for open education in Hamilton County. If he is writing for *Harper's,* he may want to know about open education's hopes nationwide.

Above all, the interviewer knows exactly what he wants to get from his interview. He is like a chess player; he does not move a piece—or ask a question— without a purpose, a plan.

"When you start asking questions," says Dr. George Gallup, the famed pollster, "the other person immediately wonders, 'Why does he want to know?' Unless your purpose is clear, he may be reluctant to talk, or he may seize the opportunity to tell you all about his problems."

ARRANGING YOUR QUESTIONS

How many questions should the inteviewer prepare? That can vary dramatically—from a lone question to flesh out a minor statistic in a business story (usually done by phone) to an array of hundreds of questions scattered over days or weeks for a *Playboy* interview. Generally, the more questions the writer prepares, the more thorough his interview and story will be.

Some believe the professional interviewer should memorize his questions, like a CIA agent who memorizes his instructions, then puts them to the torch. But it seems more sensible to keep handy a list of essential questions, lest one forget. It's incurably human, and embarrassing, to come away from an interview with an opera singer with some terrific, unexpected material about her child-hood—but nothing about her current production.

Don't strip mine in an interview—dig deep. The temptation to cover *every-thing* yields only a blurry interview studded with intriguing, but isolated, tidbits. Devise your angle, and build your interview around it.

Check with your editor; he may have an angle in mind. Omer Henry tells of one editor who had heard of a firm that was using a new wage-incentive plan for its mechanics. "He wanted to know how the plan worked. Knowing exactly what this editor wanted, I was able to draft a set of questions, the answers to which gave me the facts I needed to write and sell the article."

Meticulously arranging your questions can be deranging. "The list of ques-tions and the logical sequence invariably disappear very quickly," notes Edward Linn. "If they don't, you're in trouble." Even so, a good interview is sensibly structured. It begins with easy, rather mechanical questions; shifts to knottier, more thoughtful questions; moves back out with mechanical questions (favorite writers, future projects) and closes with a query that offers a ring of finality (one effective question: how would you like to be remembered?). If the interview has logical structure—a sense of beginning, middle and end—it will have emotional structure as well. The interview as a whole will have an impact that exceeds the sum of its parts.

The interview outline need not be dictatorial, or detailed, or even committed to paper. It can be a single, tacit purpose. In fact, the simpler it is, the better. It is only a device to give the interviewer confidence, and his questions, momentum. It gives the interviewer the reins of the interview.

KNOW YOUR FUNNELS

The interview outline may take two shapes: one, like a funnel, and the other, like an inverted funnel.

The *funnel-shaped interview* opens with generalities—"What are the benefits of nuclear warfare, Mr. President?"—then pins down the generalizations— "When and where has it produced those spectacular sunsets that you mention?" It appeals to the thoughtful, creative interviewee, because it allows him some say in the direction of the interview. Freelancer Edward Linn opens each topic with a broad question "so that the subject can take it in any direction he wants. If you make each question too specific, too direct, too narrow, you run the risk, I think, of ending up with an article that reflects your own preconceptions; an arti-cle that you have written in large measure before you leave home. If the guy I'm interviewing takes that opening question and goes off in a direction that never oc-curred to me, I figure I'm way ahead; I'm finding out what interests *him* most, rather than what interests me."

The wide-open question not only gives the interviewee room to breathe; it gives the interviewer room to grapple. Alex Haley says he's interested in ab-stract questions because "I value being able to go to the subject almost ignorant of him. Then, I have a feeling I represent more nearly Mr. Average Reader who doesn't know much about this person. I want to meet him, form an impression of him—which I hope will be fair, honest and accurate—and try to communicate this to the reader. I have never known anybody beforehand."

Open an interview with a question as broad as the Dakota hills, though, and your subject may cut you off at the pass. Hal Higdon once started an interview with, "Why don't you tell me a little bit about what you've done?"

"If you don't know," retorted the subject, "what are you doing here?"

Adds Higdon: "It took me about ten minutes before I recovered and steered the interview back onto safe ground."

Sherlock Holmes would have been fond of the *inverted-funnel interview;* it opens with hard, fast, specific questions, then ascends to more general ground. It's effective for interviewing that frankest and most baffling subject—the child. He may be stymied by a wide, world-weary question like, "Are you ambitious?" unless the ground is broken by specific questions like "Do you try to make straight A's in school?"

"A child may not be able to say, 'I dislike the authoritarian personality,' " says one veteran child interviewer, "but, if asked which teachers he likes and which he dislikes, he will be able to say."

The inverted-funnel technique makes getting answers from a former IRS agent as easy as taking candy from a baby, as Max Gunther found one wintry day in New York.

"When I walked into that interview, I wanted that ex-agent to tell me everything interesting that had ever happened to him in his tax-collecting job," recalls Gunther. "But how could I get him started? I *could* have asked a vague, general question: 'Has anything exciting ever happened to you in your IRS job?' But I didn't. It was too broad."

Instead, Gunther asked the revenuer to itemize: "When you were auditing people's tax returns, did anybody ever try to bribe you?"

"That question wound him up—in fact, very nearly overwound him," recalls Gunther. They talked for four hours. "I barely asked another question the whole time, and I came out of the interview with a wealth of fascinating material about the inner workings of IRS. My broad question—Did anything exciting ever happen?—had been fully answered without my asking it."

When shrewdly handled, the to-the-quick question can convince the subject that the interviewer speaks his lingo. A. J. Liebling, a legendary and acerbic journalist, said that one of his best preparations was for a profile of jockey Eddie Arcaro. Liebling brought some horse sense to the interview: "The *first question* I asked was, 'How many holes longer do you keep your left stirrup than your right?' That started him talking easily and after an hour, during which I had put in about twelve words, he said, 'I can see you've been around riders a lot.' "

How do you know whether to bet on a funnel or an inverted-funnel interview? Generally, if your subject is at home with words and ideas, lead him out with an open, general question. If he is ill at ease, make him comfortable with a question about the concrete, the easily explained.

The interviewer can establish rapport with open questions, then strengthen it with closed ones. The open question is like an essay question on a test: It gives the subject his head. "What do you think of Women's Liberation?" does not suggest a "yes" or "no" answer. It suggests an opinion; and the flattered subject would be hard put to withhold his.

The open question produces generalities, though, which are not enough to carry the story. In nonfiction, generalities whet the reader's appetite; he must be sated with anecdotes, details, hearty facts. So the interviewer must follow up an open question with closed questions—"Could you give me an example of that?" "What do you mean by . . . ?"

GETTING ANECDOTES

Insist on anecdotes, although the subject may seem more comfortable spinning generalities. If he says, "I owe my forty years of marriage to absolute understanding and compatibility," ask him, "What do you mean by understanding and compatibility? Can you give me some examples?"

Follow-up questions do more than secure specifics—they brace rapport. They indicate that you are genuinely curious about the subject's life and charred times. With sufficient rapport, the writer can even get away with a hard-bitten closed question. An interviewer asked George Frazier, the late and stylish columnist for the *Boston Globe,* "Which comes first—friendship or work?"

"That's phrasing it a little harshly," replied Frazier. He paused. "I make no bones about it. I'm a lonely man. The column precludes friendships."

A quote like that resurrects Frazier more acutely than a half-page of recitations in *Who's Who in America* ever could. "Your purpose in conducting an interview is partly to get facts," says Max Gunther, "but you also want color; you want anecdotes; you want quotes; you want material that will give readers an impression of the interviewee's personality."

Gunther gains color by structuring his interview loosely. He asks a few questions to get the interview rolling then sits back and allows the subject to tell his own story, at his own pace. Meanwhile, Gunther looks around. "If everything goes well, the starter questions wind him up like a clock, and I quietly fall back from the status of questioning to that of listener. If he omits some area of subject matter that I want to hear about, or if he explains something inadequately, I resist the temptation to interrupt him. I wait until he winds down, then wind him up again by asking the questions he has left unanswered."

One key word will incite anecdotes: when. "When did you realize you would need open-heart surgery?" Like a slow pan in a movie, "when" takes the subject to a scene, a setting, and thence to a story. The reporter's four other W's, of course, are also solicitors. "Where were you when you heard John F. Kennedy had been shot?" "Who told you your house was on fire?" "What are some of the most unusual questions children ask about sex?" "Why did you run away from home on Christmas Eve?"

"One way of obtaining anecdotes is to recite an anecdote you have already collected on the subject at hand," suggests Hal Higdon. "Often the person you're interviewing will respond to this challenge by trying to top you with a still better example." It may be unwise, however, for *you* to attempt to top your subject's anecdote.

The writer should never lose sight of The Definitive Anecdote, which he instinctively knows will give his article a rousing beginning or a thoughtful ending. "Quite often, in the course of interviews about a subject, a writer will stumble upon the single telling anecdote that either sums up the character or illumines one facet of it compellingly," wrote Richard Gehman. It may occur to him as soon as the research has begun, or during a follow-up phone call after the research has effectively ended. No matter. "If that anecdote 'feels' right," said Gehman, "he ought to write it at once and put it aside for later use."

DUMB IS SMART

To elicit eye-opening anecdotes—or eye-opening anything, for that matter— the interviewer does not have to impress his subject, to put on a natty and knowledgeable front. In fact, he may well learn that playing dumb is not dumb. "Stupidity is a reporter's greatest asset," said Cornelius Ryan. "Don't be afraid to say, 'I don't understand.' You'll be amazed at the help people are willing to give, once they know you are being honest with them."

And you may pay later if you feign understanding. "For fear the news source will think they are dumb or especially thick-headed, many beginning reporters fail to ask enough questions, even though they don't clearly understand what has been told them," says John P. Jones. "In such cases they may learn by bitter experience that the dumbest thing they can do is return to their office with unanswered questions in their minds."

When a subject rambles or is unclear in his answers, draw him out by putting the onus on yourself: "I'm sorry, but I don't understand"; "That's not quite clear to me. Could you give me an example?" If he still fumbles, move on to another topic, and try the original question later, from a different direction. Don't make the subject feel he is unable to get his point across, no matter how hard he tries.

Toward the end of the interview, if you still need an explanation of a certain point, volunteer a summary of what you think your subject has said, and ask him to correct you.

OPENERS CAN BE CLOSERS

Innocuous, even trivial questions at the outset can put the subject (and interviewer) at ease. "A human being likes to stick his toe into water that isn't cold," Red Barber once said. "I always start with a pleasantry."

On the other hand, people who are busy, and who are likely to be interrupted by business during an interview, often prefer that the initial question get right to the point.

Regardless: Nobody likes a smart-aleck—not even a professional smart-aleck. A *Rolling Stone* writer showed up for an interview with Don Imus, whose radio show is called *Imus in the Morning*, with dirty Levi's and a risky opener. "Imus in the morning," he said, "I want you to meet Sidney in the flesh." "It was downhill from there," recalls Imus.

The premeditated quip betrays a wily, merciless enemy of any exchange: the interviewer who is out to steal the show. He hangs out in multitudes at 1600 Pennsylvania Avenue, according to Dr. Joyce Brothers, who says this about Presidential press conferences:

> *Far too many of these questions are thought up on the way to the conference not for the purpose of getting information but in order to put the President on the spot or the reporter himself in the spotlight.*
>
> *Even before he asks a question, body language betrays the newsman more interested in impressing the television audience than in pressing for information. He beams when the President calls him by name. He smiles broadly, squares his shoulders and adjusts his tie. These are the body signals of someone about to make a speech. And that is often what he does, under the guise of asking a question.*

Dr. Brothers adds that at a televised press conference, questions weigh in at fifty words apiece, and are rarely related to the previous query. "When there are no cameras around, questions average fourteen words and tend to develop one subject until probed in depth."

LESS IS MORE

Which is not to say that hot camera lights alone spawn the filibuster question. It breeds wherever the interviewer gropes aloud, or is determined to hold the floor, and is mindless of the Law of Diminishing Returns: the longer the question, the shorter the reply.

And there is a point of no return. When one reporter persisted in asking George C. Marshall involved questions, Marshall said "Would you mind repeating what you have just tried to say?" If you *must* ask a complicated question, and the subject seems puzzled, never ask, "Did you understand that?" Instead, ask "Did I make myself clear?" You don't want to seem condescending.

Keep your questions short, even if unsweet. If your question requires background, give it to your subject as concisely as possible, then keep your question short and separate from that pack of facts. "Busing means that thousands of white students will be attending predominantly black schools. (Pause.) How will you recruit those students?"

Don't short-circuit your interviewee: Ask him one question at a time. I once asked Gay Talese a long-winded, two-part question in the midst of a discussion of celebrity interviews. "Sinatra is known as a man who is not very cooperative with journalists," I began, "and you say in your introduction to *Fame and Obscurity* that DiMaggio started to cooperate with you on the profile you wrote, then had a reversal. When this happens—when you run into someone like Sinatra who is insulated from journalists, or when you run into a reluctant subject like DiMaggio—how do you get in there close enough to do the story anyway?" Ouch.

"Let's take the Sinatra one first," began Talese—and, of course, the discussion of DiMaggio was bypassed. A two-part question is often like a baseball pitcher wasting a pitch: A discriminating batter just won't go for it.

LEADING THEM ON

As the pitcher must peel off each pitch with studied skill, the interviewer must pick his words with care. The power of suggestion is too easy to trigger by a blunt or loaded phrase. Pollsters do not ask "How old are you?"—which invites a Jack Benny fib—but "What year were you born?" or "What is your date of birth?" Name-dropping may also color a reply. In 1940, when Charles Lindbergh was unpopular in America, the American Institute of Public Opinion asked subjects, "Lindbergh says that if Germany wins the war in Europe the United States should try to have friendly trade and diplomatic relations with Germany. Do you agree or disagree?" Forty-six percent agreed. The same question with "It has been suggested" replacing "Lindbergh says" garnered 57 percent agreement.

It is best to plan the wording of key questions with care. Few interviewers leave the wording to the spur of the moment; under battlefield conditions, the interviewer's prejudices may be irrepressible. If you are doing a story on a possible strike at the local pet food factory, you will have to interview some of the employees who might abandon their duties—and the Alpo generation—if union demands are unmet. You will want an untainted cross-section of opinion, because ultimately the decision to strike or not to strike will depend on the members' vote. A simple, carefully planned question like "Would you go on strike if a call is issued?" should do the trick. But a Johnny-on-the-spot interviewer with a secret sympathy may blurt, "As a member of the union, you would be obligated to go on strike if a call were issued, wouldn't you?"—which stops just short of answering itself.

That is, of course, a leading question, i.e., one that suggests the answer in tone, inflection or phrasing. The leading question may be more statement than question: "You don't care a fig about Roger Ackroyd, do you?" "Dr. Livingstone, I presume?" An interviewer who likes to lead when he asks may do so by merely using the definite article "the" rather than the indefinite "a": "Did you see *the* body?" instead of "Did you see a body?" is provocative.

Exactly what the leading question provokes may depend on the rapport the interviewer has established. A subject tiring of the interview may blurt something he does not mean; and an edgy subject may say something he means all too well. In a terse, talk-to-my-agent interview with Warren Beatty, Rex Reed began a question, "Well, then, would you say —"

"*No!*" Beatty cut in. "I wouldn't say. I only say what *I* say."

Alfred Kinsey, the D.A. of sexual research, was a proponent of leading questions, preferably served up in rapid-fire fashion. "The interviewer should not make it easy for a subject to deny his participation in any form of sexual activity," he wrote. "We always begin by asking when they first engaged in such activity."

When they are not gracefully abandoned, however, leading questions can deteriorate from bulldogging to badgering, and produce nonanswers. Consider this exchange between Theodore Irwin and *Playboy*'s Hugh Hefner, in *Cosmopolitan* magazine:

Irwin: At what age do you believe a woman becomes undesirable to men?
Hefner: There's no such age.
Irwin: At what time? At what stage in her life?
Hefner: It simply doesn't exist. In other words, it depends on the woman and it depends on the man.

Yet leading questions can also lead to lively, pointed quotes. Here's Hefner again some years ago in a robust bout with Mike Wallace.

> Wallace: Chicago *magazine quoted you to the effect that sex will always be a primary ingredient of the magazine. Isn't that what you're really selling— kind of a high-class dirty book?*
> Hefner: *No, I don't think so at all. There's an important distinction here. Sex always will be an important part of the book, because sex is probably the single thing that men are most interested in . . . we think that's a healthy way to be. But I would estimate that no more than five percent of any issue of* Playboy *is concerned with sex, and we seem to be devoting an entire half-hour program to it here tonight. . . .*
>
> Wallace: *What's wrong with the muscular men's magazines?*
> Hefner: *Nothing at all. I think—*
> Wallace: *What's wrong with outdoor sports? With hunting and fishing and he-man adventure?*
> Hefner: *Not a thing. But I felt there was a good-sized male audience that was a little more interested in urban living—in the nice things about an apartment, hi-fi—wine, women and song. And these are the things that* Playboy *concerns itself with.*

The leading question requires a subject with a sense of spirit and fight—and an interviewer with a sense of timing. When injected into a touch-and-go exchange, it may disrupt rapport. But in secure surroundings, it may spark a surprisingly honest answer. The difference, perhaps, is in whether the subject sees his interviewer as closed-minded or simply unpersuaded. The success of the leading question—and the success of much of interviewing—is a matter of trust, of rapport.

OFF ON A TANGENT

Although the interviewer is in charge of the interview, there are times when he should follow his subject's lead. Following a tangent, for instance, is often more productive than trying to rein the subject back in. NBC's Red Barber once asked superslugger Willie Mays if he spent much time in the batting cage taking practice.

"I asked him this as the first question," recalls Barber, "just to start things smoothly. All players, even pitchers, love to hit. They won't give their mothers a swing in batting practice.

"I counted on Mays smiling and allowing as how he certainly did, and that this would break the ice and get us going. Instead, he replied to the effect that he hit well, so he didn't fool around the batting cage much, but spent his time working on what he didn't do 'good.'

"Well, we went on from there, for suddenly he had put his finger on one reason he is a star—he works on what, as he put it, 'I don't do good.' That remark opened up a fine interview." Follow that tangent.

FOLLOW-UPS

Following up on a tidbit the subject dangles before you can also yield fine quotes. In a *Playboy* interview, Howard Cosell referred to Curt Gowdy as "the best play-by-play announcer in the business," then added, "Don't ask me who I think is the best color man in the business."

"Howard, who do you think is the best color man in the business?" asked the interviewer.

"Thank you for not asking me," said Cosell. "I really believe *I'm* the best, for I have sought to bring to the American people a sense of the athlete as a human being and not as a piece of cereal-box mythology. My relationship with the men who play the game—*all* games—is probably unparalleled in this country, and I bring information about them to the public."

One of the most potent follow-up questions is a nonquestion: the Sympathetic Noise. "You feel very strongly about that, don't you?" "Sounds like you had a tough time of it, cleaning barrooms." On its face, the Sympathetic Noise may seem to do little but stall the subject until the interviewer can think up a *real* question. Actually, it takes account of the fact that subjects, like human beings at large, are cautious soul-barers; they are reluctant to confess until they have proof positive that their interviewer is sympathetic. (Then they are all too willing.) The Sympathetic Noise—which is often simply reinforcement, or a gentle rephrasing of what the subject has just said—can unlatch a torrent of anecdotes and naked quotes.

The late William J. Lederer (coauthor of *The Ugly American*) once told his interviewer, Frank Ensign, of "some little thing I had done."

Ensign lifted his eyes with surprise. "Honest?" he said enthusiastically. "Did you do that? Gee, that's wonderful."

Reflected Lederer: "I thought, here's a guy who understands my problems. I shot off my mouth for two hours, telling him things I never planned to tell him."

SURE-FIRE OPENERS

You can also persuade a reluctant interviewee to change his plans by feeding him a Day-in-the-Life question. "Whenever I sense that the interview has hit an unresponsive snag and I am stuck with an inarticulate interviewee," says Mort Weisinger, "I resort to a gambit which has worked wonders. I simply say, 'Mr. Jones, could you describe to me what you do on a typical day in your life, from the moment you get up until going to sleep at night?' Brother, does this question move mountains!"

Even small talk can move mountains. A tired, almost trivial question can pry open the soul of a politician, for instance, if it hits home. "Ask him how he handles the risk of disappointment when campaigning for office," advises Barbara Walters. "We've all wanted something desperately, but only the daring or the tough try for it so publicly. Ask him about the pressure on his family to be model people because all eyes are on them. Ask him if he was a leader when he was a small boy. Ask him what taught him the most about succeeding in life. Ask him if politicians with opposite views ever become close friends. Ask if he feels an obligation to be trim, neat, and barbered at all times. Ask him if he can manage the time to have a hobby. Ask if he has a hero."

SOUNDS FROM SILENCE

Don't interrupt your subject, unless his house is burning or you are running out of time. Barbara Walters, who is not too shy to cut into a subject's ramblings if time is short, introduced Mercedes McCambridge on the *Today* show as a fine actress who once had been an alcoholic. "Not *was* an alcoholic," said McCambridge. "*Is* an alcoholic." She then delivered a moving monologue on her battle with the bottle, consuming the entire time slot. At the conclusion, Walters spoke for the first time since the introduction: "Thank you, Miss McCambridge."

Silence is golden as an interviewing technique. "The single most interesting thing that you can do in television, I find, is to ask a good question and then let the answer hang there for two or three or four seconds as though you're expecting more," says Mike Wallace. "You know what? They get a little embarrassed and give you more."

Silence by omission can elicit information perhaps impervious to the most pointed query. Kap Monohan, a drama critic for the *Pittsburgh Press,* once heard a rumor that Clara Bow—the "It" girl of films—was going to retire at the height of her popularity to marry and raise a family. When the head of Bow's studio came within Monohan's range, the writer boned up on his man and requested an interview.

"How are Patti and Connie?" Monohan asked as they shook hands. The man's face lit up at the mention of his granddaughters.

Then Monohan ticked off the names of the stars the man had discovered—purposely omitting one.

"You forgot Clara Bow," the studio head said. "You've heard about her retiring, I guess?"

"Oh, yes, but that's a lot of hooey—press agent stuff." Monohan tried to change the subject, but his subject was insistent.

"If you think she's not quitting, you're crazy," he finally said. "She is."

By the end of the interview, Monohan had a world exclusive on Clara Bow—without asking a single question about her.

TAKING STOCK QUESTIONS

Finally on follow-up: pursue the details, but don't run them into the ground. "If you make a man stop to explain everything," wrote A. J. Liebling, "he will soon quit on you, like a horse that you alternately spur and curb."

Some subjects, of course, curb themselves at the drop of a pretext. You: "How do you spell your last name:" He: "Talk to my lawyer." This is the Difficult Subject. He is stingy in stories and spirit. He requires special handling.

Often the Difficult Subject requires no more than an open-minded interviewer. "Interviewers are like actors," Warren Beatty, notorious as an impregnable subject, told Lawrence Grobel. "An interviewer can ask you a cliché question, but you can tell what he's either capable of hearing or what he's really searching for by his inflections. You can almost tell physically what someone is going to intend to do to you by his face, his body type or his body language. And most interviewers have their story written when they show up, and they want you to do something to prove they're right or to fill it in for them."

Celebrities are often drained by the persistent, yapping pack of stock questions. "It's always the same old stuff," laments Ava Gardner. " 'Tell us about the dancing on the table tops. Tell us about the bullfighters. Tell us about Sinatra.' God, haven't any of them got any imagination at all?"

Maybe not. But they do have team spirit. Billie Jean King: "Before the Riggs thing I had 300 people who wanted exclusive interviews. And each of them wanted at least a few hours. So, a few hours times 300 was ten years as far as I was concerned. That's the trouble. And when you interview all the time, people keep asking you about your feelings. How did it feel to do this? How did it feel to do that? I want to get away from it. I want to get out of myself."

Moral: Know thy subject—and know her/his predicament. Avoid prime-time interviewing—the first days after an Event, when the subject is waylaid by cameras and clamor, when he will dispose of interviews like Colonel Sanders shoveling out chicken parts. Avoid questions that leap too easily to mind; they have leapt to too many minds before.

Concentrate on the celebrity not as a celebrity, but as a human being. That is a novel angle, for the celebrity as well as the reader. And it produces. *Boston Globe* columnist Bud Collins tells of the cold, morose night at a deserted Toronto race track in 1961 when he and George Frazier combed the barns for Floyd Patterson. The heavyweight champion was hiding out before his bout with Tom McNeely.

"Floyd was as talkative as Mona Lisa," recalls Collins. "But George, wincing at the strains of Mantovani from Patterson's record player, got the champion talking. About music. About jazz when he spotted a Charlie Parker album. . . . George, who had known Parker and began to tell stories about 'Bird,' got the album on. 'Repetition' was playing. Floyd dug the strings behind Parker's sax. He talked. We both got good stories."

Whimsy works, as Barbara Walters found when she interviewed Sir Laurence Olivier. She had recently taped an interview with Lord Lambton—a member of Parliament who had been caught in bed with two women—when she went to see Olivier. "I knew Sir Laurence was a shy man, hard to interview," recalls Walters in her excellent *How to Talk with Practically Anybody About Practically Anything*. "So when I met him I said, 'Sir Laurence, I'm afraid I didn't have time to write my questions, so I'm going to ask you all the questions I asked Lord Lambton.' He burst out laughing, and everything went fine after that. We spent the day together. He talked about his childhood, his insecurity. And he finally read a Milton poem. It was a love poem, and I looked at his wife and there were tears rolling down her face.

" 'Are you crying?' I asked, and she said, 'I always do this when he reads.' "

SURE-FIRE, GUARANTEED QUESTIONS (MAYBE)

Walters once revealed to *The New York Times* her five "foolproof" questions for the over-interviewed:

> 1. *If you were recuperating in a hospital, who would you want in the bed next to you, excluding relatives?*
> 2. *What was your first job?*
> 3. *When was the last time you cried?*
> 4. *Who was the first person you ever loved?*
> 5. *What has given you the most pleasure in the last year?*

Walters says that question three is "an especially good one for comedians. They're hard to interview because you're always the straight man."

When the *Times* asked Walters how she would answer her foolproof questions, though, she demurred, "Uh, well . . . I don't think I want to. It would take too long to think of some good answers." (Which may confirm that the most difficult interviewees are often interviewers.)

Walters' foolproof question #1, and many similar icebreaker questions, are hypothetical. And the interviewer skates at his own risk.

Walters recalls the time she asked Prince Philip of Great Britain if, in the event England elected a president, he would have enjoyed being a politician. Philip replied, without warmth, that this was a hypothetical question, which he normally didn't answer.

"I was crushed," says Walters, "but I learned a valuable lesson about talking to people in very high places: Avoid the hypothetical question, of the sort that usually begins 'What if . . .' and then departs into some fanciful situation that never happened and never will. That type of question can be asked of creative people, for whom imaginary situations are intriguing, but practical, crisp people dismiss it as a waste of time."

When the subject is inventive and in the mood, however, hypothetical questions are fecund. Kenneth Tynan asked Richard Burton, "If you had your life to live over again, would you change anything?"—a question that is as worn out as vaudeville. But Burton's reply was fresh and revealing: "I'd like to be born the son of a duke with 90,000 pounds a year, on an enormous estate. . . . And I'd like to have the most enormous library, and I'd like to think that I could read those books forever and forever, and die unlamented, unknown, unsung, unhonored— and *packed* with information."

Tynan's *Playboy* interview ended, in fact, with a string of hypothetical questions:

> Tynan: *You meet a man at the end of the world, and he asks you three questions which you have to answer spontaneously and immediately. The first is: Who are you?*
> Burton: *Richard, son of Richard—for I am both my father and my son.*
> Tynan: *The second question is: Apart from that, who are you?*
> Burton: *Difficult, devious and perverse.*
> Tynan: *And the third is: Apart from* that, *who are you?*
> Burton: *A mass of contradictions. As Walt Whitman said, "Do I contradict myself? Very well, I contradict myself. I am large, and I contain multitudes."*

There are multitudes of hypothetical questions, most of them of the office party strain. Some that may work in the rare, playful interview are:

> *What three books (records, movies, Presidents) would you take with you if you were stranded on an island?*
> *If you were fired from your present job, what sort of work would you undertake?*
> *If you could live any time in history, what age would you choose?*
> *If you could be anyone you wanted to be today, whom would you be, and what would you do?*
> *If someone gave you a million dollars, how would you spend it?*
> *If your house were afire, what would you grab on the way out?*

Such questions may not set an interview on fire—particularly with a Difficult Subject—but they should elicit an irreverent, penetrating detail which will enliven your article. Of course, you can gather such sparks with more direct and realistic questions. Mrs. Dorothy Schiff, publisher and editor-in-chief of the *New York Post*, once suggested these human interest questions:

> *What person influenced you most in life? What book, if any? What do you do for relaxation?*

What was your greatest opportunity?
What do you believe about people—can they be changed for better or for worse?

Indeed, a question about beliefs can be an intriguing icebreaker. "One thing I have found out is that almost any person will talk freely—such is human frailty—if you ask him the measure of his own accomplishment," said John Gunther. "One effective question is to ask a man what he believes in most; I have collected an interesting anthology of answers to this."

Above all: Ask. Pursue the blind alleys; voice your human—as well as professional—curiosities. Ask intriguing, innumerable questions, with enthusiasm and only civil restraint. In the end, interviewing is less a technique than an instinct. An interview is simply a lively and thoughtful conversation. The more life and thought you invest in your questions, the more answers you'll get.

BY L. PERRY WILBUR

Draw Your Readers In with Titles

Titles are the calling cards of your articles. They are most useful for catching the reader's attention. Learn to come up with fresh and appealing titles and you'll give your article writing much more chance of being successful.

TITLES ARE HEADLINES

Think of titles as headlines for your articles. You'd be surprised how many readers check over only the titles of the articles in a publication before deciding which ones to read. I do it myself. It's only natural to want to read first those articles with the most interesting or promising titles.

TITLES MAKE PEOPLE BUY

Dynamic titles captivate readers and can make them so eager to read a given article that they start the piece on the spot, even before they've paid for the magazine or newspaper. Many magazine buyers buy because of the title interest alone. It may be something curious, compelling, or newsworthy indicated by the title. The better the title list, the bigger the magazine sales.

Editors will sometimes change a title because they want the strongest one possible. A title may change any number of times, right up to an article's publication deadline. Strive to write a title that grabs the reader. It's hard to do this consistently, but it's worth the effort. Over a period of time, training can help you attain more sales.

STRONG TITLES

Here is a list of some effective titles. Look them over and see if you think you could improve them. Place a check-mark beside those you especially like, then ask yourself why they appeal to you.

"How to Watch TV Without Losing Your Mind"
"Why Do Fat People Eat So Much?"
"The Lure of Faraway Places"
"The Amazing Psychic Powers of Doc Anderson"
"How to Handle Blue Mondays"
"Horror Movies Are Hot Again"
"Frightening Facts About Fat"
"The Superwoman Squeeze"

"The Things You Learn After You Know It All"
"The Marines Who Beat the Odds"
"Buying and Selling a House: The New Rules of the Game"

HOW TO CREATE FRESH TITLES

One of the best ways to come up with a strong and fresh title is to read the finished article over several times. You can often derive a good title from the material itself.

1. Look for key phrases in the article that seem to sum up what it's about.

2. Stay alert at all times for snappy lines, short and to-the-point questions, expressions, and sentences that seem to sparkle and leap out at you. Any of these can originate one or more good titles.

3. Practice examining the titles of already published articles to see how you might word them. You can also borrow the idea behind a title and express it in fresher words. A title cannot be copyrighted. You have free rein to experiment with those you come across for your own articles. It would not, however, be good practice to use exact titles already published. Editors might rightfully frown on this. Strive instead to come up with your own original and strong titles.

I once wrote an inspirational article on the deep meaning of Christmas. I wondered how to treat the birth of Jesus in a fresh way. After much thought and several attempts at a beginning, I hit upon an effective analogy. I began the article, "It was fifteen minutes past midnight. Not far from five beaches lay the greatest fleet of warships the world had ever known." I went on to describe the courage, bravery, and fear of June 6, 1944 (D-Day), when the Allied forces invaded Normandy.

After finishing the D-Day description I wrote the following paragraph:

"There was another day on which an invasion took place. There were no warships in this invasion, no guns, no thousands of men waiting to land on a beach. This invasion had a Supreme Commander too—a Supreme Commander of love. His invasion sign was a star of faith, hope, and redeeming love. The entire armada in this invasion was the birth of a child; a child named Jesus who became a man."

I wrote the entire 1,500-word article before coming up with a title. After completing the article, I read the entire piece through several times and let my mind wander. Eventually, the best and strongest title I could've hoped for hit me—"Earth's D-Day."

MORE TITLE TIPS

Here are some useful pointers for creating more effective titles for the articles you write:

Don't worry if you complete an article without a title. There's still time to come up with a good one. Reread the material and think about it. Should you fail to get a title you like, it sometimes helps to put the article away for several days, but to continue thinking about the material you have written. When you look the article over again, you may find that you know just the title to give the piece.

Titles may be short ("Speak Out") or long ("An Effective Way to Save on Your Food Bill"). Long titles can work well. Articles published in newspapers often use them. Long titles may be used to create a novelty effect or grab attention because of the sheer length. Generally speaking, however, most writers agree that a title shouldn't be too long.

Question titles are sometimes good attention grabbers. Here are some examples: "But Do You Inspire Your Employees?"; "Why Make a Marriage Encounter?"; "Can You Really Trust Your Lawyer?"

Don't be too quick to settle on a title idea. Unless you're absolutely convinced that you've chosen the best possibility, see what other alternatives you can create. When and if you find it hard to choose alternative titles you've created, test them by seeing which ones keep popping into your mind. Visualize the titles in published form at the top of your article. Which ones stand out and look most inviting on the screen of your mind? You can also test your title ideas on friends or relatives.

TITLES LEAD TO ARTICLES

A lot of writers begin an article only when they have a strong title in mind. I once wanted to do an article about the amazing versatility of Thomas Jefferson. I didn't have a definite title in mind, so I used a dummy title (a temporary title) while working on the piece. The substitute title I wrote at the top was "The Incredible Versatility of Thomas Jefferson." This wasn't a bad title, but I felt I could come up with a stronger one. About halfway through the 2,000-word article, it suddenly dawned on me that a fine title for the article would be "The Genius of Jefferson." And that's the title that appeared above the published article in *PHP-International* magazine. Don't rule out doing an article simply because you don't have a four-star title for it.

AN IMPORTANT EXTRA PLUS ABOUT TITLES

Staying alert for titles can add to your cash profits in article writing. How can you do this? One way is by reading your old articles from time to time (those you haven't sold yet) and giving them fresh new titles. Professional writers do this all the time. In other words, if an article won't sell under one title, another one may be just what's needed to click with the next editor.

You should make a definite point of resubmitting your unsold articles every now and then. Give each one a new title and send it to a new market. The results of this step will certainly increase your article sales and overall profits.

TITLES ARE OFTEN FUN TO WRITE

Since a title often sums up the entire idea and scope of an article, there's a continuous challenge to come up with high quality ones. Many writers find this title game most interesting.

You may find in time that you've become a title collector. No matter where you go or what you do, your mind will be alert to any and all possible title ideas for future articles. Many will be useless to you, but you're certain to come up with a number of gems if you keep at it long enough. I've been saving and collecting titles for over fifteen years.

Another way to stay alert for titles is to review the list of the various kinds available:

Shock titles
Surprise titles
Command titles
Question titles
Punch line titles
Alliterative titles
Statement titles
Dramatic titles
Place titles

Trick titles
Catch-phrase titles
Musical titles
Short titles
Long titles
VIP name titles
Sad titles
Happy titles

POINTS TO REMEMBER

• Titles are the labels, headlines, or calling cards of your articles.
• Magazine buyers often read the list of article titles before deciding whether to buy.
• Key phrases, snappy lines, pointed questions, and other ideas in your articles can lead to an effective title.
• A title cannot be copyrighted. Titles of existing articles can be paraphrased, updated, and otherwise changed into new titles.
• A good title can suggest itself after the article has already been finished, but the title comes first (or fairly soon) for many writers.
• It's a good idea to come up with several titles for an article and choose the strongest.
• Writing fresh titles for old articles (those you haven't sold yet)—can increase your sales and profits.

BY MICHAEL J. BUGEJA

Making Your Article Leads Sparkle

The writer, like the salesperson, has only so much time to close a deal. So if you want to peddle your prose to an editor, you had better make your pitch fast—in the lead of your article.

The pitch delivers the first impression of you and your work, and if yours is wordy or trite, the editor will react as you might with a gabby salesperson: *sorry.* . . .

To sidestep that, you must recognize several varieties of lead problems. The no-frills newspaper-like lead is a good device to show common weaknesses and the ways to overcome them. Hang all the ornaments and accessories you need on that basic frame, and your feature or nonfiction lead will succeed.

IMPROVED FORMULA

The lead is the eye-catcher of an article. In it, you present your best piece of information in the "hot spot"—the first ten words.

Improper Beginnings

Begin your lead with a proper noun, and you bore the reader:

The Department of Game, Fish and Parks reports that winterkill has spoiled what some anglers hoped would be a banner year for bass at area lakes. But a little help from hatcheries can ease the problem this spring.

When you put the news in the hot spot, the lead thaws:

Winterkill at area lakes has spoiled what some anglers hoped would be a banner year for bass. But a little help from hatcheries can ease the problem this spring.
The Department of Game, Fish and Parks. . . .

Greater Definition

A salesperson would not make a pitch by defining the product—"A vacuum is a device to clean carpets"—and neither should you. The typical "definition" lead is as exciting as a dictionary:

The American Agriculture Movement is an organization of hundreds of family farmers who want to have a say in US farm policy.

Such methods belittle the reader because the leads begin at square one. Worse, they don't inform. The reader takes note when you perk your lead with news.

Farmers who recently returned from protests in Washington are bouncing atop tractors again at harvest, but woe to the politician who tries to take them for a ride.

The Preceding Has Been Brought to You by . . .

Akin to the definition lead is the "background precede"; information that's timely and factual but too weak to lead into a feature. Too much emphasis on the time element can kill a story, especially if it is intended for a magazine:

Vocational Education Week, Feb. 12-18, is being recognized by the three vo-tech facilities that serve county students.

When you rewrite or edit such a lead, look to the second through fifth paragraphs in the body of the story for lead material. Put the "background precede" high in the article, but obscure the time element:

Students who do poorly in the classroom but who work well with their hands often gain confidence in their potential at area vo-tech schools, county educators say.
 Vocational Education Week was recognized this winter by the three area vo-tech facilities.

In each of these revisions, the writer wants to keep us reading just as a salesperson wants to keep us listening. Dull material is excised from the hot spot.

BETTER PACKAGING

Sometimes, however, an otherwise salable story may arrive in unattractive wrapping. . . .

Say What?

The "say-nothing" lead is as alluring as a plain brown wrapper. This type of lead promises much but delivers little, usually only the topic of the story:

The reorganization of the telephone company has caused some interesting rate changes in long-distance calling.

To test if you have a say-nothing lead, read the first paragraph aloud as a broadcaster might and then stop (a tactic Chevy Chase often used for laughs on the mock news segment of the old *Saturday Night Live*). A say-nothing lead will sound humorous because it is woefully incomplete. Usually, the real lead will emerge in the second or third paragraph of the original story. Adapt it for a lead:

The best times to call long distance are listed by the telephone company in the current directories. Yet that information actually may increase your monthly bill, because rates have been affected by the recent reorganization.

Brand X

More incomplete than the "say-nothing" is the "label" lead, usually one word. Manufacturers cut costs when they tag generic labels on their products, and writers cut corners when they resort to this type of lead:

Violence.
  A problem that affects nearly 20 percent of dating couples, says a nationally known sociologist.

Writing one-word leads is easy because the reader does the brainwork, imagining the range of possible meanings. Typically, a label lead produces another fragment that the reader must connect with other information for meaning. To correct this problem, make the fragment an appositive and look lower in the story for more material to complete the sentence:

Violence, a problem that affects nearly 20 percent of dating couples, ranges from shouting to rape.
  Dr. Brenda McKinley, a nationally known sociologist, . . .

Amazing Stories

Sometimes the wrapper is so colorful that we question the quality of the product. Simply, the claims on the label are too amazing for belief. This occurs with leads that overreach:

Oklahomans are eating so much these days—and dying because of it—that soon nobody will be around to do the cooking, doctors say.

Apart from being clever, this lead exaggerates fact. The writer who misleads his reader is as crooked as a salesperson who bilks his customer. No lead, no matter how astounding, will salvage a story. Play it straight:

Too many Oklahomans are fat and unhealthy, no longer dying from old age as their pioneer forefathers, but from heart attack and stroke, doctors say.

Keep the reader in mind and you will overcome problems with boredom, brainwork and misinformation.

A NEW LINE

You will also succeed by avoiding clichés and tired expressions, which no writer should pitch to an audience.

Wearisome Prose

The weary salesperson wastes our time. So does the writer weary of his topic. Nobody would read an article that begins:

Well, it's done.
*   At a gathering in the local Holiday Inn, Sister Mary Teresa won the million-dollar lottery that everyone has been making such a fuss about.*

Such leads tell us more about the writer than the topic. Moreover, they do not convey truth—what it felt like for the person who experienced an event. Leads that focus on human interest capture our attention:

Sister Mary Teresa considered it gambling, but she kept the lottery ticket her father gave her last summer. Now she's a millionaire who plans to give her winnings to Catholic charities.

Questions and Answers

Readers anticipate the next word in a sentence, the next turn of phrase. If you surprise them—exceed their expectations—they become excited about the topic. But if you express ideas in customary ways, readers say: "I've heard it all before." Editors who see "question" leads have heard them all before:

What do you do if one day the federal government tells you it intends to confiscate the land your family has farmed for five generations so it can build a lake?

The question begs a silly answer: "Bury toxic waste in your fields." The reader anticipates a punchline, which eliminates the element of surprise. You are forced to switch from the second person to the third person in the body of the story. To fix this, combine the best elements of the question and punchline. Keep the lead in the third person:

When the government evicted Tom Hadley to build a lake on land his family farmed for five generations, he went to court—not to keep the acreage but to haggle for a price.

MORE POWERFUL INGREDIENTS

Occasionally, the writing itself is the stumbling block of a lead.

In Reverse

You must sell the subject of your story quickly and creatively. You can't afford to back into the lead:

He's known by many names: "The Hunting Hero," "Mr. Deer," "Joe Williams."

*If he isn't the finest hunter in Oklahoma, then he is as close as one can
get. . . .*
This is a man who only recently held a rifle for the first time.

If you seem to be backing into your lead, resist the urge to create a new top
and scan the second through fifth paragraphs of your story. Often you will find
sharp sentences you can combine for a lead:

*If he isn't the finest hunter in Oklahoma, then he is as close as one can get.
Not bad for a man who until recently never held a rifle.*

Mixing It Up

When writers try hard for a creative lead, they usually rely on metaphors.
When they rely too heavily on metaphors, they usually mix them:

*Would-be tycoons made thousands of requests this year to drill oil wells in the
state, each hoping to sprout a gusher-producing derrick but no one struck
gold.*

You can't compare one object—oil derrick—to two others—plants and gold
mines—in your lead. If you must use metaphor to create your lead, be consis-
tent. Use words in keeping with the idea you are trying to sell to an editor:

*Drillers hoping their wells would spout gushers made thousands of requests
this year for state permits, but each bid came up dry.*

Sometimes experienced writers pitch leads so well that they (and even copy
editors!) take them for granted. Here's a lead that contains strong verbs typical
of good writing, but nevertheless could use some final touches:

*Earthen scars concealing ten miles of new waterline now snake through a
Cherokee village south of Oklahoma City. Creeping along, it sidles up and
bumps to a stop at the house where Sarah Walkingstick lives with her daughter's family.*

In the above example, an "earthen scar" cannot snake, creep, sidle, and bump
without mixing metaphors. Also there is subject-pronoun disagreement. All,
however, are relatively easy to touch up:

*An earthen scar concealing ten miles of new waterline snakes through a
Cherokee village south of Oklahoma City. It coils to a stop at the house where
Sarah Walkingstick lives with her daughter's family.*

PARTING SHOT

After you rewrite your lead, make sure the rest of your story is as polished
and lively. A good lead cannot guarantee a sale, but a bad lead can lose one.

BY LORENE HANLEY DUQUIN

Setting a Good Example

When you learned to add, a teacher probably wrote $1 + 1 = 2$ on the blackboard and then showed you that 1 apple plus 1 more apple equals 2 apples. The teacher was using apples as an example to make an abstract concept seem real and interesting. It was better than just telling you $1 + 1 = 2$. It was showing you.

You use this same powerful tool when you incorporate examples into your work. Examples answer the questions: *How? Why? When is that the case?* They create pictures in readers' minds.

Good examples can be analogies, real-life anecdotes, or fictional scenes. They also can be a specific sample of something that explains or elaborates on what you're trying to say.

Let me give you some examples.

• An *analogy* likens one thing to another, which helps the reader understand your point. For instance, when you create an analogy to explain the human heart, you could say the heart is like a pump. I used an analogy in an article for *Mothers Today* to show how a babysitting co-op works:

> *A babysitting club can work like a savings account. But instead of money, members deposit the number of hours they spend babysitting and they withdraw hours when another member babysits for them.*

• An *anecdote* is a short, real-life narrative, which illustrates the point you're trying to make. I used the following anecdote in an article for *Modern Bride* to illustrate my point that men and women can have strong personal preferences on something as mundane as bath towels:

> *Sheila and Bill had to compromise on their bath towels, for instance. He liked a slightly rough, textured towel that stimulates the skin, while she preferred the soft, terry velour towels.*

• A *fictional scene* is a short, made-up narrative that illustrates your point. It is usually written in the second person, and places the reader in a "let's suppose" situation. I created this scene in an article for *Campaigns & Elections* as an example of how endorsements can hurt a candidate:

> *For example, if you are endorsed by the local senior citizens' lobby in a race for a school board seat, your opponent might go to the PTA and say, "This man's endorsed by the very people who consistently vote against school budgets."*

• A *sample* can be one or more aspects of something that will elaborate your point. In an article for *Seventeen* on how to run for class office and win, I used the following sample to show the kinds of high-contrast colors that work best on campaign posters:

> *For example, black lettering on a pale-pink background has higher contrast than yellow lettering on a white background.*

LIVELY WRITING

In addition to helping your readers understand, good examples can make your writing come alive. Several years ago, I wrote a dramatic narrative for *McCall's* about a little girl named Shanda Baldwin, who slipped into a deep coma after she had been accidentally poisoned with carbon monoxide. The doctors couldn't predict when or if she would wake up. The family had to wait and see. In my rough outline of the story, I wrote:

> *Shanda's grandfather didn't like the idea of just waiting to see what would happen. He thought the family should talk to Shanda and try to wake her up.*

When I went back to the transcript of my interview with Shanda's grandfather, I found that this former dairy farmer had used a powerful example of how he had dealt with sick animals on the farm when he talked about trying to wake Shanda up. Look at the difference adding Warner's example makes:

> *The uncertainty bothered Shanda's grandfather. A former dairy farmer, Albert Warner remembered when his animals were sick and he had to nurse them back to health. "A sick calf can't tell you what's wrong, but you don't give up trying," he told Linda, "and you don't give up trying to comfort it. I think we should talk to Shanda and try to wake her up."*

FINDING EXAMPLES

There are two ways to find examples—from first-hand sources and from second-hand sources.

• First-hand sources are the people you interview. Whether you're talking to an expert, a public relations person, a victim or a friend, look for colorful descriptions, anecdotes and analogies that will enliven your writing.
• Second-hand sources are books and newspapers, television and radio programs, public relations information, and magazines and newsletters.

First-hand sources are *always* preferred.

Chances are you'll never get the opportunity to listen to a professional writer conduct an interview. If you could, you'd find that the writer constantly asks for examples throughout the interview.

Here is an excerpt from an interview I conducted with psychologist Warren Keller for an article I was researching for *Working Mother* on why it's important to get to know the parents of your children's friends.

Keller: I feel very strongly that it's important to know the parents of your children's friends because there's a strong tendency in children to adopt the value system of their parents. The strategy of getting to know the other parents will depend on the age of the children.

Me: Can you give me some examples for working mothers who have young children?

Keller: Working mothers. It can be more of a problem for working mothers because they're not home as much and probably don't have as much opportunity to meet the parents. It does take time to get to know the parents of your kids' friends, and everyone's short of time but I think there are some very simple things a parent could do. For example, if you're home on a Saturday, you can invite parents in when they drop their kids off or you can stay for a few minutes to talk when you drop your child at a playmate's house. You can also seek out other parents when you attend school or community functions. Even introducing yourself over the phone is better than no contact at all.

Me: Can you think of anything else working parents could do?

Keller: Well, they could take their child's friend along with them on a family outing. Spending that time with your child's friend is going to tell you a lot about what that child is allowed to do and how things operate at his house. The child has probably adopted the value system of his parents.

Me: Adopted the value system of his parents? Can you point to an instance where that could be a problem?

Keller: Well, it's going to be a problem if you have a different set of rules for your child than the friend's family has. Or you might suspect a problem such as an alcoholic parent and you might decide you don't want your child to play at that friend's house. Or maybe you find the kids aren't being properly supervised. There's nothing wrong with exerting some control over your child's relationships.

Get the idea? If I hadn't probed for examples, I would have had little to tell my readers. The next time you hear a radio or television talk show host interview someone, listen for the way they probe. They're after the same thing you are— good examples.

But sometimes even the best interviewer will come up empty-handed. At that point, you must turn to secondary sources.

That happened to me when I was working on an article for *Weight Watchers Magazine* on what to do when you lose weight and your clothes are too big. I interviewed a professional seamstress who advised checking each garment for good quality and construction before going to the trouble of having it altered. Writing the article, I realized that I needed some concrete samples of "good quality." I found just what I needed in several sewing books. My final draft read:

Now examine the quality and the construction of each item in your closet. Everyone's definition of quality differs, but if the garment was expensive, is

made from high-quality fabric, or has a designer label, chances are it'll be worth altering. Here are some other examples of high-quality construction:
- Straight, even machine top-stitching with no broken threads.
- Finished seams to prevent raveling.
- Good-quality buttons and well-made buttonholes.
- Pattern designs, plaids and stripes matched up at the seams.
- Reinforced stitching in the arms, sleeves and crotch.
- Zippers that work well and lie smooth.

Newsletters are another good source of examples. In an article I was writing on head injury for *Kiwanis* magazine, I found some perfect examples of different types of head injury in a newsletter that was published by a rehabilitation center. If I hadn't found what I was looking for in the newsletter, I would have called the newsletter editor or a public relations person for the hospital. Such people can be a big help in finding examples because they're familiar with the subject.

Radio and television are also good secondary sources. If I know that an interview show or news segment will be aired on a subject that I'm writing about, I tape it. Often such programs will contain the examples I need to flesh out my article.

But sometimes, even secondary sources won't give you a perfect example. When that happens, you must make up your own. It requires some thought and a lot of imagination. In an article I was writing for *Mature Outlook* on how lonely people can get ripped off by dating services, my interviews turned up several anecdotes from senior citizens who had had bad experiences with professional matchmakers. But I needed a concrete example that would tie everything together.

To find that example, I did a little brainstorming. I came up with the idea that someone who joins a dating service is lonely and willing to take a risk, a gamble. The idea began to take shape. In my example, I showed the readers that dating services exist for the same reason Las Vegas casinos do: Everyone knows that most people will lose, but lots of people are willing to gamble that they'll be one of the few lucky winners.

It's OK to make up an example if, as in the above, you're drawing an analogy. It's *not* OK to make up an anecdote and lead readers to believe that the incident really happened. If you really need an anecdote and can't find one, turn it into a fictional scene by using the second person.

For example, suppose you're writing an article about auto breakdowns and you want to give the reader some examples of cars that don't start. You're tempted to write:

> *For instance, Jane Montgomery turned the key in the ignition and nothing happened. Not even an r-r-r-r-r.*

Don't do it. Just change that example from the third person to the second person:

For instance, you put the key in the ignition and nothing happens. Not even an r-r-r-r-r.

Now you've created the same effect. But by using the second person, you are not deceiving readers.

WRITING THE EXAMPLE

Whenever I begin to write an example, I think of an Irishman I know named Tom Flynn. He is a master joke-teller. His jokes are concise. He doesn't waste a lot of words leading up to the punch line. The words he uses all create emphasis and expectation. In the end, he makes a point.

A good example is just like that.

Each time I write an example, I ask myself:

- Is this example necessary?
- Is it overstated?
- Could I tell this more simply and still make a point?

Suppose you're trying to explain that in some cases, collision insurance for your car might not be necessary. You need an example to show the reader when the extra coverage isn't necessary. You could write:

Sometimes, collision insurance isn't necessary. For example, if your car is more than five years old and in bad condition with many rust spots and several dents, you probably don't need collision insurance because if you were in an accident the cost of repairing the car or replacing it would probably cost less than what you'd pay for the insurance.

Not a bad example. But lousy writing. Tighten it:

Sometimes, collision insurance isn't necessary. Suppose your car is more than five years old and in bad condition. If you're involved in an accident, the cost of repairing the car or replacing it would probably be less than what you'd pay for insurance.

Did you notice that in tightening the paragraph, I eliminated the phrase, *For example*? There are a number of ways to lead into an example. When I write my first draft, I usually start every example with a *for instance* or a *for example*. But then I look to see if that phrase is necessary. In many cases, it's not. The context of the example will tell the reader its function. Many of the examples in this article aren't specifically identified as such. And that last sentence is an example of an example that isn't identified as such.

An example can be introduced simply with a colon: like this.

In other cases, I still need a lead-in, but I can alter the position of the phrase in the sentence. It doesn't always have to go first, for example. I can also change the phrase for variety or to better fit the rhythm and tone of the article. Instead, I might use: "Here are some examples" or "Let me give you an example."

A NEVER-ENDING PROCESS

Finding examples and fitting them into your article is a continuing process. It's not something that becomes automatic. You must think about it every time you write an article. But sometimes, even professional writers miss: Last week an editor from *Childbirth Educator* called. "I like your article on how to produce a slide show," she told me. "But there are a couple of places where I'd like to see some more examples."

No better example of my point: Good examples often make the difference between an article that sells and one that doesn't.

BY BARBARA BISANTZ RAYMOND

Give Your Writing the Midas Touch

Remember Midas?

His touch turned wine glasses into golden goblets, copper pennies into sovereign coins. A writer can employ a kind of Midas touch, one that is just as magical—a light touch that makes writing sparkle as brightly as Midas' gold.

How? By taking the leadenness out of writing, and letting it take flight. Making its point as simply, succinctly and interestingly as possible, light writing entices the reader to continue. A light touch transforms explicit sentences into subtleties that surprise and engage the reader. It exhibits poise born of confidence and flair. Trimmed of ponderous words and empty phrases, of needless pointing and overlong description, light writing glitters on the page.

Light writing means understanding when to avoid using the unnecessary adjective and when to eliminate an adverb whose meaning is implicit in its verb. It means knowing when to let the sound and rhythm of language carry some of its meaning, and when to stop giving information and let a reader figure out a point for himself.

Light writing means including every necessary word or fact.

And not one more.

Spareness keeps light writing lively. Spare, powerful, light writing signifies a writer sure enough to let his reader do some thinking. It shows rather than tells, implies instead of explains, and says more than it seems to.

Light writing is more readable, more enjoyable, more intriguing—and more attractive to editors. Like Midas' gold, it glitters and shines. And it's valuable.

So why don't we write light? Because we're afraid. Unsure of our ability and burdened by the awesome responsibility of our task ("This could be read by millions!" or "Someone's actually paying me for what I think"), we overcompensate, using five-syllable words when plainer ones would do. Nervous that our readers won't understand us, we become over-explicit, padding our writing with extra phrases that slow it down and make it dull.

Based on the principle that what's left out of writing is as important as what's included, the light approach is a paradox: It's the art of knowing what not to do.

ON TIPTOE

Light writing looks easy.

So does ballet. But just as a dancer's graceful movements belie aching muscles and years of practice, achieving light writing's "effortless" language is much harder than it seems. Often, three or four drafts are necessary to lighten and breathe spontaneity into a piece. I learned this while writing my first article, "He Was a Giving Father, and It Didn't Cost a Cent."

Though I was enthusiastic about my project, my first attempts were stilted and lifeless. See how my article, which I sold to *The Buffalo News,* changed through successive drafts:

First draft:

> *An extremely talented man himself, Dad conveyed confidence in our ability. We learned to use his brightly colored poster paints before we could even groom ourselves.*

Second draft:

> *My dad was very talented, and convinced all of us that we had ability. We learned to paint before we learned to groom ourselves.*

Final draft:

> *My dad was talented and convinced us we were, too. We learned to paint before we learned to brush our teeth.*

Notice how removing stuffy-sounding words like *groom* and *conveyed* lightens the sentences? See how the more specific *brushed our teeth* adds strength? Light writing is close to the bone. Stripped of phrases and clauses that can be summed up in a word, its readability is heightened in proportion to the unnecessary words eliminated. So toss out modifiers like *brightly colored* and qualifiers like *extremely.* Rely on nouns and verbs to carry your piece.

This "less-is-more" philosophy means eliminating not only individual words, but also facts, like those in bold type below.

> *That month, there were twenty-three burglaries on the* **tree-lined** *city block.* **Police efforts were futile**, *and elderly residents were afraid to go out at night.* **Dark-haired** *Emma Tillman,* **an active church and community volunteer and mother of three teenage boys, had been shy as a child.** *But she was tired of feeling like a victim.*

Though the bold type details might be relevant later in the piece, packing them together is distracting, and robs the paragraph of focus. Here's the actual lead to my profile commissioned by *Parents* (for $1,300):

> *She lives on a street where crime had become common, and elderly residents were afraid to go out at night. There had been twenty-three burglaries during the past month alone. And Emma Tillman was tired of feeling like a victim.*

Clean and concise, this paragraph has impact. The lack of extraneous details makes those that remain stand out, and propels the reader into the body of the piece. Spareness has power to make readers wonder, to make readers think. Even to make readers feel.

I forgot this when I began writing the lead for a *USA Today* article on how divorced people cope with the holidays. The details I added to make it touching made it heavy and flat. Two revisions later, I'd reduced it to this:

> *In the year since Marianne and Tom's divorce, their three children hadn't seen much of their father. For that reason, and to hold onto the past, Marianne invited Tom for Christmas dinner.*
>
> *In the candlelight the children's eyes sparkled with questions: Would their parents get back together? Would they be a family again?*
>
> *At 6:00 Tom passed out his presents, and left. The kids went to their rooms. Marianne broke down and cried.*

Marianne's tears, the children's sparkling eyes and their subsequent return to their rooms tell the story. They depict divorce's pain more graphically than would statistics, information about Marianne's Christmas menu, or generalities about the sorrows of separation. The lead's spare setting gives those facts I did include attention and dignity.

Don't bury important information in irrelevancies. The purpose of much of your laboriously gathered research will be simply to add authority to what you're saying. Experiment with putting in less hard-core information than you're used to—you'll be surprised at how much can be left out.

Where's the fine line between too much and too little information? To help identify that imaginary border, put away your notes, close your eyes and "daydream" your piece. Or outline your article without consulting your research. Which facts figure in your daydream or outline? These are probably your (few) vital points. Beginning with them, add only the information readers need to draw the appropriate conclusion. (If you find it hard to be objective, write one or two sample pages, then ask a relative or friend to "figure out" your work.) Use only those facts, quotes and statistics that do real work. Write them as succinctly as possible, and never state what you can suggest.

READERS CAN READ

When I was sixteen, I read a novel in which the villain was repeatedly characterized as having long, grasping, scarlet nails. By the fourth reference, I'd had enough. "Red nails again?" I sputtered. "We already know the woman's a manipulative creep!"

Writers who underestimate their readers think they have to hit them over the head to make a point. But, though readers may tolerate writers who trudge deliberately to their destinations, they'll delight in those who, relying on nuance and implication, arrive there as if by accident, pause a moment to let readers "discover," then tiptoe ahead.

Writing light requires nerve. There's always a chance readers won't get your point. But writers who provide enough clues for their readers can be confident they'll be understood.

"You were always the good girl. What could I be but bad?" asks Lynn, as we sit in the living room surrounded by my children's drawings, my husband's law books, appointments of my "perfect" life.

Though even as a child I knew my sister and I were polar opposites—I the shy, dutiful "A" student; she the flirtatious, defiant under-achiever who'd later move 3,000 miles to forget her roots—I was in my twenties before I realized we'd been defined by our opposition.

"I couldn't compete with your successes, and so I did everything you didn't," says my sister. While I learned what not to do by watching what Lynn did.

This excerpt from an article I'm writing on "sisters as opposites" doesn't give many specifics of Lynn's and my personalities. It doesn't drone on about the rivalry that may dog us till we die. It doesn't spell out Lynn's defensiveness, or the guilt that's always plagued me.

But you got it, didn't you?

You read between the lines.

If I'd written the above passage like this, I would have cheated my readers:

My sister and I are opposites, and I think she blames me for it. I was always good. I was also shy and a good student, while she was a flirt who defied authority. As an adult, she even moved 3,000 miles away.

But even though I knew we were different, I never realized that we had helped form each other's personalities. Lynn, for example . . .

The magic is gone. So is the reader's attention. Recall the excitement you've felt when you discovered a "truth" through reading? And remember your satisfaction at discovering it yourself? Leaving "space" between the lines you write is important because it acknowledges that the reader can contribute, can think. About what you *say* and what you *imply*.

Don't be so explicit that your reader becomes bored and passive. Don't think you must do 100 percent of the work. Allow and encourage readers to make a few jumps.

I did, when I wrote my first *Good Housekeeping* article, which detailed my seven-year struggle to get doctors to test and treat me for an illness I'd already diagnosed. The lead that propelled my query from slush to assignment went like this:

The illness crept up on me slowly, and for a while I was able to ignore it. But one day shortly after my fourteenth birthday I had to admit something was wrong.

Three friends and I were hurrying to meet the bus that would take us to our high school, when one girl noticed the bus slowing to a stop a block ahead. "Run!" she shouted. "I can't be late for homeroom again!"

In a flash my friends were off, and I stumbled after them. But try as I might, I could not make my legs move in anything but slow motion. Horrified, I realized my recurring nightmare of being slowed down was becoming reality. I felt like a rat in a maze, a person on a treadmill going faster and faster but not covering any ground.

I arrived at school late that morning, and tried to sneak into study hall unnoticed. . . .

I received $1,500 from *Good Housekeeping* and an award from *Reader's Digest* for the piece because, said John M. Allen, then *Digest* managing editor, "it made people care. You had me involved from the very first sentence, and by the end, I wanted to punch those doctors out."

His comments show that writing that allows input is writing that involves the reader. Because I didn't ramble on about how frustrated I felt that morning— about, say, how the school bus, and my friends, left me "in a cloud of dust"— readers like Allen had room to make the leap that spells commitment, to decide on their own to care or not about my piece.

YOU'VE GOT RHYTHM

Writing that is logical and well-thought-out will always be superior to writing that is not. But light language goes one step further. It pulls readers along with words that flow and roll and toss the reader, that crest to a climax, then drop. Light writers, who attempt to "hear" their writing as if read aloud, strive to make their melodies harmonious, their rhythms appropriate to the mood of the piece. And they realize that awareness of the sounds of language can free them to be more subtle: Why rattle on about a subject when a word can "sound" it all? For example:

Her novels deal with romance and intrigue. She writes at night, to the strains of Spanish guitars. Dark hair frames the face of a fragile storybook heroine. But Rosemary Rogers is tough.

Juxtaposition of the unexpected "tough" with the melodious "strains of Spanish guitars" gives this excerpt from a *USA Today* article snap, and allows me to introduce succinctly the theme (that Rogers, like all writers, works hard). That *romance, intrigue* and *tough* sound like what they mean only helps.

Watch what happens when I forget that:

Her novels deal with romantic relationships. She writes at night, with music in the background. Her dark hair and small face make her seem delicate. But she works hard.

The two passages seem to say the same thing. But the second is flatter, less compelling than the first.

"The good writer of prose must be part poet, always listening to what he writes," says William Zinsser in *On Writing Well* (Harper & Row). He must know how to "end with a phrase that will linger," how to choose one word over another "because of a certain emotional weight." He must make use of the difference between "*serene* and *tranquil*, one so soft, one strangely disturbing because of the unusual *n* and *q*."

Develop your sensitivity to language by reading your work aloud, or asking someone else to read it to you. Observe how other writers use sound. Note that (unobtrusive) alliteration can make words melodious. Pay attention to the "beats" of the language you read. Note how the rhythm of parallel construction adds impact and formality, how long sentences can sound soothing and short ones abrupt.

The sound of language can also convey meaning, as I realized while writing an article for *McCall's* about a family's attempt to boost the confidence of their facially disfigured daughter and her chances for a normal life. I was concerned that the description of the child's reconstructive surgery could upset my readers. Yet I wanted to describe the surgery honestly and convey some sense of what these—and all—parents feel when a child undergoes surgery.

In the second draft, I realized that by using the rhythm of parallel construction and by contrasting the activity outside the operating room with the activity within, I could lighten what had been a heavy, rather technical exposition of the medical procedure. And I could report the "gory" details in a matter-of-fact, yet sympathetic, way. I wrote:

Irene and Jerry sat on a blue vinyl couch in the hospital waiting room, their moods alternating between expectation and panic as they waited for the nine-hour surgery to begin.

And so they waited, while Dr. Whitaker cut their daughter's scalp in an arc over the top of her head, then pulled the soft tissues of her face out and down, leaving attached only the nerves and blood vessels that linked Annie's eyes and nose to her brain. They agonized while the surgeon, working at times less than an eighth of an inch from Annie's optic nerve, cut her orbits loose like picture frames, then moved and wired them into proper position.

They clutched each other's hands while, using the rasp of a power saw and showering a spray of bone dust around the room, Dr. Whitaker molded the pieces of Annie's ribs he'd use to build up her cheekbone, nose and forehead. They counted the seconds as the surgeon wired the inner corner of Annie's eye higher up, so that her right eye would be more symmetrical with her left. They waited as the longest day of their lives inched by.

Then it was over. The Spiegels leaped to their feet as Annie was wheeled from the operating room. . . .

Notice that I didn't spell out the obvious by writing: "The operation seemed to take forever" or "The Spiegels could hardly believe it was over."

I didn't have to. The sound of the language freed me to be more subtle and succinct. I let the rhythm of the parallel construction ("They waited . . .", "They agonized . . .", "They clutched each other's hands . . .") help convey the eternity of the parents' vigil. And the short "Then it was over" brings it abruptly to a halt.

You can also use language's absence as a tool. White space. It can speak, as comparing two versions of a passage from my first *Good Housekeeping* article reveals:

> *My voice deepened, my tongue thickened, and in winter I was so cold I sat on radiators for warmth.*

> *My voice deepened. My tongue thickened. And in winter I was so cold I sat on radiators for warmth.*

The subtle but effective difference in the above examples is caused by the different lengths of the pauses symbolized by commas and periods. The longer stops in the final version give impact that the shorter ones do not.

Be aware of the different "sounds" of dots, dashes and spaces, and use them to maximum effect. Experiment with using the rhythms of words and punctuation marks to convey meaning—substitute a dash for a semicolon, a period for a comma, and see what a difference it makes. And don't worry that anyone will criticize your "strange" sentence structure. Write what seems most logical, effective and economical.

THERE WAS A TRAVELING SALESMAN

Anecdotes are one of the light writer's most valuable tools. By making the general specific and by making otherwise stale writing come alive, anecdotes help your writing become more engaging and fun to read. Look at the following anecdote, from a recent *USA Today* piece about soap operas; besides setting the tone for the article, it gives a capsule summary of what goes on in soap operas and introduces the theme of the piece—why "ordinary people" watch them:

> *It's 1 p.m. in Niagara Falls, New York. Darlene Petro tucks in her son, turns on the TV, and sinks into her favorite chair.*
> *The music swells, and a Galanos-clad villain plots against her arch-rival, concludes a $1-million business transaction, and swoops magnificently down a circular staircase. Darlene sighs in satisfaction.*
> *"I love to watch her operate. She does all the things I can't."*

Utilitarian as anecdotes may be, readers expect them to be light and interesting, too. See how the addition of superfluous phrases slows and flattens the same piece:

It's 1 p.m. in Niagara Falls, New York, and Darlene Petro's son is ready for a nap. She gives him a bottle, and tucks him in.

Now Darlene has time to relax. She takes off her shoes, turns on the TV, and watches her favorite program, a soap opera about a rich and powerful woman who . . .

Everybody has an Uncle Max (or James or Henry) who fancies himself a joke teller, but who drones on for minute after tedious minute, leaving his listeners exhausted and forgetful of the point of the story. Like jokes, anecdotes must move. They must point to the punch line, and contain nothing but the information necessary to get the reader there.

Hone your anecdotes even more carefully than the rest of your writing. Reduce each story to its essence before you use it, then write and rewrite your anecdotes to make them crisp. Anecdotes are a microcosm of light writing. And the same rules—brevity, logic and interest—apply.

So does moderation. Don't clutter your work with pretty but pointless stories. Use anecdotes only when useful—to illustrate a point, or introduce a new one, as this excerpt from a *USA Today* article on self-destructive people shows:

Point:

Since many self-destructive habits have been with us since childhood, we seldom recognize or question them. And because we feel most comfortable with the familiar, it often takes a personal crisis to precipitate change.

Anecdote:

Bob's crisis came in 1982, when a routine physical revealed pre-malignant growths in his mouth. Suddenly realizing "the cigarettes I smoke today could kill me—tomorrow," Bob stopped smoking that instant. And even after his lesions disappeared, he avoided his self-destructive habit.

New Point:

Not all people can. Experts speak of women who stay with physically abusive husbands, of cancer patients who smoke through their tracheotomy tubes. Why do we persist in behavior we know is self-destructive? The answer to this question eludes experts even now.

But, in an effort to shake us out of the "play now, pay later" syndrome, many researchers are. . . .

The anecdote justifies the words spent on it, for it does real work. And because it flows logically from the preceding paragraph, it keeps pace with the rest of the piece.

THE SENSE OF AN ENDING

Have you ever held a conversation with a person who didn't know how to end it?

Light writers don't rattle on forever. They know just when to say goodbye. When they've finished giving the reader new material, they don't build up to the obvious ending, or summarize what they've already said. They stop.

And, though ease and smoothness of transitions are important, light writers aren't afraid to be a little abrupt. "Like a good blackout line in a play, an ending should take a reader by surprise," says William Zinsser. "He didn't expect it, but now that it's here, it's undeniably the right ending."

There are no hard and fast rules for writing endings. "Use whatever works," says *McCall's* managing editor Don McKinney. He considers endings so important he often skips from the first page of a submitted article to the last, just to see how the writer has closed it. But there is agreement about how endings should make readers feel: "Good." "Uplifted." "Like they've learned something about the world."

"Seconds From Death," my *Good Housekeeping* article about a woman who fell into the Niagara Falls rapids, included a sidebar titled "A Talk With a Hero." It ended like this:

> Though John has led an adventurous and exciting life—he's broken horses nobody could ride and received an award for his rodeo riding—he says snatching Sherry from certain death has been his greatest satisfaction.
>
> "Driving along that road to work now, I stop and look out at that swirling water," says John. " 'What if . . .' I think to myself. 'What if . . .' "

Endings that allow the reader to fill in the blanks (or the ellipses, as above) can be particularly effective. So can leaving a word or phrase open to interpretation, as the following example from a *Parents* article about a woman who was foster mother to twenty "incorrigible" teens illustrates:

> . . . The girls were treated like family: they did homework, helped with the chores, and read stories to then-three-year-old Jonpaul. "We grew very close," says Fran.
>
> So close that many of the now-grown "girls" still visit, and Fran's been matron of honor, Lamaze coach and godmother for the children of more than a few. "The more you give, the more you get" is her explanation of the rewards of volunteering.
>
> "Those girls aren't with me anymore. But they're never really gone."

Letting the reader decide what "gone" means not only keeps the ending from being heavy-handed—it makes it richer and more memorable.

So let "the wonderful" happen. Leave room for your readers to participate. And whether you end with a thought, a statistic or an anecdote, leave readers with a sense of discovery. For the most satisfying endings are those that let readers feel they've gone, with the writer, on a journey.

And have done some of the driving themselves.

BY ROBERT L. BAKER

Twelve Ways to End Your Article Gracefully

Reams of copy have been written about leads, story organization and development. You will find very little in our professional literature, however, about closes, possibly the most significant and the most *memorable* segment of any feature article.

This is both puzzling and unfortunate.

We may be adept at snaring our readers with brilliant graphics, tempting heads, and exciting leads, and we may have the writing talent to keep them enthralled through paragraph after paragraph of body copy. But if there is a letdown at the end, if we fail in fashioning a strong, *memorable* finish, all could be for naught and readers will lay our work aside with a shrug and wonder why they read the piece.

It adds immeasurably to the pleasure of a new musical if you can leave the theater with at least one catchy tune to whistle. It is equally satisfying to finish reading anyone's editorial piece with at least one useful and stimulating idea lodged in your mind. And it is my personal contention that the close is where this mental implantation is most likely to occur—not in the lead, not in the body.

What we must understand, particularly in our feature writing, is that we are basically storytellers. A feature article should be more than a drab recitation of facts. It should embody all the characteristics of an essay, a play, a short story. The basic framework is clear and obvious. We start with a theme, an idea, or a news peg. We develop this theme or idea point by point in the body of the story. And then comes the ending, the conclusion, the close.

"Your article must have a theme, make a point of some kind, drive toward a conclusion," author Max Gunther advises. "It must lift the reader up, carry him along, and set him down with a satisfying thump—and he must end with a strong sense of having arrived somewhere, of being in a different place from the place where he started."

If we could convert article-writing theory into a visual form, it might look something like the diagram on page 110 (we're assuming a feature that builds gradually to a high point or climax).

The lead, of course, is the "show window" of any article; a promise of great things to come; a pacesetter and moodsetter for the story and facts that follow, the match that lights the fuse of interest.

We all realize how critical a lead can be. We all know it needs to be clear, concise, provocative, vigorous, and true to the facts that follow. The mood and manner of the lead should predict the mood and manner of the story.

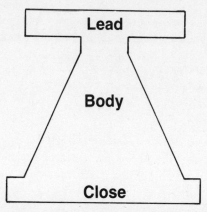

Another fact in writing leads that is seldom considered: A good lead paves the way to a good "close." One "teases" the reader into the story; the other "teases" the point of the story into the reader.

A transitional statement or paragraph carries you out of your lead into the body of the story where you can elaborate as space permits on the lead's promise and develop the storyline through employment of all the various devices of the article writer—anecdotes, quotes, specific examples, lively presentations and verifications of fact and opinion, even dialogue.

The readers, as they read, begin to feel that the story, if it is properly and excitingly written and paced, is building in fascination and merit, that it's leading somewhere to their benefit, driving toward a significant and worthwhile conclusion.

So, finally, we come, we hope, on an upbeat of interest and with great expectations, to that final statement or paragraph, the climax or coda of your work.

Your close should represent some of your keenest thinking and your finest and most carefully prepared prose.

Just as it pays to be constantly "lead sensitive" when you are assembling facts and photographs for a story, so it helps to be "close conscious." Many writers will slug at least one page of their notes "lead" in hopes that inspirational lightning will strike long before they start composing page one. The same procedure should apply for closes. Keep a page of notes slugged "close" and, as your editorial research progresses, jot down thoughts as they come to you.

There are undoubtedly some editors and writers who believe that no connection need exist between an article's lead and its close. Possibly so, but it is my conviction that the lead ought to be written with the close not entirely out of mind. In my many years behind a typewriter, I have relied on three primary sources of inspiration for my closes, in this order: 1) the lead, 2) the story objective, 3) ideas that germinate from body copy, usually body copy in the paragraph or two preceding the closing paragraph.

There are no mechanics, no rules, no magic blueprints to follow when writing your close. If, however, you know the various ways of ending a manuscript, you can select and work with the one that best suits your article. Here then are twelve types of closes I have identified. (Most of the examples that follow were pulled from a single publication—International Stanley Corporations's *Inside Story*, a magazine for railroaders and grain trade readers.)

THE LEAD REPLAY

As the name implies, this is a duplication or a rewrite of the lead, occasionally with some amplification. Or it could be simply a repeat of the lead's theme as in this example from an article on railroad lore.

Lead

As she flies through Colorado
She gives an awful squawl
they tell her by her whistle
—the Wabash Cannon Ball.

Why, that train went so fast, after it was brought to a dead stop it was still making 65 miles an hour!
Then they speeded up the schedule.

Close

Though the big laughers may have now passed on, on balmy nights when the stars are high in the heavens, if you listen hard, you'll hear a whistle that laughs like a man and keeps the hills echoing with wild laughter as the train races by . . .

THE PROXIMITY CLOSE

Tap the material immediately preceding your final paragraph for a closing angle, like this example written by Richard F. Janssen for "The Outlook" column in *The Wall Street Journal:*

Preceding Paragraph

What worries Ralph Bryant of the Brookings Institution, a liberal bastion in Washington, is that inflation will remain high for several years, causing "a period of disillusion" and Reaganite resort to traditional "austerity" policies after all. In relying mainly on expectations, he frets, the administration is relying mainly on "hope."

Close

That hope, at least, is widely shared.

Another example from an article about a grain grower and exporter in the Pacific Northwest:

Preceding Paragraphs

As one grower said, "There is nothing so satisfying as growing food in the Pacific Northwest."

"And," he added, "we do it well."

Close

Behind that simple statement is the reason why North Pacific is now able to embark on its second half-century of moving food from its "little corner of the world" into the bellies of the hungry all over the globe.

THE RESTATEMENT OF PURPOSE

Every article has a purpose, or it should have. Occasionally, a vivid and colorful restatement of that purpose makes an effective close.

The purpose of the article about the Union Pacific was to show new efficiencies and economies in moving large volumes of grain from the Midwest to the West Coast. Here's how the article closed:

Whether it's "Westward Ho!" for a 75-car grain train, or an overnight 25-car domestic shuttle, the U.P. has one goal in mind: the movement of far greater quantities of grain as economically as possible and with far greater dispatch and efficiency.

By every statistic, success in meeting this commitment has been achieved.

U.P.'s grain trains have, indeed, turned into "gravy trains" for everyone involved.

And this article, the purpose being to show how important the Federal Grain Inspection Service (FGIS) is to US standing in world grain markets. It closed:

To reach a level of performance and product quality unmatched by any other country supplying grain to the food markets of the world, our nation must do more to develop and preserve absolute integrity in the inspection, weighing, handling and certification of US grain.

And for accomplishing this mission, the FGIS is the best tool at our nation's command.

THE PLAY ON WORDS

You can get too cute, of course, but sometimes alliteration, sloganeering, catchy phrases, etc., make the most vivid impression and stick longest with the reader.

This hobby story for an oil company publication about a budgerigar (an Australian parakeet) that preens for hours in front of a mirror shows both a definite connection between lead and close and a good example of The Play on Words ending.

Lead

Your first indication of something unusual would be a whirr of wings, a streak of blue, a tiny object using your cranium as a landing field, and the sound of those beautiful words:
"I love you!"

The Close

He will stand for hours preening himself and rubbing his beak furiously against the mirror, all the time muttering to himself like a tuned down Donald Duck.

It might not be all vanity. Perhaps it's because the little lovebird has no lovebird to make love to.

Or this profile of ConAgra, an Omaha-based agri-business giant. It closed:

But, a famine-threatened world's hunger for food continues to grow. And as the world's need for food grows so grows the need for companies like Con-Agra, the uncommon company that handles "common" business so uncommonly well.

THE QUOTE CLOSE

Use a quote taken from a subject, from history, even from a sign on the scene, as in this example from an article about the Minneapolis Grain Exchange.

"American consumers are willing to pay more for the best," Wilkens says, "and American producers deserve to earn a premium price for a premium product."

At one sample table, some wag had tacked a small sign to the wood that phrased this marketing philosophy on a different plane.

"Quality is like buying oats," the sign reads. "If you want nice, clean, fresh oats, you must pay a fair price. However, if you can be satisfied with oats that have already been through the horse . . . that comes a lot cheaper!"

THE ADD-ON

The close can be used to make a point never made before in the story. Sort of a "saving the best for last" theory. It could be a "shocker" withheld deliberately until the last editorial moment, or, more commonly, an add-on that just seemed a natural for making your final point.

This example is from an article about railroading in Alaska. The best in this case, was definitely saved for last.

Then there is always the dream that someday there will be a land rail connection through the Yukon and British Columbia to the "lower 48."

When that happens—and studies are underway proving that it could—the old "moose gooser" will achieve its ultimate destiny.

THE ANECDOTAL ENDING

Using this approach, you can either end with a complete anecdote or use the split-anecdote technique in which you start telling an anecdote early in the article, maybe even in the lead. Halfway through your anecdote you stop. You then carry on with the rest of the article, completing the anecdote in your close. These two examples, one about the nation's first Secretary of Transportation (Alan S. Boyd) and the other about the current president of the Union Pacific Railroad (John C. Kenefick), show the use of the pure anecdote (in humorous form) and a reasonable approximation of the split anecdote. In the latter case, however, the soccer anecdote in body copy was not interrupted but used to wrap up the story.

Boyd's story for the day at a recent transportation confab was about the missionary who went to Africa without the usual survival equipment, relying entirely on faith. Shortly after his arrival in the jungle, the minister encountered a lion. Without a moment's delay he got down on his knees, and the lion sat back on his haunches. After a brief silence, the lion said: "I don't know what you're doing, but I'm saying grace."

The story undoubtedly has no application whatsoever to the Department of Transportation.

The profile of John C. Kenefick, a not-too-effective soccer goalie in his school days, closed in this fashion:

But for Kenefick nothing much has changed his thinking since he was tending that soccer goal in high school. His mind then, as the ball went whistling by, must have been on railroading.

And it still is.

THE NATURAL CLOSE

Do as the storyteller does. Let your story end naturally. No sweat. No strain. You've told your story. Stop.

An example from an article about wooden railroad crossties:

Once the treatment is completed, the ties are transported, usually by rail, to their final destination at trackside. They don't remain unused for long. Track crews, outfitted with a rail armada of mechanical equipment, remove old ties that have "done their time" and insert the newcomers for their long tour of duty as an unsung but vital element of support in moving the commerce of a nation.

THE SUMMARY CLOSE

The summary close, as the designation indicates, attempts to distill highlights of the story, or tie up all the loose ends. It often points back to the lead or comes through as a summarizing quote.

An example from a profile of Farmland Industries, a giant, Kansas City-based, farmer-owned co-op:

> *Farmland's utter size and power in the marketplace; its dedication to building a better, more economically secure life for farm families, has undoubtedly kept thousands of American farmers "down on the farm" being where they want to be—the Good Lord willing—and doing what they want to do.*

THE STRAIGHT STATEMENT CLOSE

This could also be called the "assessment" or editorial close. It consists of a few sentences or a final thought about the subject in your own words, often right "out of the blue" without duplicating your previous prose in the article. It is not a summary. It is seldom long-winded. It is generally short and straight to the point you want to make about the story.

An example of personal editorializing from an article profiling Peavey Company of Minneapolis:

> *Peavey Company, in maintaining such a philosophy [emphasis on maintaining good relations with "rural people"], may have grown in 104 years to a company of considerable size and complexity, but at heart, it still functions as a small family enterprise at its finest.*

Another example from an article on the world food crisis in the mid '70s:

> *"People who know where to grab the tiger can make it squeal," is a favorite saying of Dr. John A. Pino of the Rockefeller Foundation.*
>
> *It is now time for the leaders of the world to grab the terrible tiger of famine by the tail and make it squeal in terror as it retreats forever from the lives of the living.*

THE STINGER

An unexpected conclusion, or an ending that startles, surprises or shocks the reader, is The Stinger. An example from an article called "Eighteen Ways to Kill Yourself in Traffic":

> *Excessive speed, failure to yield the right-of-way and the sixteen other "mistakes" pictured on these pages are dangerous driving habits. If you are*

guilty of any one of them, you're gambling with death.
And it only takes death a split-second to become a winner.

THE "WORD OF ADVICE" CLOSE

One last admonishment, warning or word of advice—a verbal finger pointed straight at the reader—is a blunt but effective way to get one final, all-important point across, like, "The next time you think about smoking—don't!" for the close of an article on cigarettes and health.

There are undoubtedly other types of closes in addition to the twelve we have covered here. We've heard one writer refer to an "Echo Ending" in which you pick some word or phrase that has been repeated often and prominently and weave it into your close in a meaningful, surprising or clever way.

Closes, whatever the approach you use, rate among the most fascinating, frequently frustrating and exasperating elements of an article. Fascinating because they offer you the few words of greatest potential to inform, persuade or affect your reader. Frustrating and exasperating, not only because they often are the most difficult portion of a story to write, but also because none that you write will ever satisfy you.

BY MARSHALL COOK

Revision: Seven Steps to Better Manuscripts

I have a confession to make: I like to rewrite.

I know. That's like admitting you like green vegetables. You're supposed to eat spinach and revise manuscripts because they're good for you, not because you like them.

But when I rewrite a manuscript, sticking to a seven-step process I've developed during my twenty years as a writer and writing teacher, I can see my work growing stronger and clearer. That's all the reward I need.

The secret is to revise with a purpose, with specific objectives for each step in the process.

STEP 1: KEEP YOUR INNER EDITOR IN ITS PLACE

Writing is art. Rewriting is craft. Mix the two at your peril. If you let your inner editor (who, according to popular theory, lives in the left side of your brain) into the process too early, it's liable to overpower your artist, blocking your creative flow. When that happens, you squeeze out technically competent but uninspired work. You may even quit in frustration, thinking, "I'm just not in the mood," or, worse, "I'm just not a creative person."

Write your rough draft freely, with little thought to form and less to style. You can always fix mistakes. What you can't do is breathe life into a stillborn manuscript. Lock the editor out and let the artist create; then you'll have something worth revising.

Writing that seems effortless—the homespun musings of Erma Bombeck, the folksy wisdom of Andy Rooney, the barstool philosophy of Mike Royko—usually represents hours of sweat. The easier it reads, the harder it was to write. That's where purposeful revision comes in. You do the struggling so your reader doesn't have to.

STEP 2: READ FOR ASSURANCE

Read your manuscript as soon as you finish writing it. Assure yourself that the words you wrestled onto the page haven't gotten back up and walked away. Give yourself a mental pat on the back.

If you spot changes you'd like to make, jot notes to yourself in the margins. Don't do any editing yet, and be tolerant of your mistakes.

As you read, you may hear the siren song of ecstasy. "Alert the members of the Pulitzer Committee," a voice deep inside you purrs. Or you may hear the dirge of despair. "This isn't a manuscript," a rasping voice informs you. "It's garbage. It should be burned." You may even hear both voices at once.

Ignore them. Your work is neither the best nor the worst ever created. It's simply your work, with potential, but needing repairs.

STEP 3: LET IT COOL

There's just no way you can effectively revise your writing immediately after you've created it. You know exactly what the words are *supposed* to say and how they're *supposed* to affect readers. Instead of reading them critically, you'll simply project the meaning and the emotion that are supposed to be there onto the page.

Put your work aside and go on to something else. I try to have two or three writing projects going at the same time, so I can leave a rough draft of one to revise or research another.

Your cooling-off period may cover weeks, days, perhaps only a few hours. Just make sure to put some distance between creation and revision, but not so you can gain "objectivity" about your work. If you were truly objective about what you've written, you'd probably revise all the juice out of it—if you bothered to revise it at all. If your words don't engage your emotions, they surely won't engage your readers'.

You'll still be subjective about your baby, but time will allow you to shift from artist (right brain) to editor (left brain).

STEP 4: USE YOUR CRITICAL CHECKLIST

As you read your manuscript, ask yourself a series of large and small questions about content and style.

That's where your critical checklist comes in. You may not have written your checklist down, but you've been developing a sense of what makes good writing work for as long as you've been reading, and developing an awareness of your strengths and weaknesses as a writer for as long as you've been writing.

Here are the items on my checklist for a nonfiction article such as this one. I can't hope to offer a complete discussion of each item. Lead-writing, for example, deserves an article, or even a book, of its own. But I can suggest the questions you ought to be asking about your writing and offer examples of how I've answered the questions in my own writing.

Large Questions

1. *Does your lead promise the reader a specific benefit?* There are really only two reasons to read: for information and for a good time. If you don't promise at least one and preferably both in your lead, readers will never get past the first twenty-five words.

In my first draft of an article for *Business Age* profiling a successful small business, I developed a lead that I thought lead clearly and firmly into my topic:

This isn't your typical small-business success story. It's two success stories, neither of them typical. The first concerns a federal government program that works, a program that converts taxpayers' dollars into productive research and makes sure that small businesses get their share of those research dollars.

The second is about one of those small businesses. . . .

When I revised, I realized that I had promised useful information in only the most general terms. And I'd also promised all the fun of reading a dry textbook.

In my second draft, I introduced my subject more specifically, and with a lighter touch.

Legend tells of the alchemist who discovered a method for turning lead into gold.

If he were around today, he'd probably be working for Bend Research, where membrane research is making lead-into-gold look like a parlor trick.

But that wizard would need more than magical abilities in the laboratory to get by at Bend. He'd need to be a wizard at the word processor as well. . . .

2. *Does your lead offer a clear, specific focus?* Newspaper editors call it the "angle"; magazine editors, the "slant." It's the first and most important element they look for in your articles and queries. For example, this article promises not simply "some information about how to revise a manuscript" but a seven-step process for effective, purposeful revision. Revision is the subject. Purpose and process are the slant.

I recently interviewed Peter and Olaf Harken, expert sailors and builders of Olympic-champion boats, for *The Yacht.* As I expected, I learned a great deal about their achievements, but I also developed an appreciation for their ability to laugh at and learn from their failures.

This became a major element of my profile of them. I began, not with anecdote or quote attesting to their greatness, but with a scene in the City Cafe in Lake Shore, Texas, the day after the Harkens had wrecked a boat called *The Slingshot* attempting to set a world's speed record. The first words we hear are Peter Harken's rueful, "Here we are, right in there with NASA."

3. *Is your slant fresh and imaginative?* If you've read it before, your readers probably have, too.

My first several drafts of an article about harness racing for *Wisconsin Trails* began with a "they're off and running" lead: I used the voice of the track announcer to punctuate my opening observations about the sport.

A kind but firm editor helped me realize that the voice of that track announcer came from a score of old movies I'd seen as a kid. I was writing a rerun. So I came up with a new slant, building on my observation that most of the race drivers and horse owners I interviewed were friends. My new lead: "It's always best to beat a friend."

4. *Does the body of your article flow smoothly from point to point?* Does your ar-

rangement of material make sense? If not, some minor shifting may solve the problem, or you may have to perform major surgery. You may even have to start over. It's worth the effort. If the material isn't well organized, it won't flow, and probably won't sell.

Beginning my Harken article in Texas got me into some trouble midway through the piece. I could cover only so much material while the brothers were still in Texas. I needed to get them back home to Pewaukee, Wisconsin, to describe other important aspects of their lives.

After shuffling and reshuffling my material, I finally went with a technique borrowed from the movies, the "jump cut."

> *. . . The run for the record will have to wait. The Harkens are heading for home.*
>
> *Two weeks later, Olaf sits amidst the creative clutter of his office in Pewaukee, sips coffee to soothe the sore throat that is probably a souvenir of* The Slingshot, *and tells the story of Peter and the Bear, or the Day the Russians Invaded Pewaukee.*

It's quite a jump indeed, but I sealed the seam by referring back (*Slingshot*/run for the record) and looking forward (story about the Russians), so that the paragraph works as a hinge.

5. *Have you led your reader from point to point smoothly?* Transition words and phrases are no substitute for solid organization, but those *howevers* and *on the other hands* can help your readers catch your train of thought without getting derailed.

In the case of that Harken article, I wove anecdote and exposition by using matching actions and repeated words, and transitions like these:

> *"While at the University of Wisconsin . . ."*
> *"But boatbuilding had to wait . . ."*
> *"By the time Peter finally graduated in 1964 . . ."*
> *"Despite the difficulties . . ."*

6. *Have you supplied the right amount of information?* Your reader needs enough background to process the information you're providing. Anticipate reader questions. Plug the holes. Remember, the readers weren't there when you interviewed your subjects.

At the same time, make sure you haven't given readers more than they need. Irrelevant information can destroy the focus and unity of your piece.

For an article on the founder and president of a fast-growing PR firm, I told of his experiences as president of his college social fraternity, not only because I thought it a good story but also because it revealed the germ of his desire to own his own company.

But I edited out all the other stories from his college days and before because they weren't relevant to the focus of the piece.

7. *Have you supported every general statement?* You'll seldom "prove" anything in a magazine article the way you might prove a theorem in logic. But you must supply illustration or example for every generality, to help readers understand and to encourage them to believe. Specifics make for more vivid, memorable and believable writing.

If I tell you the Harkens employ unusual techniques to build their boats, you nod and flip the page to search for something more interesting. If I tell you how they designed a boat by imagining themselves as water molecules trying to get from the front of the boat to the back as rapidly as possible, I have you emotionally involved and ready for more stories.

8. *Have you shown rather than told?* Use anecdote to reveal your subjects in action. Let your subjects speak for themselves by quoting liberally. For sailors, a good sailing breeze isn't a good sailing breeze. It's "blowing like stink." Share such flavorful language with your reader.

Make your writing vivid through selective use of description. Choose what is unique about your subjects. Describe thematically, so that the physical details support the focus of the piece.

9. *Have you provided a strong conclusion?* The conclusion is the second most important part of the piece. Those last few sentences leave a lingering impression.

The techniques that work for a compelling lead—quote, anecdote, startling statement, arresting statistic—also work for your conclusion. In fact, you can use your conclusion to complete your lead and reinforce your slant. If you began with an anecdote, come back to it in the conclusion and carry it a step further. If you began with a quote, let the speaker add a final reflection.

In a piece I did on writer Herbert Kubly for *Writer's Digest,* I began with a quote from his father. In the conclusion, another quote completed the idea that the nurturing father had enabled the son to develop as a writer by giving him "permission to write." By coming back to that quote, I reinforced my slant and gave readers a sense of completion. I constructed this frame only in the final draft.

Small (But Still Very Important) Questions

1. *Have I written in active voice?* Compare these statements:

"The passive voice is avoided by good writers."
"Good writers avoid the passive voice."

They mean the same thing but the second is more vigorous and concise. Passive voice makes for passive readers. Turn passives into active voice whenever possible.

2. *Have you built each sentence around a specific, active verb?* Verbs are the primary meaning carriers in our language. If you settle for a weak, vague verb, such as *walked,* you must shore it up with an adverb or adverbial phrase. He walked with a limp. He walked through the door sideways, as if reluctant to enter

the room. He walked proudly, head held high. Substitute a stronger verb and watch the adverb flab melt away. He limped. He sidled. He pranced, strolled or strutted.

But don't get carried away. An exotic verb at home only in the thesaurus will call attention to itself and render your manuscript "cutesy" instead of creative. Be especially careful with verbs of attribution. It's often best to stick with good old *said,* because the reader's attention remains focused on the quote, where it belongs.

3. *Have you provided each verb with a specific, tangible noun?* The noun is second in importance to the verb.

To most of us, a boat is a boat. But to readers of *The Yacht,* there's a world of difference between a 470 and a Finn. Make sure you understand your reader's language, and then use it precisely, especially when you name things.

4. *Have you used a minimum of modifiers?* Mark Twain once advised, "If you can catch an adjective, kill it." Rene Cappon, author of *The Associated Press Guide to Good News Writing,* calls modifiers "the great deceivers." They give the illusion of specific meaning without its substance.

Write with nouns and verbs. Use modifiers sparingly, as needed. Create vivid writing through selective use of detail.

5. *Have you chosen the short, simple word over the long, obscure one?* Have you ever been to a "conflagration sale"? Probably not. But you may have attended a "fire sale."

Words are hobby, vocation, even passion for you. You can't assume the same level of commitment from your readers. How hard are they willing to work on your article? Will they look up every word they don't understand? Or will they simply quit in frustration?

6. *Have you kept your sentences and paragraphs relatively short?* Don't mow readers down with machine-gun bursts of prose. And don't make every sentence the same length. But short sentences and paragraphs make it easier for readers, not because readers are stupid and must be talked down to, but because your reader is as busy and preoccupied as you are.

7. *Have you cut out every unnecessary word, sentence and paragraph?* The poet says, "Every slaughtered syllable is a good deed done." That doesn't mean your writing should sound like a telegram, but that every word in your manuscript must convey information, establish tone, or both.

Search your rough drafts for throat-clearing, those two or three paragraphs of warm-up before you get to your point. Look for "baby puppies," those unnecessary adjectives that crop up in phrases such as *general consensus, past history* and *original founder.*

Chop out any sentence that begins with *In other words.* Rewrite the sentence in front of it.

Finally, check for redundant or irrelevant examples. This may be the most painful cutting, because the writing may be clear, sharp, even witty. But cut you must. Irrelevant material has no place in your manuscript.

STEP 5: GET YOUR COMMAS FLYING IN FORMATION

Now that you've trimmed your manuscript to fighting weight, give it a slow, thorough reading for accuracy. Check all facts, quotes, spelling and grammar. This is important because if you lose the readers' trust in one matter, you may lose it in all matters.

If you aren't sure, look it up. If you find yourself looking up the spelling of the same word over and over, make yourself an "idiot card" and list all your tormentors. If rhymes and slogans help you remember, use them. "Your attendance is requested at the dance" finally enabled me to get attendance off my idiot card. Your reader doesn't have to know how silly you are when you revise. Only the quality of the finished product counts.

STEP 6: REVISE BY EAR

Now you have a competent, clear and concise manuscript. You've checked the oil and tires and are reasonably sure your vehicle will carry your idea where you want it to go.

But you want more than serviceable transportation. You want adventure.

Read through again, this time out loud. That 187-word sentence looks fine on the page, but reading it aloud, you'll perish before you get halfway through. "The latest in convenience" says exactly what you want it to say—until you read it aloud. "He threw his mother from the train a kiss" provokes laughter when you hear it.

Reading your work aloud also enables you to feel its rhythm and flow. By varying sentence and word length, you can speed up or slow down your readers, but only if you let your ear play its part in the revision process.

STEP 7: GET HELP IF YOU NEED IT

Nobody can tell you what your words mean to you. But others can tell you what your words mean to *them,* and that's the best feedback you can get. Show your work to others, but only when it—and you—are ready. Showing a rough draft wastes your time and your reader's. Show polished work that may be one draft away from being as good as you can make it with a little help.

Be sure you're ready for criticism. It isn't fair to ask someone to evaluate your work if all you really want is praise.

Ask specific questions. Don't ask, "How do you like it?" (with its unstated "Pretty good stuff, huh?"). What's an honest friend to say? Ask instead, "Tell me what you think this means" or "Does this dialogue sound natural to you?"

A BONUS STEP 8: KNOW WHEN TO STOP, AND WHEN TO START AGAIN

One more revision will almost always make your manuscript better, but know when to quit. At some point you must make the compromise between the ideal manuscript you could have created and the real-world demands of deadlines, bills and other projects. When you can read your work with a blend of pride and satisfaction, send it off and get busy with something else.

And be prepared to do still more rewriting. An editor's objective and educated eye may spot things you were too close to see.

These revisions—like all those that went before—should be done for an underlying purpose: your vision of what you want your finished work to be and what you want it to do for your reader. Guided by that vision, you may even find yourself saying, "I *like* to rewrite."

BY PHILIP BARRY OSBORNE

Writing the "Art-of-Living" Article

The only kind of writing E. B. White said he could accomplish with minimum effort was about the small things in his day. In many ways this also produces some of our best writing, because it touches the readers right where they live.

Consider Martha Sweeney, who recently had her first article in *Reader's Digest*. Not long ago, Martha was in a coin laundry outside her hometown of Stonewall, Texas, when half a dozen young motorcyclists roared up to the gas station next door. They were all a boisterous, rough-looking lot, and one of them—younger than the others, no more than seventeen—was the loudest and roughest-acting of the bunch. Then something about this older woman observing him, something about this small, rural town in which he found himself—something caused the boy to hesitate. After his friends had gassed up their cycles, he told them his starter was on the blink and to go on without him. He said he would catch up. After the others went roaring off, the boy brought some dirty clothes into the laundry and glanced at Martha.

"His shoulders sagged as if he were terribly weary," Martha later wrote.

Dust and grease and sweat stained his shirt and jeans. A beginning beard faintly shadowed his chin and lean cheeks. He turned, and briefly our eyes met. Emotion flickered across his face—doubt, longing, pain?

The boy ran his clothes through the washer and dryer, then disappeared into the men's room. When he emerged ten minutes later, he was wearing clean pants and shirt, and he had shaved his scraggly beard, scrubbed his hands and face, and combed his hair. He grinned in Martha's direction and, jumping on his motorcycle, zoomed away. Not following the others, but going back the way he had come.

This type of writing, an inspirational narrative, falls into the broad category we call art-of-living. Also in this category are inspirational essays, inspirational articles on faith and religion, and self-help articles. As a group, art-of-living articles are a staple of general interest magazines—and represent one of the widest-open markets for new writers. All it takes to be an art-of-living writer is uncovering some common experience or concern that touches all our lives and emotions in a special way—and the discipline to get it down on paper. You don't have to be a best-selling poet or author. All of us have these everyday experiences, if we just learn to turn on our mental Geiger counters. From *Reader's Digest*, here's a brief sampler of titles: "Help for Your Hardest Decisions," "A Legacy of

Rainbows," "A Little Hammock Time," "Safe in a Father's Storytelling," "Thoughts Upon a Devil Wind," "Make a Friend of Change," "A Carillon of Prayers," "Love That Lasts a Lifetime," "Why I Go to Church," "A Rose for Miss Caroline."

The secret of these articles is their personal immediacy. Self-help articles help us deal with the world around us by showing us how to improve ourselves and grow in new ways and directions. Inspirational articles—narratives, essays and articles on faith and religion—deal more with our inner world of personal feelings; this kind of writing tends to surprise us with the familiar, revealing old, sometimes forgotten truths in a fresh, vivid way. It's been said that the obvious is that which is never seen until someone expresses it simply. And so it is with inspirational articles. The writer must startle us with what we often know and, in Stendhal's words, be "a mirror walking along the main road"—a "life watcher" in the way, for example, that French author Colette was.

"She heard, she touched, she breathed the world in, she stared with intense care, hypnotized," Helen Bevington writes of Colette in *Beautiful Lofty People.*

> *"Look at flowers, she would say. Look at the white gardenia that after three days resembles a 'white kid glove that has fallen into a stream.' The tulip—a painted Easter egg, its heavy posterior sitting on its stem. The black pansy— the velvet of it. She looked at love most of all, determined to define its nature and worth. 'The heart can begin again,' she said with authority."*

Richard Armour mastered this lesson well—because his writing, like all good inspirational writing, comes straight from the heart and emotions. In his book, *Out of My Mind,* he writes about one of the houses he grew up in. It had water stains on the ceiling, and as a child, he would gaze up at them when he lay sick in bed:

> *"The stains looked like animals, an overhead zoo that helped me pass many an hour. These memories inspired me to write a book for children,* Animals on the Ceiling. *What made the effort seem worthwhile was a letter I received from a little Mexican-American girl who said she had three brothers and four sisters. 'We have lots of animals on our ceiling,' she wrote. 'But the rich kids don't have any.' "*

The key to such writing is its power to move people. Art-of-living articles make a *difference* in people's lives—whether it's teaching them the healing miracle of forgiveness or simply helping them stretch a dollar. After reading "Dare to Live Your Dream" in *Reader's Digest,* one woman wrote us:

> *"In the article the author suggested making oral-history tapes of some of the old people around town. I went one step farther. I not only make the tapes, but also transcribe them and our local newspaper prints them for me in a weekly column. Besides writing the weekly column, I have started writing my first novel, and it's all because of* Reader's Digest."

Another letter, this one a little startling:

"I was planning to kill myself early today with an overdose. I just couldn't seem to cope with life. Then I happened to pick up a Reader's Digest *and read the article, 'Before You Kill Yourself.' I felt as if someone were talking directly to me. After reading this article I made a decision that I needed help. I phoned a psychiatrist and made an appointment. Tomorrow I'm going to a mental-health clinic to talk to someone. Maybe there is hope for me."*

That one word, *hope*, is central to all four types of the art-of-living article:

INSPIRATIONAL NARRATIVES

Like Martha Sweeney's article about the young motorcyclist, these are "stories" with a strong inspirational message. They anchor in the mind the way no other type of article can. Sherwood Anderson saw this; while he was dealing with fiction, what he had to say about storytelling applies just as much to the nonfiction narrative:

"What I really want to do—my purpose in writing—is to grow eloquent again about this country. I want to tell how the streams sound at night—how quiet it is—the sound the wind makes in the pines. I have written a few stories that are like stones laid along the highway. They have solidity and will stay there."

Good "stories" are all around us, but it takes more than simply *hearing* them. You have to develop an active curiosity for them—the way a child does. "Long before I wrote stories, I listened for stories," Eudora Welty recalls in *One Writer's Beginnings*. "Listening *for* them is something more acute than listening *to* them. I suppose it's an early form of participation in what goes on. Listening children know stories are *there*. When their elders sit and begin, children are just waiting and hoping for one to come out, like a mouse from its hole."

In her *Reader's Digest* article, "You Must Go Home Again," Ardis Whitman tells of traveling to Nova Scotia and visiting the house she grew up in many years before. This was more than a sentimental journey, however. It was a pilgrimage of spirit, reaffirming who she really was and giving her back again the blessed peace of belonging that we all need.

As Ardis writes:

"Contrary to Thomas Wolfe's famous lament, 'You can't go home again,' we must *all go home again—in reality or memory. When we don't, our lives lose their structure. Nostalgia is not simply a wistful exercise in sentiment. Rather, it is an illumination of the present; an invitation to re-examine oneself; to know the nature of the seed that started the tree; yes, and to remember what it was to be a child. Even if the past was not kind to you, turn it to account, to understanding."*

On her voyage of self-discovery, Ardis found something within her—a hidden and half-forgotten treasure—that suddenly enriched her life. In another narrative we published, Betty Weiss found inspiration outside herself, in a chance encounter of a very American kind. Working for Travelers Aid at the Los Angeles airport, Betty met a man from French Africa who had spent the better part of a year earning the money to visit this country. Then, while he was taking a nap in the airport lounge after his arrival, all his belongings had been stolen—passport, money, return ticket. Travelers Aid would need a few days to replace the travel documents. Meanwhile, the man was one of the most forlorn people Betty had met. "All I wanted was to see the United States," he said. "But this place is not for me. I want to go home."

That evening, Betty thought more and more about this man with a dream, who had come all the way from Africa just to see America. As she wrote in her article for the *Los Angeles Times*, later reprinted in *Reader's Digest*: "To return with only ashes for memories didn't seem right." So the next day Betty phoned the caseworker who was helping the man, and arranged to take him on a day's sightseeing tour. What he saw opened his eyes—and Betty's, as well. Together they saw our tall buildings, our ethnic variety, our hamburgers, discount stores and many of the other things that make this country what it is—and that we all tend to take for granted.

"It is too much, madame, too much," the visitor kept murmuring. "If I never see anything again, it will be enough for the rest of my life." It was easy for Betty to catch his enthusiasm. "I had seen things afresh through his eyes," Betty discovered. "He never saw the graffiti, trash or weeds, never saw the violence. Yet he was right. Most of it is beautiful and wonderful. We forget, harping about the bad, just how well it does work."

At the end of the day, the visitor thanked Betty again and again. Then he took out a tiny Statue of Liberty pin that she had bought him and told her that he would wear it when he got off the plane in Africa. She asked if he knew the significance of the statue.

"*Oui*," he answered. "*Liberté*."

"I believed then," she wrote, "that he had seen what he came here to see." And by then, of course, the reader had also seen it.

These stories tend to work best in first person. But that doesn't rule out third-person narratives, if they're done right. That's how Jack Fincher handled one of my favorite art-of-living narratives, "The Boy Who Remembered."

This story centers on a youngster of ten, living in Minneapolis back in 1932. His name was Tony Yurkew, and his parents were too poor to buy him decent shoes. So young Tony's school teacher, Mrs. Hansen, took him to a local store and bought him some shiny, new black brogans. Dumbstruck and shy, the boy couldn't find the words to express his thanks; but he vowed that one day he would. Then soon after, the school was closed, its pupils and teachers were scattered—and the years passed.

Finally, in August 1984, Tony Yurkew tracked down his former teacher. By then, Tony was a grandfather, and it had been more than half a century since

Mrs. Hansen's kindness. She and her husband were now living in retirement in San Diego. After flying to the coast, Tony at last said thanks—with roses, dinner for the Hansens and a kiss for this teacher who had remained all those years in his memory.

INSPIRATIONAL ESSAYS

These articles tend to be more difficult to write than inspirational narratives. Unlike a narrative, which deals mainly in a chronology of facts, an essay deals more in essence. It is more philosophical, more ruminating, more interior—a set of propositions that develop out of a single theme. You don't listen to the words or bare facts of an essay. You listen to the music. You experience a sensation— not the fact that it's raining, says novelist E. L. Doctorow, but the *feel* of being rained upon.

Here is Peter Steinhart, writing about the spell of a moonrise:

"I learned about its gifts one July evening in the mountains. My car had mysteriously stalled, and I was stranded and alone. The sun had set, and I was watching what seemed to be the bright-orange glow of a forest fire beyond a ridge to the east. Suddenly, the ridge itself seemed to burst into flame. Then, the rising moon, huge and red and grotesquely misshapen by the dust and sweat of the summer atmosphere, loomed up out of the woods. Distorted thus by the hot breath of earth, the moon seemed ill-tempered and imperfect. Dogs at nearby farmhouses barked nervously, as if this strange light had wakened evil spirits in the weeds."

The appeal of an inspirational essay is that it unlocks the mystery of some feeling or memory we all share—or would, if we ever thought about it: the joys of solitude, the stillness of a summer afternoon, the meaning of friendship, the soothing delight of daydreams, the importance of childhood memories. These things are a part of all of us—and the challenge of an essay is to come as close as you can to the *total* word or the total feeling on the subject. As Aldous Huxley once put it: "The essay is a device for saying almost everything about almost anything."

Sometimes, the subject will turn up where you least expect it. This happened to Jean George, a writer who lives in New York. After a winter storm several years ago, Jean was asked to check a friend's Long Island beach house while the friend was away. Jean expected to find a "dreary scene—an abandoned cottage set among pines, stirred by mournful winds." But the instant she climbed from her car, she found a world of harsh beauty, drama and discovery.

"The air smelled clean as I looked out on a brilliant landscape," she wrote. "The sea was a violent blue, the sky turquoise, and the beach, which last summer had sloped gently, was now steep, scooped-out and luminous. Crabs scurried for burrows and gulls spiraled down on them, like paper airplanes

against the sky. At the water's edge, empty shells that whisper when summer waves turn them now made shrill, whistling sounds."

Teased and tempted by what she found, Jean started thinking more and more about winter beaches. And soon, like any good writer, she was writing about them. She called her essay "Lure of the Winter Beach." This article glories in the many moods and alterations of the winter beach—and their effect on her and others:

> *"I saw a couple walking hand-in-hand. The man leaned down and wrote something in the sand. I smiled at his age-old act, the epitome of transience: romantic declarations written and so quickly erased by the sea.*
> *"Not so. When I came upon his sand message—one word only, his companion's name—the erosive winter waves were sweeping it, etching the letters more sharply and deeply until they fairly shouted of their permanence. They will be there forever, I thought . . . or at least until the next high tide."*

Change is a powerful theme—changes in nature, changes in ourselves. Where our personal lives are concerned, in fact, change is probably the biggest single challenge we all face. So ultimately, some of the best inspirational essays explore our transitions in life—if only to encourage us to accept ourselves in some new context, or as we are becoming. In "The Girl Inside the Woman," which we reprinted from *Ladies' Home Journal*, Peyton Bailey Budinger probes the two directions that she and so many other women are being pulled today. One moment, a woman may be yearning for a homespun past, the next she might be determined on a career-oriented future. She wrote:

> *"I have an image in my head, an image of a woman (me) whose life is calm, ordered, nourishing. My days are spent in rich simplification. I roll out a pie crust, arrange flowers in an ironstone pitcher, frame a favorite snapshot for the family picture wall. The woman in this image is the woman I would be. There was going to be no divorce (I am now married for the second time), no career conflict (I've tried in vain for twenty years to find a workable balance between home and my writing career) and an infinite number of children (I have one daughter of my own, a stepson and a step-daughter)."*

This lurching back and forth between the old and the new can create conflicts for a woman—as parent, spouse and money-earner. "It would help if we could simply accept the ambivalence in us, since the ambivalence is not likely to go away," the author concluded. "There will always be a part of us that swoons over a romantic novel. But we are also women with spunk who can do—and *do* do—some of the toughest jobs on earth. We are, like men, both strong and vulnerable. We are a blend of the old images and the new. Both parts of us are valuable. Both parts are worth hanging on to."

INSPIRATION ARTICLES ON FAITH AND RELIGION

Evelyn Waugh, that gifted but curmudgeonly writer who sometimes savaged people with his words was once asked by a brave woman: "Mr. Waugh, how can you behave as you do, and still remain a Christian?" He answered with blunt sincerity, "Madam, I may be as bad as you say, but believe me, were it not for my religion, I would scarcely be a human being."

Today, after twenty years indicating decline, polls show that more and more Americans are embracing some form of faith or religion. Ninety-five percent of those surveyed profess belief in God or a universal spirit. Sixty-six percent perceive God as a being who watches over and judges them personally, and to whom they're answerable. Eighty-seven percent say they pray sometimes during their everyday lives. This figure includes 75 percent of those who are *not* members of a church or synagogue, and half of the people who subscribe to no formal religion.

So *Reader's Digest* is always searching for general interest articles on faith and religion. They're a challenge to find, however. We don't want sermons and preachiness. We want articles that will be read by church-goers and non-church-goers alike. These cover everything from worship, the Bible and personal revelation to the simple act of prayer—in church or otherwise.

In "One Hour That Can Change Your Life," which we reprinted from *Catholic Digest*, Barbara Bartocci described how she set aside an hour a day for quiet prayer and meditation. The idea, suggested by a friend, came out of Barbara's need for filling an emptiness in her life. On the first cold, winter morning when she tried to meditate, various thoughts kept intruding—about an argument with her son the previous day, about problems in the advertising agency she managed. But gradually, the thoughts faded and her breathing slowed, until Barbara sensed a stillness within. Soon she grew aware of small sounds—the refrigerator hum, her dog's tail slapping the floor, a frozen branch brushing a window.

"Then I felt the warm presence of love," she wrote. "I know no other way to describe it. The air, the very place in which I sat, seemed to change, as the ambience of a house will change when someone you love is home." All her life, Barbara had been *told* God loved her. "On that cold February morning, I *felt* his love, and the immensity of it was overwhelming. All through the rest of that day, I felt warmed by the memory of that love."

As a young girl just starting out in the theater, actress Helen Hayes was bothered by all our prayers that ask for something. "I worried that perhaps nobody ever thought about sending a prayer of *thanks*," she observed in an article reprinted in *Reader's Digest*. "So one day after rehearsal, I raced back to my room and wrote out a prayer full of thanksgiving. I was sure God would be so grateful to receive it, amid all the prayers asking for help, that he would do something wonderful for the world."

Even to this day, looking from the window of her Hudson River home in Nyack, New York, Helen Hayes still gives prayers of thanksgiving for the shapes and colors that gloriously surround her house. "Not a day passes," she wrote, "that I don't whisper thanks."

Ardis Whitman calls this "spontaneous worship." In the sight of dawn breaking or the sound of music or the thousands of other personal happenings that enrich our lives, Ardis wrote in "This, Too, Is Worship," there can be moments of reverence that transcend the experience of church and temple. She defined this kind of worship as an attitude toward life, a response to the universe around us, the recognition of worship as simply the essence of wonder.

"When I think of spontaneous acts of worship," she observed, "I remember a musician who lived in my city. One brilliant summer day he and his wife visited the tower that stood on the highest peak of the Mohawk Trail in the Berkshire Mountains. Three states—Connecticut, Massachusetts and New York—spread before them, the sun blazing down on valleys, forests and lakes."

The musician was so moved by the grandeur of the scene that he rushed back to his car, grabbed his cornet and climbed back up the tower. "There," Ardis continued, "he played with all his heart—for his own delight, for the passing tourists, and for the glory of God."

Such narratives or essays needn't be long. They can be short, with a simple—but meaningful—message. In a two-page article entitled "Mother's Bible," Marjorie Holmes wrote about how her mother, having died at an old age, left behind a final message of love that healed some old divisions between two members of her family. The dying woman did this by marking two passages in her Bible that said so eloquently what she herself had trouble conveying when she was alive. The message is in the last paragraph of the article: "The peace that night was to last. Mother's passing had spanned their arrangement. The bridge of death had become the bridge of love."

SELF-HELP ARTICLES

Alex Haley, the author of *Roots* and a longtime contributor to *Reader's Digest*, has a picture in his office, showing a turtle sitting atop a fence. The picture is there to remind him of a lesson he learned long ago: "If you see a turtle on a fence post, you know he had some help." Says Alex. "Any time I start thinking, 'Wow, isn't this marvelous what I've done,' I look at that picture and remember how this turtle—me—got up on that post."

All of us need help now and then, and that's where the self-help or self-improvement article comes in. These offer readers help for everything from shyness, poor memories and overeating to keeping cool in a crisis, raising a happier child, landing a higher-paying job, or simply getting along better with a wife or husband.

In "Lessons From Aunt Grace," Nardi Reeder Campion describes a time in her life when she was down in the dumps—and then discovered a diary that had been kept more than forty years before by a maiden aunt who had gone through some bad times herself. Aunt Grace had been poor, frail and forced to live with relatives. "I know I must be cheerful, living in this large family upon whom I am dependent," Aunt Grace wrote. "Yet gloom haunts me. Clearly my situation is not going to change; therefore, *I* shall have to change."

To help hold her fragile world together, Aunt Grace resolved to do six things every day: 1) something for someone else, 2) something for herself, 3) something she didn't want to do that needed doing, 4) a physical exercise, 5) a mental exercise, and 6) an original prayer that always included counting her blessings. From there, the article explores how these six steps helped change Nardi's life, just as they had helped change Aunt Grace's life many years before.

"Can life be lived by a formula?" Nardi asks in her article. "All I know is that since I started to live by those six precepts, I've become more involved with others and, hence, less 'buried' in myself. Instead of wallowing in self-pity, I have adopted Aunt Grace's motto: 'Bloom where you are planted.' "

Such self-help articles must teach without lecturing—and the best ones come straight out of the problems or concerns of daily living. This happened recently with Kenneth Gilmore, our editor-in-chief at *Reader's Digest*. One day, Ken received a phone call from a close friend, informing him that the friend's wife had been killed in a car accident. Startled and shocked, Ken offered what comfort he could—but later worried that his words fell short of what he had felt and what he should have conveyed. That afternoon, Ken suggested doing an article that would help readers deal with this most universal of experiences—comforting those who grieve.

In her article, published shortly after the *Challenger* disaster, author Barbara Russell Chesser showed how even a giant government agency like NASA recognizes the importance of knowing just the right thing to say or do for somebody who has lost a loved one. Following the fire and explosion that destroyed the space shuttle in January of 1986, the families of each one of the seven astronauts who perished had another astronaut family at their side soon after the tragedy. The support families were there to help the *Challenger* families with everything from food and travel arrangements to boarding the family pet. Especially moving was a comment Barbara picked up from Clarke Covington, manager of the Space Station Project at NASA's Johnson Space Center in Houston. "With all the vast technology of our space age," he told Barbara, "there's still nothing more powerful than one human reaching out to another."

That probably summarizes—better than anything else—what art-of-living is all about.

BY CHARLES V. MAIN

Writing and Selling the List Article

If I were asked to list the components of the nearly perfect article from the writer's point of view, I would say:

- The article would be easy to research.
- The article would be easy to write.
- The article would be easy to sell.
- The article would appear in a list format.

The "list article" is one that unifies several units of information under a single theme. After selling about 50 such articles to national magazines ranging from religious publications to inflight magazines, I have found the list article one of the most profitable. Over the past five years, I've picked up checks ranging from $25 to $500 for list articles that have taken only a few hours to research and write. You can do the same.

LIST ITEM #1: THE IDEA

Good writing is important in a list article, of course, but at the core of the article is *information*. List articles are designed to solve problems, present information, and otherwise help the reader. *This* article is, of course, a list article. Keep the information angle in mind when looking for ideas for this type of article. Ask what problems must be solved, what procedures must be explained, what needs must be fulfilled.

First ask those questions of other people. One conversation I had with a friend, a sales trainer for an insurance firm, once resulted in a $100 sale. I asked him what problems he would like to see addressed in print. He said that one of the biggest problems new salespeople face in closing a sale occurred when customers said they wanted to think about the deal. Two months later *Specialty Salesman* magazine bought my article, "Handling the World's Toughest Objection," which listed several ways to encourage a buying decision when the customer is unsure.

Ask those questions of yourself, too. Your own problems, concerns and pet peeves can produce ideas for list articles. A couple of years ago I was bothered by the fact that many churches gave their youth little opportunity for creative expression. So I wrote an article that listed ten forms of creative worship activities to be used with church youth groups. The article sold to a church magazine on the first submission. Ask yourself, "What things bug me that I've been able to handle effectively?" The answer to that question may result in a sale.

By far the best source of list article ideas is the magazine you want to write for. Study a few back issues and note the titles of all list articles. Then change the titles by substituting a word here and there. For instance, a house-and-garden magazine may carry an article titled "Ten Ways to Improve Your Lawn." You could change this to "Twelve Ways to Improve Your Vegetable Garden." Assuming the magazine doesn't have a similar article in stock, and assuming the information is sound, the editors will probably be interested in your variation on the theme of outdoor improvement.

In fact, I've found several list article title formats useful in gathering ideas. These are:

_____ Ways to Improve _____
_____ Ways to _____ Better
_____ Ways to Save Money on _____
The # _____ est _____s

LIST ITEM #2: RESEARCH

I said earlier that the nearly perfect article would be easy to research. Again, the focus of the list article is information. Where that information originates is relatively unimportant, as long as it is fresh, useful and accurate. Your most important sources are:

● *Yourself.* I have drawn on my experiences as salesman, advertising consultant, Sunday school teacher, and drama coach to write articles for a variety of specialized publications. You don't need to be a "recognized expert" to write for specialized publications, as I proved with my "Toughest Objection" article for *Specialty Salesman.*

● *Experts.* Don't think you must find someone with a long list of formal credentials. The purpose of a list article is to convey information. The purpose of your interview is to collect that information. You are less interested in finding quotable quotes than you are in finding valuable information. With this in mind, the definition of an expert changes from a person with certain credentials to a person who has the information you need to write your article.

Thus, your expert could be a friend whose hobby or job relates to the subject you're writing about. Your expert might work for some governmental or quasi-governmental agency like the police or fire department, the Consumer Protection Agency, or the post office. Or your expert might be a college professor who has studied the subject in question. Schools are repositories of experts on all sorts of subjects. If no one at the university or college can help you, someone can probably tell you where to go for the information you need. A few months ago, I was writing an article about shyness. As it happened, the nearby university employed a professor who made a special study of shyness and worked with people to help them overcome their own shyness. The information I gained from an interview with her resulted in two articles. One was a list article for *American Way*. The two articles based on that interview have already brought me more than $800. If you want to know if a university has a resident expert on a certain subject, either call the appropriate department or call the school's public information center or news bureau.

• *Published sources.* An afternoon in the library can often provide you with enough information for certain kinds of articles. For instance, if you were writing an article on "Ten Organic Ways to Protect Your Vegetables From Insects," you could probably find all the information you'd need in textbooks on gardening. If you have trouble finding the information you need, ask a librarian.

When doing library research, learn to look beyond the obvious for sources of information. Many libraries have cassette tape libraries that contain information on all kinds of subjects. Others have computer terminals connected with data bases that allow you quick and easy access abstracts of difficult-to-find information. Microfilm files often contain otherwise unpublished information. And some major university libraries are depositories for US government documents.

LIST ITEM #3: WRITING THE ARTICLE

List articles consist of four parts:

1. The introduction
2. The theme
3. The list
4. The conclusion

The introduction should entice the reader to read the article and tell the reader what the article will be about. Your introduction should be short and to the point. For instance, the lead to my article for *In Business*, "Eight Ways to Cut Advertising Costs," emphasized the main benefit of reading the article—saving money.

> They say it pays to advertise, but the truth is that you pay to advertise. As a salesman for several advertising media, I have discovered eight ways the average small-business person can cut advertising costs substantially without reducing advertising effectiveness. By using these cost-cutting techniques, you can conserve your cash flow and increase your profit.

This introduction not only gives the reader a reason to keep reading, but it also sets forth the theme of the article. Most list articles state the theme within the first few paragraphs. The theme is the entire thrust of the article stated in one sentence. In the above example, the theme is "I have discovered eight ways the average small-business person can cut advertising costs substantially without reducing advertising effectiveness." The rest of the article is designed to support that assertion. Stating a theme orients your reader toward what is to come and gives you a focus for your article.

LIST ITEM #4: THE LIST

The list itself forms the bulk of the article and its structure varies with the type of article you are writing. Of the four common types of list articles, each has a slightly different structure.

1. *The Helpful Hint List.* This is perhaps the most ubiquitous of all list articles. I found five such articles in just one issue of *Good Housekeeping.* The helpful hint list consists of short tips on how to save money, do a better job, make improvements around the house, and generally live a happier, healthier, more prosperous life.

The lead of a helpful hint article should appeal to the self-interest of the reader. For instance, I recently sold an article, "Nine Ways to Make Your Typing Service Special," to a regional business opportunity magazine. It began:

> *Nearly every home has one. Yet very few people realize that a typewriter can be a gold mine with keys. You may think that the typing service field is overcrowded. But with some careful marketing and by providing specialized services, you can develop business that other typists don't.*

This lead immediately engages readers' interest by promising them a way to make money at home.

Each entry in your helpful hint list should start with a short imperative sentence that capsulizes the hint. Then briefly explain the hint. For instance, the following hint comes from a sidebar to an article on business fraud I wrote for an inflight magazine. The article was a modified list article describing various forms of business fraud. The sidebar discussed ways businesses could protect themselves against such fraud, such as the following:

> Deal with companies you know. *Acquaint yourself with the major firms that sell the supplies you use. If a new firm places an order, investigate whether the firm is legitimate by checking with the Better Business Bureau in the hometown of the company.*

In organizing the helpful hint article, I like to place my two strongest hints at the beginning and end of the list so the reader is enticed to keep reading at the start and feels satisfied at the end.

2. *The Problem-Solving List.* This is similar to the helpful hint list and some problem-solving lists can be considered forms of the helpful hint list. However, the problem-solving list generally takes a little different approach. In the lead, you set forth a common personal, family or even societal problem. This is followed by a description of the extent and nature of the problem. Next comes your list, which suggests how the problem can be solved. My article on shyness took this form. The first half of the article discussed the latest research on shyness, focusing on the nature and extent of the problem. The last half suggested ways the reader could handle shyness.

3. *The Step-by-Step List.* This list article style differs slightly from other list articles in that each component is necessary and the order of presentation is vital to the article.

When organizing this type of article, break down the process you are describing into individual steps. Each of these steps should describe a single procedure in such a way that the average reader of that publication can duplicate it. You want to keep your steps as simple as possible, considering the probable skills possessed by your readers. For instance, you could write, "Make a dado joint," if you were writing for a carpenter's trade journal. However, you would probably have to break the process down into simpler steps if you were writing for a more general magazine. Under each step, explain any procedure that might be necessary to complete that step. Anticipate any problems that may arise in completing each step, and explain the solutions to these problems.

If the process you are describing produces a physical product, accompany your manuscript with artwork (either photos or drawings) illustrating each step in the process.

If you are in doubt as to the clarity of your instructions, let someone else read the article before you submit it. After he or she reads it, ask, "Would you be able to do this if all you had to go on was this article?"

4. *The General Information List.* Some list articles round up general information about people, places, lifestyles, trends, new products and events. Travel magazines run articles on restaurants, campgrounds, tourist attractions and events. Home and garden magazines list new products for the home. Consumer publications evaluate different brands of the same product. Many of these articles might be called "best of" lists. They describe the best places to go, the best things to do, the best products to buy. When writing a "best of" list, be specific. Why are the items you choose the best? Why should they be included in the list and not others?

LIST ITEM #5: THE CONCLUSION

There are four basic ways to conclude a list article. The first is to relate the conclusion to the lead. For instance, my article on advertising costs began with reference to the old adage that "It pays to advertise," and concluded:

It's true. You pay for advertising and in turn advertising pays off for you. But, by keeping these eight cost-cutting tips in mind, how much you pay can be substantially reduced.

This method of concluding gives readers a sense of completeness when they come to the end of the article.

The second way of concluding a list article is to restate your theme. I call this the "And so . . ." conclusion. For instance, the theme in my article, "The Principles Are Few" (written for a trade magazine), was "There are principles of selling that transcend the considerations of time and product." My conclusion read:

Methods are many; principles are few. Methods change; principles never do. Success may be temporarily gained by studying the methods. But long-term success comes from mastering these five principles that never change.

The third type of conclusion I call the "go-to-it." This conclusion is especially useful with the problem-solving and step-by-step lists. The "go-to-it" conclusion simply encourages the reader to take the advice presented in the article and apply it in his or her personal life. For instance, I wrote an article for a publication for church youth directors, on how to use Bible games in their youth meetings. My conclusion read:

Bible games are educational and inspiring—as well as fun. So if you haven't played a game in some time, there's good reason to have one.

The last way to conclude a list article is to skip a formal conclusion altogether. Many times the last entry in your list can act as your conclusion. To let your reader know that you are ending the article, simply precede your last list heading with the word *finally*. I used this approach in the article I wrote on shyness. My list consisted of four ways to overcome shyness as suggested by the expert I had interviewed. My last entry seemed to be a natural place to end the article, since it encouraged action on the part of the reader. It read:

Finally, Act First, Feel Later. *Don't wait until you feel less shy to strike up a conversation with someone. . . . You'll never get over that shy feeling until you've had some successes, and you'll never have successes until you act. As Dr. Glaser says, "It's easier to act your way into new ways of feeling than to feel yourself into new ways of acting."*

LIST ITEM #6: THE PERFECT QUERY

Even though list articles are generally short (800-1,500 words), I recommend that you propose the article to an editor in a query rather than taking the time to write the complete article.

I begin my queries with the lead I plan to use in the article. I follow this with a transition line that explains the working title, the theme of the article, and a proposed word length. Then I briefly describe the segments I plan to cover in the article. If I haven't worked with the editor before, I conclude with a brief list of credits and any special qualifications I have for writing this article.

LIST ITEM #5, REVISITED: ANOTHER CONCLUSION

Now you know just about everything I know about writing and selling list articles. You know:

- How to generate ideas.
- How to research your subject.
- The types of list articles.
- How to organize and write the article.
- How to sell the article.

In keeping with my previous advice, go to it.

BY NANCY KELTON

How to Write Personal Experience Articles

Paula, a former student of mine, recently sold an article she wrote in my class last semester. Paula's article discussed her college boyfriend's suicide and what she experienced during and after her relationship with him. The piece could have been as depressing as the subject, but it wasn't. It was serious and poignant, but not maudlin. I read it more than six months ago, yet it lingers in my mind. I suspect it will for a long time.

Quite the opposite is true of an article that Stuart, an acquaintance, recently asked me to read. The subject was his divorce and its aftermath, and since I have sold both serious and humorous articles about my own divorce, he thought I could be helpful.

I wanted to like Stuart's article. I didn't. It was tedious. It contained a lot of mundane details about lawyers and custody battles. And now, just a month after reading it, I can't remember much about it, except that the tone was so very angry.

Why did Paula's article come alive while Stuart's fell flat? And what, in short, makes a personal experience article successful?

Three components:

A point of view. This is the author's unique or special way of viewing his experience.

In the first paragraph of her piece, Paula talks about how she felt before the funeral, deciding what to wear. She draws her readers into her world and, as she flashes back to her first encounter with her boyfriend and traces the relationship, we are right there beside her. In capturing her experience, *she got under her own skin, showing* us how the experience affected her.

Stuart's article, on the other hand, rehashes the events of his divorce proceedings—the consultations with lawyers and visits to therapists—without ever looking at the experience or saying how he felt about it.

In my article "A New Mother's Confessions of Ambivalence" (which appeared in *The New York Times*), I get my point of view across in the first sentences:

Sometimes when I walk down the street with my child in her carriage and my husband beside me, I feel so detached from them that I want to turn around and race off in the opposite direction to be alone with my thoughts. At other times, in the same situation, I feel we are so close to one another that I want nothing more than to continue walking along in silence, sharing what is ours alone.

In "Travels With a Novice," a piece about my first trip to Europe (which I sold to *The Student*), I begin:

"It was just fantastic!" Or so I told my parents who had been waiting two days at Kennedy International Airport for my delayed charter plane to return from Europe. How else would you describe eight hot weeks of rushing around with fifty pounds of luggage, blistered fingers, lower back pains, engraved circles under the eyes, and Leslie Birnbaum?

The arrival at some basic truth. As a result of the experience, *something should become clear* to you. You should reach a new level of understanding that you convey to your readers.

Stuart did not reach a new level of understanding in his article. Paula, through her anguish, came to realize that no matter how much she loved her boyfriend, she couldn't have prevented his suicide, thus arriving at the truth that each of us is responsible for his own life.

What became clear to me in "A New Mother's Confessions of Ambivalence" is that the demands and frustrations and responsibilities of motherhood are necessary to experiencing its joys. I say this in my last paragraph:

Suddenly my sobbing turned to laughter. I picked up my daughter and held her tightly, realizing that there will be many more times in our lives when we will unwittingly inflict pain on each other, and many more times when we think we understand each other but don't. And it won't always be easy. But nothing worthwhile ever is.

Emotional involvement. To make readers care about your experience, put them at the center of it.

At the beginning of Paula's article, we see her standing in front of her closet, trying between sobs to decide what to wear to the funeral. She opens herself up as she opens the closet door and we feel as if we are standing there with her.

In "Waiting for Daddy," a *Parents* article about how I have felt during the last several years sending my daughter to her father's every other weekend, I am right there going through the experience with her. Here is the second paragraph of the article:

As we ride down in the elevator, Emily bends down to play with a wire-haired terrier and proceeds to tell its owner that at home she has no pets but at her Dad's she has goldfish. I listen to the matter-of-factness and ease with which she discusses her two parents' homes as if it were as commonplace as having two eyes or two ears, and I feel an enormous wave of emotions swelling up inside me.

Note that there must be a universality in the emotions you dramatize, not necessarily in the experience.

PUTTING THE COMPONENTS TO WORK

People read for several reasons: to learn, to grow, and sometimes to be amused. If you put yourself at the center of the experience, view it in your own special way, and arrive at some basic truth, you will educate and touch your readers. And if you have a sense of humor and see your experience with a twinkle in your eye, you just might tickle them, too.

Here's how to go about doing that when turning your experience into articles:

Pick an experience you care about deeply. "How do you decide what to write about?" a friend recently asked me. I thought about that. I know I write about the things in my life that obsess me, that play over and over in mind and heart.

"I don't pick my subjects," I told her. "They seem to pick me."

"Waiting for Daddy" was one of the few pieces that burst right out of me. The pain and sadness I felt about the breakup of my family were acute. Sending my daughter off to her father's was difficult for me. Always. Yet, I learned how to handle this incredibly delicate situation—and that was the point of the article.

"A New Mother's Confessions of Ambivalence" actually began as random notes I was writing in my journal. I was so overwhelmed by my profoundly conflicting feelings—the intense love I felt for my daughter on the one hand and the fear of the awesome responsibility of raising her on the other—that I was literally jumping out of bed in the middle of the night to jot them down. These feelings continued to pour out of me. I played with them, cutting and adding and switching things around, and eventually an article evolved. To this day, I still think that this and "Waiting for Daddy" are my most deeply felt articles.

You should have the same feelings when you write a personal experience article, because if you don't really care about your subject, neither will your readers.

Don't make publication your primary goal in writing your article. Although you eventually hope to see your work in print, don't set out to write about a topic just because you think it would be suitable for a certain magazine. Your initial satisfaction should come from the writing and the discoveries you make in the process.

When I began jotting down my feelings about motherhood in my journal, I didn't know I would shape them into a finished article that I would eventually send to *The New York Times*. I was bursting with a whole new set of emotions I felt compelled to look at and understand.

The same is true with my other articles. If I'm not compelled to write about a certain experience, I obviously didn't learn much from it or have anything worthwhile to say about it. And if that is the case, why should an editor be interested?

Don't write a personal experience article to vent anger, indignation or other negative emotions. We all have had experiences that have angered or hurt us: painful experiences such as illness, death and divorce, and less painful ones such as being the butt of inhumane or shabby treatment.

Having anger to vent is *not* a reason to write an article. It is a reason to consult a therapist, write letters to editors or keep a journal. Stuart's divorce article was, as I saw it, a vehicle for letting off steam about his situation. But I didn't learn anything from his experience, because he didn't or couldn't communicate what he learned.

I admit that with "Waiting for Daddy" and other articles on my divorce, anger was one of the feelings that came out. But I also examined the anger and—partially through my writing—I came to understand that my anger masked other more profound feelings. In other words, I went beyond my anger to look deeper at the situation so I could learn something that would be useful to me and eventually to my readers.

Except for your therapist and loved ones, no one is interested in hearing you whine and complain.

Have the courage to reveal yourself honestly. I am often asked how I have the nerve to write about certain things for publication. "A New Mother's Confessions of Ambivalence" was my first article to generate this sort of response. In it, I captured the darker side of motherhood. Yet, this article brought me more fan mail and more positive feedback—including letters from magazine editors asking me to write for them and an invitation to appear as a guest on a television talk show—than I had received for any of my published work.

My answer then to those who ask how I can say certain things in print is this: My job as a writer is to deliver to readers the truths they subliminally know, and these truths are often the darker, unmentionable feelings we have about people and situations in our lives.

To write successful personal experience articles, therefore, you must face reality head on. You must be courageous enough to reveal yourself honestly.

Don't tell what you went through. Show it. Showing means dramatizing. It means putting yourself there in the scene at the heart of what's going on so the reader can actually see you and feel what you are going through.

I started "Travels With a Novice" with my arrival at Kennedy with a host of lighthearted complaints, establishing a humorous tone for the piece.

Here's how I begin "Waiting for Daddy":

It's 6 o'clock on Friday—a warm, spring Friday evening. I just finished packing my 5-year-old daughter Emily's overnight bag and she is now putting in her favorite stuffed animal and her new fruit-flavored lip balm. Her father is coming to pick her up for their weekend visit, and she wants to wait outside where Jamie and Katy, her friends from the building, are trying out Jamie's new bike.

In these pieces, I am, in essence, saying: "This is where I am. Now I am going to show you what I went through. Why don't you come along and see what I discovered?"

If I had begun "Travels With a Novice" by saying I was exhausted rather than showing my blistered fingers, engraved circles under the eyes and lower back pains, I wouldn't be drawing anyone into my world. If in "Waiting for Daddy" I had said only that it was hard to see my daughter go to her dad's, it would not have the emotional impact it does when readers actually see me packing her special things and taking her to the lobby.

But don't show everything—don't write about the mundane details of the experience. Unless they are essential to the story and to the point you are driving home, don't include things like how many streets you crossed to reach your destination, which bus you took, and how many stores you searched before finding the mauve scarf.

To justify such inclusions, students often tell me, "But that really happened," to which I respond, "So what?" When I tell my students to write about an experience that affected them, I tell them to begin the article *after breakfast*: unless their scrambled eggs had polka dots or unless they fell in love over the wheat toast, no one cares what they ate or said with their morning coffee.

THE BOTTOM LINES

It all comes to this: As writers of personal experience articles, we must look at our worlds as honestly as we can, seeing the truths—both the dark and the light—within our experiences so that we can share them with other people who will nod and say: "Yes, that's how it is. I've been there, too."

BY DON McKINNEY

How to Write True-Life Dramas

Many people think of fiction when they hear the word *story*, but a true story is just as much of a story as a short story is, and often a more compelling one. For example, early in 1984 *McCall's* received a query from a California writer, Paul Bagne, about a young woman who, when she was 14 years old, had been told that she had leukemia. I still remember how that story began:

> *Cindy Walters listened intently to the carefully measured words of Dr. William Lande. "At first it didn't hit me that anything was seriously wrong," she says. "But his voice was shaking and that began to scare me. You know you're in trouble when the doctor is almost in tears."*

The doctor went on to tell her that her prognosis was not good unless she was willing to try a radical new combination of drugs that would make her very sick but might help her. She and her parents decided to take the risk, and eventually her disease went into remission. Several years later, Cindy fell in love and married. She wanted a child, but was told that pregnancy—if she were able to get pregnant at all—sometimes caused the disease to return. Cindy did become pregnant, and both she and the baby came through with flying colors.

At *McCall's*, we call such stories human interest narratives; other editors refer to them as true-life dramas. Whatever they're called, they are accounts of dramatic experiences in the lives of real people. And, like fiction, they are told in narrative form. These stories have always been popular with readers, in part because we all love to get caught up in a good story. And beyond that, such stories often perform a real service. Not only can readers identify with people who have confronted serious problems and overcome them, but also they often can gain hope and courage from someone else's triumph.

We thought the story Bagne wanted to tell sounded like an excellent human interest narrative, and even though we didn't know him and had never seen any of his writing, we told him to go ahead. *McCall's* is constantly looking for these stories, and we've tried to run at least one in every issue. Our research tells us that they are invariably among the most popular with our readers, even in issues containing stories of far more importance, or interviews with major celebrities. Human interest stories are also increasingly in demand by a great many other magazines, from *Life* and *Reader's Digest* to most of the women's magazines. They sometimes lead to book contracts and even movie and television sales.

Let me give you a few more examples of the kind of stories I'm talking about, and then I'll give you some hints on where to find them and how to go about writing them.

Shortly after we had heard from Bagne, we talked to two young reporters from Chicago, Rick Soll and Gene Mustain, about a story they had uncovered for their newspaper. It involved two women. One had severe birth defects and at age three months had been labeled as retarded and placed in a state institution because nobody else wanted her. A few years later an idealistic young nurse came upon this little girl. She found the child bright and inquisitive. The nurse took an interest, fought the indifference and even hostility of the institution, and finally succeeded in having the child retested and found to be normal. The little girl was eventually placed in a foster home, grew up and graduated from high school, married, and had a child of her own. Soll and Mustain wanted to tell us how the nurse and the woman she had rescued had been reunited many years later, and what that meeting had meant to them both.

A writer from North Carolina, Glenn Joyner, came to us with the story of a remarkable woman named Kathleen White who had developed multiple sclerosis, and subsequently lost the use of her legs and most of the use of her arms. Then, through a fluke, she saw a doctor's report on her condition. The doctor had concluded that Kathleen was in the terminal stages of her disease and had not long to live. Angry that she had not been told, and determined to prove her doctors wrong, she went on a grueling program of exercise and training that not only put her back on her feet, but also enabled her to run in—and finish—a 26.2 mile marathon.

Barbara Raymond, a writer from Buffalo, New York, wrote us about a family named Spiegel, whose youngest child, Annie, had been born with severe facial damage. The Spiegels had raised Annie as normally as possible, but her appearance was shocking to strangers, and as their child grew older they came to realize that it would become harder and harder to keep her from feeling like a freak. They finally found a surgeon who could help her and, after several operations, Annie was restored to nearly normal appearance.

THE OUTSIDE ADVANTAGE

And just so you don't think that all of these stories involve medical disasters, I should tell you about the writer from a small town in upstate New York, Lorene Hanley Duquin, who wrote to tell us about what happened the previous Christmas in the nearby town of Ripley. A severe snowstorm had hit the area, stranding hundreds of travelers on the highways. The people of Ripley not only rescued these families but also found them places to sleep, fed them, got Christmas presents for them, even found a Santa Claus for the children, and ended up giving them all a Christmas they would never forget.

These writers all had several things in common. They did not live in New York City. We had never met them or even heard of them before. We bought every story and in each case it was the first sale the writer made to *McCall's*. And human interest narratives can be an excellent way for you to break into a national magazine, too.

Of course, these markets demand excellence, and the standards for narratives aren't any less than for our other articles. Some of these writers were inexperienced in writing for magazines, and their first tries were pretty rough. But because they had good stories to tell, we wanted very much to have them succeed. We gave them detailed rewrite instructions, talked to them a number of times about their articles, helped them through one and sometimes several rewrites.

Let me emphasize another important point about the stories I've just mentioned: *We did not know about them.* New York editors read the New York papers, and sometimes a few other big city papers; we read most of the national magazines and we watch television, and when we spot a story we think would work for us, we assign it. Competition for such stories is fierce, and we know from experience that if we don't move quickly, some other magazine will. I can't tell you the number of times we've heard about good stories in other parts of the country and assigned them, often using a New York writer, and have gotten the story in print without ever hearing from a local writer—a writer who might easily have gotten the assignment if he or she had brought it to us.

So if you live outside the New York area, you have an advantage—you may be able to find out about events and people we will never hear about. But what kinds of stories should you be looking for?

An extraordinary experience. Such stories often involve some sort of disaster (fire, flood, earthquake) that places a person in jeopardy. Then they go on to tell how he or she pulled through. A woman survives the crash of a light plane. She is badly injured and the pilot is dead. She doesn't know where she is, but she knows she cannot survive long without aid. After waiting several days to see if help will arrive, she starts crawling down the mountain. . . . That was a hell of a story, and we ran it in the magazine a number of years ago.

A common problem. This kind of narrative describes how a man or woman or family dealt with the sort of experience many of us have faced or might face, and thus helps us to understand how such problems can be handled, and perhaps how we might behave in similar circumstances. An older couple whose grandchild had been separated from them because of their son's divorce and his former wife's remarriage decided to fight for the right to see the child. They finally went to court—and won. The story of how they were awarded visitation rights has great meaning for others in their situation, as well as being a heartwarming story for everyone. Think of some universal problem and try to find one person or family whose story will make it vivid and alive for the reader.

A national issue. A few years back, we ran an article about a woman in Alsea, Oregon, who had suffered a miscarriage and found reason to believe that it might have been caused by a chemical herbicide that had been sprayed in her area. Working virtually alone for the next three years, she managed to gather enough evidence to convince the authorities to suspend spraying until further studies could be made.

When Love Canal was in all the newspapers, we ran the story of one woman's family and what they had suffered because of the toxic wastes that had been buried near their home. By telling of her children's birth defects, her husband's blinding headaches, and her own serious illness, her story brought this national problem home to our readers. (Incidentally, this was one of those stories that wasn't proposed to us by a writer in the area; we learned of it through the national press and assigned an outside reporter.)

WHERE DO YOU FIND SUCH STORIES?

I asked each of the writers I have mentioned where they found their material, and they offered some pointers that you can use, too. Paul Bagne found out about the young woman who had recovered from leukemia by working as a volunteer for a local branch of the American Cancer Society. "It's good for a writer to stay involved with the world around him," he told me. "That's where the stories are."

Rick Soll and Gene Mustain, the two reporters who told us about the "retarded" child and the nurse who rescued her, found their story by looking through back issues of the newspaper they worked for. One of them came upon a report of a girl who had sued her parents for abandonment, and they were curious to learn the story behind it. They eventually wrote it up for their paper, and later for us.

Barbara Raymond heard about her story on a local TV show. Glenn Joyner discovered Kathleen White and her fight against MS in a newspaper column in a North Carolina paper. "I always check the columns when I'm in a strange town," he says, "because you often find human interest stories there." Lorene Hanley Duquin, who told our Christmas story, read about Ripley's "miracle" in her local paper. She called the town clerk in Ripley and got the details she needed to write her query.

"Finding ideas for true-life dramas is easy," she said in a recent letter. "The newspapers are full of them. Attorneys are another good source—especially if they have a hot court case that is based on some social issue. Once you become established in your community as a freelancer, people come to you with stories. In fact, I just got one the other day. I've met people on vacation that I've done true-life dramas about. And I try to keep in touch with friends and acquaintances who might lead me to a story because of where they work. For example, I have one friend who works in a hospital emergency room, another who is the assistant New York State attorney general in the Buffalo office, and another who is involved in local politics. I've gotten story ideas from all of them."

With a little imagination and a lot of legwork, you can sometimes discover a human interest story that hasn't been in the papers at all. When we learned, for instance, that new medical techniques were being used to save the lives of premature babies that once would have died, we asked a writer to go to a hospital that used such techniques and see if she could find a couple that had seen their baby saved because of this. She interviewed doctors, talked to a number of couples, and finally found one whose story illustrated the point perfectly. She spent several days with them, recreated their experience, and wove the medical facts into a gripping narrative.

The same approach has been used to illuminate such heartbreaking problems as finding a baby to adopt, or to illustrate the new choices available to infertile women. We have used it to dramatize the new treatments that are saving so many more cancer patients. If there is some dramatic breakthrough in medical knowledge, think about how it might be made even more compelling by using the story of one person or one family as the narrative framework.

HOW DO YOU WRITE THEM?

The narrative form is comparatively easy for the beginning writer because the structure is largely dictated by the facts of the story itself. Every story has a beginning and a middle and an end, and when a writer asks me how to handle a narrative, I usually tell him or her to begin at the beginning and simply tell what happened—to get out of the way and let the events themselves carry the story along.

The only real decision you have to make is about the lead, because the most effective way to introduce your readers to the story may not be with the first incident in the chain of events you're describing. There is no "right" lead, of course; no formula I can give you that will guarantee a successful article. But however you choose to begin, remember that your lead has a single, simple purpose—to lure the reader (and this includes the editor, who will decide whether the reader gets a chance at it or not) into your story and to capture that person's interest so that he cannot put it down until he learns how it comes out.

For Maxine Rock, whose story of one woman's fight to save her son from paralysis and death was published in our June '85 issue, the lead went this way:

Most of all, Alana Shepherd remembered the blood. It came gushing out of her son's throat when a tube, placed there by doctors because the young man was so paralyzed that he couldn't breathe on his own, slipped out. She recalls a horrible hissing sound, and suddenly the hospital walls were splattered with red. It cascaded over her hair, her face, her chest. Blood puddled in her lap. It shot higher and higher, erupting like an angry volcano. It was the only time, whispers Alana, her hand trembling at the memory, when she really thought her son might die.

From there, Rock went back to the beginning, describing the boy's near-fatal accident, how his mother learned of it and what happened next.

Soll and Mustain began in the present, years after the drama they were going to describe, with the reunion between Karen and the nurse who rescued her:

Karen Boldt, a tiny, attractive woman of 32, hesitates a moment, then leaves her crutches in the car. Struggling into the icy wind of a winter day in Detroit, she limps toward a motel coffee shop. Inside, she scans the room until she recognizes an older woman sitting several booths away. Approaching her from behind, she cups her hands over the woman's eyes and kisses her cheek. The woman turns, and they embrace. It is an emotional moment for them both.

Their long and special relationship began 27 years ago in Dixon State

School, a cruel and dehumanizing institution in rural Illinois. Karen, left there by her parents when she was three months old, was Dixon's youngest inmate.

Glenn Joyner used a somewhat different technique. Using the marathon itself as his narrative framework, he interwove the current action with the story of Kathleen White's fight to get to the starting line. It began, dramatically, this way:

The Starting Line: It is a brisk Saturday morning in Charlotte, North Carolina, and 1,002 runners are nervously jogging and stretching as they wait for the start of the sixth annual Charlotte Observer Marathon. At exactly 10:01 there is the crack of the starter's pistol, and the pack surges forward. At the very rear, her heart already pounding, is a 35-year-old housewife wearing lavender shorts and shirt and a railroad engineer's cap. Waving to her four excited children along the sidewalk, she appears very ordinary and totally relaxed. She is neither. . . ."

Joyner continued the action for a few more paragraphs and then cut to give some background:

Kathleen White has been battling with incapacitating illnesses for almost two decades. At the age of 17 she contracted Crohn's disease, an incurable disorder that causes severe abdominal cramps, nausea and chronic diarrhea. But, with remarkable stoicism for a teenager, she accepted her misfortune and vowed not to let it ruin her life. . . ."

Cutting back and forth between the dramatic story of her fight back from paralysis and her agonizing effort to finish the marathon, the first she had ever run, Joyner shaped a compelling narrative. This technique won't work every time—you obviously need some dramatic event to provide the framework—but it's a good one to keep in mind.

SELECTIVE DETAILS

After the lead, as you go back to the beginning of your story and relate the events as they unfolded, you must keep in mind that even the most exciting story will not hold an audience unless the characters are human and believable, people the reader will identify with and care about. To make someone come alive on the page, you need details—about appearance, manner, the way he speaks or she moves. You need those little human touches that may do nothing to move your narrative forward, but that will make its characters seem real.

Maxine Rock captured these details by talking at length with Alana Shepherd and her son, James, about Alana's struggle to make him walk again after the paralysis. Much of what they told her could not be used in her final story, but only through hours of interviewing did she learn the little details that made the scene she was describing unforgettable. This is Alana's memory of seeing her son for the first time after his accident: ". . . we were in a tiny hospital, staring down at the body of our son. He was too tall for the bed, and his heels were hanging over the end. He looked like a rag doll." Instead of simply saying that he was limp and unconscious, the image of the rag doll said it for her, and in a way that lets readers see it for themselves.

Later in the article, Rock describes the trip back to their home in Atlanta.

It was a long, hard trip. James burned with fever one moment, then turned icy cold the next. When he was awake, his dark eyes were wide with pain and fear; asleep, he looked ashen and skeletal. James was nearly dead when the plane touched down in Atlanta, but he opened his eyes briefly, and his lips soundlessly formed one word: "Home."

Specific details like this don't just leap at you from the person you are interviewing; they have to be dragged out with lots of questions: "What did he look like?" "What did he say?" "How did you feel?" "What is your most vivid memory of that moment?"

Under Barbara Raymond's patient questioning, Irene Spiegel remembered the moment when her daughter first became aware of her facial deformity. "Annie loved to sing and dance in front of the mirror. One night she stopped, leaned forward and looked at her image. With her fingers, she tried to tug her features into place. 'Why does my eye look like this?' she asked me."

After hours of interviewing Jeanette Cusick, the nurse, about the little "retarded" girl she had rescued, Soll and Mustain were able to recreate a touching scene that took place in Jeanette's home the first night Karen had been out of the institution.

Karen touched everything—the furniture, the carpeting, the draperies. She was mesmerized by the ordinary comforts of Jeanette's home . . . for the first time, Karen used a fork and drank from something other than a tin cup. . . . Later, after soaking in her first bubble bath, Karen snuggled into bed, then gazed intently at the painting hanging in Jeanette's bedroom. Titled "Love Is Blind," it depicted a little girl hugging a doll. Sawdust tumbled from the doll's broken foot. Jeanette, conscious of how sensitive Karen was about her clubfoot, told her, "When people see your beautiful face, no one will notice your foot."

The next morning Karen opened the first real Christmas presents she had ever received. Among them were a rocking chair and a doll. She examined the doll's perfect legs like a doctor examining a newborn baby. Then she named the doll "Jeanette."

Talk to your subjects as much as you can, even after you think you have all you will need. I've had writers tell me that sometimes the most revealing comments come after the interview seems to be over, when the recorder or the pad and pencil has been put away and everyone is beginning to relax. Over-research, over-report, learn much more than you can ever use. Only then will you fully understand the people and events you are writing about, and be able to select the details you need.

A FINAL WORD

Where do you stop? And how? In her story of Alana Shepherd's struggle to help her son recover from paralysis after his accident, Maxine Rock decided to stop with the climax, the moment everyone had been waiting for, even though much has happened to James and his mother since then.

Doctors insisted on wheeling James to the hospital doors, but James got up, folded the wheelchair and handed it to his father. "I won't need it," he said. He leaned on just a cane and pushed open the hospital doors. Then, triumphantly, he walked out.

Soll and Mustain ended by coming back to the reunion between Jeanette, the nurse, and Karen, the little girl (now 32, with a son of her own) she had rescued from the institution:

"The whole experience at Dixon," [Karen] says, "was a tragedy. But I try to find good even out of bad experiences. The pregnancy hurt, but I have Michael. I look forward to watching him grow up and accomplish things I couldn't."

Jeanette tells Karen that's what she always wanted, to watch the girl she rescued grow and become what she is now. "Karen, I loved you from the time I met you, and I love you now."

"That," Karen replies, "is what saved my life."

And Lorene Duquin ended her story of Christmas in Ripley, New York, with this lovely image:

Christmas had come and gone. But the nearly 1,000 visitors did not forget. Cards, letters and donations poured into Ripley, many from people who had not even been there that night.

Then, last spring, a man from upstate New York, whose daughter and son-in-law had spent Christmas in Ripley with their children, sent each of the women who had worked in the kitchen three beautiful rosebushes. Now, every June, when the tall shade trees form an arch over Ripley's Main Street, the townspeople will see the blooming Peace roses, and they will remember, too.

Just as there is no one right lead, there is no one right ending. But the ending should leave your readers feeling satisfied, uplifted, moved. Don't simply summarize your story, or restate points you have already made, but find some image, some quote, some anecdote that catches the theme of the piece and, by so doing, ties it all together.

It is sometimes said that good stories tell themselves; they don't, but if you have done your job well, they will read that way. You must research the situation thoroughly, talk to a lot of people, find a focus that will hold it all together. Then you must figure out the essential ingredients of your narrative and describe them as simply and honestly and cleanly as you can. Human interest narratives do take a lot of work, both to find and to write, but they are relatively less complex to put together than a profile or a straight article. They are also in great demand, and an excellent way to break into a magazine.

Let me leave you with a thought that will, I hope, inspire you. *McCall's* continues to publish pieces like the ones I have described, and if history is any guide, more than half of them will come from writers we have never heard of before.

One of them could be you.

BY GARY PROVOST

Writing the Roundup Article

If you wanted, you *could* sell a roundup article without actually doing any writing.

For example, you could telephone six local bankers and ask them if they think the American economy is going to croak next year. Type up their names, the names of their banks and their opinions, stuff it all in an envelope and mail it to the business page editor of your local newspaper, and *presto* . . . you have written a roundup article. You have "rounded up" their opinions like so many cattle and corralled them into a newspaper article.

That sort of thing, however, strikes me as being more the work of a secretary than a writer, so I'm not going to deal with it. I'm talking here about roundup articles that you *write*.

My kind of roundup article does not begin with a name in boldfaced type followed by a colon. It is more likely to begin something like this:

> *The American economy is going to croak next year. At least that's the opinion of Paul H. Percival, President of the Pumpkin City National Bank.*
>
> *"It's as fragile as an egg," says Percival, "and if I didn't have a bank to run I'd hock everything I own and hide out in the mountains for three years."*
>
> *Percival, despite an impish sense of humor that refutes the banker stereotypes, is a conservative sort not given to rash statements about the economy or anything else. His opinion is certainly to be respected, but there are at least four other bankers in the country who think he is dead wrong.*

At this point the writer has begun a roundup of banker opinion on a specific subject, but he has done something more. *He has turned a survey into interesting reading.*

In a sense a roundup article is always a survey. It might be a survey of how carnivals are run, or what being a rock star is like, or what happened to people who assumed new identities (I have sold roundup articles on all of these), but it *is* a survey. It's not a specific survey boasting the kind of statistical accuracy upon which you would base a decision to get divorced or to vote Republican. But it is a survey, nonetheless, with pros and cons, common denominators, exceptions to the rules, consensus and disagreement; and what it lacks in girth it more than replaces with charm.

CONFERENCES AND CORRALS

While you still might not be sure of just what a roundup article is, chances are you have read dozens, even hundreds of them. They appear in movie magazines

("How Important Is Oscar? Five Academy Award Winners Tell"), sports magazines ("The Nation's Five Top Football Coaches Pick the All-Time Greats"), women's magazines ("Three Up-And-Coming Starlets Talk About Beauty") and virtually every other kind of magazine you can name. Not all magazines use roundup articles, but you would be hard-put to find a *type* of magazine that doesn't. A quick look at a small stack of magazines I keep near my desk brought out roundup articles in very different magazines: "A Tale of Two Sleuths" and "Where Have All the Good Men Gone?" in which the author interviews several women about the shortage of good men. Also, *USAir*, which has my own roundup article, "Funny Business," in which I profile six top cartoonists.

By now you might have noticed a common denominator in these articles. They all bring people together to talk about something; *they are conferences on paper.* They might be the kind of conference where one person speaks, then the next, or they might be the kind of conference where all the conferees speak throughout, debating, agreeing, disagreeing.

And these national magazines I have mentioned are the smaller part of the roundup articles market. Newspapers, Sunday supplements and regionals such as the city magazines and the multi-town "shoppers" are hungry for roundup articles that bring together experts in their geographical areas.

No subject that I can think of has been immunized against the writer who wants to corral it into a roundup article (though in most cases he would really be rounding up a group of *experts* on the subject). A roundup article is defined not by the material you write about, but by your approach to the material.

I have written roundup articles about private detectives, haunted houses, pool rooms, singers, roller rinks, and dozens of other topics. With any one of them I *could* have taken a linear approach to the subject. For example, I could cover the history of pool shooting, followed by some famous pool shooters, followed by the negative attitudes toward pool, followed by the emergence of family-style pool rooms elevating the game to respectability, etc.

But I didn't. Instead I rounded up a number of specimens and dissected each to reveal truths about them all.

In the case of the pool rooms article I drove first to a sleazy smoke-filled pool room that seemed to be hiding out in a basement beneath a treacherous downtown alley. Next, I moved on to a middle-class pool room that was jammed into the back end of a suburban bowling alley, and finally (at four bucks an hour to play) I ended up in a plush new family style billiard parlor on Rt. 9, whose tangerine colored felt covered shiny new tables. At each establishment I shot pool. I spoke to players. I interviewed the manager. *I got people to talk about pool rooms.* I took photographs. When I was done I had rounded up three pool rooms, and into my notebook I had scrawled hundreds of quotes and observations about the things they had in common and the things that made them different.

I have gone through this process of taking notes and snapping pictures many times, and I usually finish with the answers to all my questions, save one: *How do I organize my notes?*

ROUNDING UP THE GEESE

Of course, with the roundup article, as with any article, the process of organizing begins long before you start glutting your notebook with quotes and observations. Your first organizational problem is coming up with a good slant.

Your slant is your particular view of a subject, the aspect of it that you choose to explore. It is the thing that makes your article about Canada geese different from my article about Canada geese. Generally, if either one of us calls up an editor and says, "Hey, how about an article on Canada geese?" he's going to say, "What about Canada geese?" The answer to that question is your slant.

However, editors tend to mellow a bit when it comes to roundup articles. If you're a beginner or you're writing for a national magazine, then yes, you probably will have to come up with a decent slant for your roundup. But if you're writing for a newspaper, a Sunday supplement or a regional magazine, and you're writing for an editor who knows your work and knows you will come up with "something," you can often suggest something vague like "a roundup article on amateur theater groups," and get the assignment. All of the roundup articles I do for regular clients are assigned on a "come up with a slant later" basis.

You will find that getting a newspaper assignment on a roundup article, even without a slant, is often easier than getting the go-ahead on something even more sharply focused, because you will be interviewing people or visiting establishments in several different towns. The editor of a wide circulation newspaper gets paid to create the illusion in each town his paper serves that reporters are scouring the streets for stories about that town. The reader's town should seem somehow special, and when you give the editor an opportunity to print something in-depth about three or four towns in one article he will be happy. Usually he will see the "rounding up" as a kind of slant in itself, and won't ask for anything more. In your query letter or phone call to an editor, tell him that you're going to round up "people who know" to comment on an issue. For example, "Everybody says winters in Iowa are getting harsher. What do the areas' meteorologists say?" But don't draw all your experts from the same well. Tell your editor, "I intend to ask men as well as women this question," or "I'll interview both black and white leaders," or "I plan to speak with people in California, Florida, and Connecticut."

In any case the roundup article, by its nature, needs a wide scope. It should not be heavily slanted, such as: "The Pool Room Ambience: Is It Really Bad for Your Kid?" (an article I sold to *MetroGuide*, a Boston-area magazine).

Ideally, the roundup article shouldn't be committed to any slant at all until after you have explored the subject and discovered some interesting way of looking at it.

THE HUEY, DEWEY AND LOUIE PRINCIPLE

The next thing to decide is: how many? How many private detectives should I interview? How many zoos should I visit? For me the answer is almost always the same. Three.

Three is a kind of magic number in writing. Both in syntax (I came, I saw, I conquered—bewitched, bothered and bewildered—Huey, Dewey and Louie) and in construction. Three is somehow enough but not too much. Three allows the possibility of a majority and minority view on any question, yet it makes unanimity convincing. And when you're bouncing around from one to the other, the reader can still keep track of three.

You could use four or five, of course, but the more you use the less room you have to explore each. As you widen the shores the water gets shallower, and as you add people or places you drift farther from the craft of writing and closer to those secretarial chores of making phone calls, listing titles, etc. Keeping the number of subjects manageable becomes more important when you consider the average length of these pieces: 1,000 to 3,000 words is a good range for the typical roundup article; anything under 1,000 could get pretty crowded.

After you have decided how many subjects to work with, figure out where to find them. That's usually easy. If you're going to round up members of a profession such as "Bartenders" (an article I sold to *Sunday Morning* magazine) or establishments, such as "The Five Best Ice Cream Parlors in the City," (which I sold to *Worcester Magazine*) all your sources are in the Yellow Pages. On the other hand, if you're seeking people and places that don't advertise, such as car thieves or haunted houses, you will have to ask around or go thrashing through old newspaper files. *But you will probably only have to find one this way.* People who live in haunted houses are being constantly accosted by other people who live in haunted houses or know someone who does. They become a kind of community of haunted house owners. Likewise, car thieves have served time with other car thieves. Your first interview can usually point you toward several more.

When I write roundup articles I choose my interview subjects with a number of balancing acts in mind. I'm usually writing for a regional publication, so I choose people in three different towns for that geographical balance that editors like. I try to find one male subject for my "female" stories and one female subject for my "male" stories. And most important, I track down subjects operating on different levels, just as I dropped in on pool rooms that operated on three different strata of society. When I did a roundup article on local rock groups I found a trio of guys who were still looking for a drummer and hadn't made a dime yet, another group of guys who worked regular jobs but were getting well-paid for weekend gigs, and a flashy six-piece band with an agent, a three-color brochure, plenty of work, and a nationally released recording.

Sometimes I do roundup interviews by phone, but usually I go to my subjects. It's important that your writing appeal to the senses, and only by going there can you tell the reader what you saw, smelled, felt.

And of course you have to go there to take the photographs. One of the best reasons for approaching your material as a roundup article is that more photographs will be used, and that means more money.

Vary your photos. Just because you are interviewing three pianists doesn't mean you should send your editor three photos of people sitting at the piano. His printed page will be more attractive with photos depicting one person performing on stage, one horsing around with his kids, and one writing the notes to a composition, for example.

You will also want to organize your questions before you go interviewing, though you should always be open to areas of discussion you hadn't considered. I always make it a point to ask many of the same questions at each stop. For example, when researching my piece on haunted houses I asked all of the inhabitants if they thought their ghosts intended to harm them. I do this because of an odd phenomenon that is one of the great attractions of the roundup article. *Several answers to the same question are interesting, whether the answers are the same or different.*

SLEUTHING FOR SLEUTHS

In her article in *Woman's Day*, Natalie Gittelson was able to intrigue the reader by eliciting from women a variety of answers to the question, "Where Have All the Good Men Gone?" Some women said the men had rushed into the arms of old-fashioned, nonfeminist gals. Others said the "good men" were being decimated by a rapidly rising standard of what made a "good man." Some said that good men hadn't gone anywhere, that there were more than ever, and the women explained why they felt that way. The women who were surveyed didn't have to agree so that Gittelson could come up with a good article. They just had to have well thought-out opinions based on their own experience and observation. Polls, even when they are unscientific, are fascinating.

By the time you finish taking notes and pictures and reading supplementary material on your topic, you will have much more material than you can use. You have perhaps decided on a slant, but you are still pestered by organizational questions. If you are rounding up sleuths who track down stolen art, as the *Life* writer did, you might ask: Do I write all about one sleuth and then the next? Or do I cover all the "how I got into this line of work" material and then all the "some of my most exciting cases" material, etc.?

If you decide to do one sleuth, then the next, your organizational problems are not severe. After all, your notes are already arranged that way, and you have only to decide who is going to say what, and try not to be repetitive. But that kind of construction gets stale in a hurry and all your stories will start to look alike. A roundup article is much livelier when all the characters are present throughout the story. You get that quality of a "poll being taken" over and over. If one teacher, for example, says that teachers are lavishly overpaid, your reader would like to know right away what the other teachers have to say to that.

In my haunted house roundup (published in the *Worcester Telegram*), similarities that would have gone unnoticed if spread over three little stories became fascinating because I had the freedom to include all of my subjects throughout the story. I wrote:

Nevertheless, there are striking similarities in the stories told by these people. All of them note the non-threatening character of the ghosts. Several mention the presence of music, though none can describe it or locate it. All of them associate the ghost with the house and not with themselves, and none of them plans to move out just because a ghost has moved in.

The illusion of the roundup article is that all of the principles have gathered in a room and discussed the subject. The reader hears a lively debate between them, even though they have never met.

GRID AND BEAR IT

To create this feeling in the article, I use a chart that organizes my material so that I have access to it in any order I want to use it.

For a roundup article on photographers in Central Massachusetts I recently sold to *Sunday Morning,* I found three photographers—two men and a woman, in three different towns—interviewed them, took pictures, read a little background material, and then I made out a chart from my notes. Across the top of my paper I printed the names of the photographers. Along one side I listed the topics I had discussed with them. I drew lines to create a grid. Then I went through all of my notes, picked out key words from each section, and plugged them in to the corresponding block (Chuck Kidd on the use of equipment, Pam Koumoutseas on her hobbies, etc.). This only takes a few minutes and it organizes all of my notes.

If I wanted to write about money first, I could follow my money line and see what notes I should be reading (or remembering) in order to get the views on money of all the photographers. If I wanted to have Pam talking about her philosophy, her family and her future, before I switched to Jack Doyle addressing those subjects—or others—I could do it. I could follow the blocks any way I wanted, to create whatever pattern of discussion seemed logical, and I would know I was not overlooking any good quotes.

The key to maintaining this illusion of three photographers (or pool room operators, haunted house owners, vacuum cleaner salesmen, whatever) carrying on a cohesive discussion is to create smooth transitions that make it seem that they are replying to issues that have been just brought up. If you want to write about something, then create the illusion that it springs logically from the last thing you wrote.

For example, to get from the "favorite subjects of the photographers" to the ethical issue of "truth in photography," I wrote:

What Pam Koumoutseas sees in young girls is perhaps the same thing Chuck Kidd sees in the farms around Hardwick—a chance to etch his artistic vision onto film without regard for client's wishes, cost effectiveness, or skirting too close to that elusive line called "truth in photography."

Sometimes the easiest way to create this imaginary group of experts is to pose the question in print. I wrote:

Again the quality. What is it that makes one picture better than another?
"Composition is what counts," says Pam Koumoutseas.
"Yes, composition," Doyle says, "framing the photo and seeing how the light lands on your subject."
"Composition," says Kidd. And though he's not ready to say with finality just what it is that makes one photographer better than another, he does add an interesting note to the eternal debate over whether the photographer is a craftsman or an artist.

Now that I think of it, Chuck Kidd's comment has a lot to say to the writer of the roundup article. Kidd said, "I suppose he's both, but more and more as I practice photography I find I know exactly what's going to happen with a picture. That, I guess, is the difference. The craftsman knows what's going to happen. The artist doesn't."

And the writer of the roundup article? Well, he is both, too. He is an artist certainly, using the mundane worlds of bowling alleys, used car dealerships, and pool rooms to draw fascinating word pictures. But he's a craftsman, too, who carefully cuts out the pieces of his puzzle, or organizes them with not a seam showing, so that the reader thinks three or four experts sat down and had a fascinating discussion and the writer didn't have to do any work at all.

BY RONA S. ZABLE

Cooking Up the Food/Recipe Article

In spite of—or maybe because of—these tough economic times, Americans are obsessed with food. We are literally devouring all kinds of stories and articles that in any way concern food—how to cook it, serve it, freeze it, grow it, stuff it, and eat right! We are, in short, involved in what a *U.S. News & World Report* cover story once called "America's Great New Food Craze."

Which is delicious news, indeed, for freelancers, because editors are more receptive than ever before to ideas for food-related articles.

But, you may wonder, doesn't one have to be a good cook to write food articles? No. Certainly, if you plan to write for *Bon Appetit* or *Food & Wine*, you must know your onions (or better, your scallions). Yet, I am only a fair-to-mediocre cook; but I have one advantage. I'm a terrific eater. My penchant for "quick, easy recipes any dummy can make without fouling up" sold my first food article to *Family Circle*. I figured that other busy single parents out there might be looking for fast and foolproof meals that don't require many pots and pans. My query, along with a brief description of some of the more intriguing recipes, whetted the editor's appetite, and I eventually sold "A Treasury of No-Fuss, No-Fail Recipes" for $650.

My second sale to *Family Circle* was a collection of other people's recipes: "Heavenly Recipes From Atlanta's Church Suppers," which earned $1,200.

Ideas and imagination are more important than great culinary skills here. Just as you don't have to be a governess to write gothics, you don't have to be a great cook to write food articles.

FOOD ARTICLES: THE BASIC RECIPE

The *food/recipe piece* is essentially a how-to service piece, with a lead or introduction and a number of recipes. It concerns food and beverages in some way—preparation, cooking, baking, serving, cleaning up, nutrition and dieting, history, usage, preserving, trends. It might be a general feature such as the one *Ford Times* did some time ago on today's new young chefs or a *Family Circle* piece on how to cut costs by learning to cut up packaged chickens properly. It might be a reminiscence about a person, a place or a product, with or without recipes. It might be as broad as a feature about twenty low-cost dinners for two, or as specialized as a feature on "Home-Made Potato Chips." It could tell how to grow herbs and spices in a window box, or how to plan a Sunday night backyard Mongolian fire pot supper.

Glance through the food sections of some major magazines on the news stands, and you'll marvel at the diversity of subjects. Readers want to learn new ways to cook old favorites, and old ways to cook new favorites. They want to know everything about every kind of cuisine—ethnic, vegetarian, gourmet, regional, low-calorie, low-fat, simplified, money-saving, body-building, natural and even sexy!

And national magazines will certainly consider food stories without recipes. For instance, some marvelous stories include: "Bake Sale Dough's and Don'ts" (how to successfully run a bake sale), "How to Set Up a Holiday Cookie Swap," "How Smart Cooks Save Money." Perhaps you've gleaned some tips on cooking equipment—new or special hints about outdoor grills and barbecues, suggestions about food processors, microwaves or cooking over campstoves.

FIRST INGREDIENT: THE IDEA

The publications that accept food recipe articles have distinctly different palates; if you plan to sell to them, send for editorial guidelines. Editors seek articles that interest *their* specific audiences. Readers of *Woman's Day*, *Family Circle* and *Working Mother*, for example, like ideas about fast, simple and inexpensive yet healthful ways to serve food. Also consider the income of the readers when you target the article. The upscale, affluent young marrieds who subscribe to *Bon Appetit* or *Food & Wine* are not looking to save money or time; they prefer elegant and frankly complicated meals.

Give your idea a novel twist. Rather than a feature on money-saving meals prepared with hamburger (an overworked theme), suggest a feature with some recipes that really stretch a pound of hamburger to feed more than four to six people. Maybe you have a way with leftovers, or your family has found some unusual and healthful eating habits. Or, in fact, take just one food—lemons, tomatoes, chocolate, pita bread—and build a story around it.

SEASONS AND SEASONINGS

Whenever possible, tie your articles to the seasons. "We're always looking for holiday food pieces," an editor from *Bon Appetit* once told me, "especially Thanksgiving, Christmas and Easter." It's easy to run out of ideas, so editors always seek offbeat themes—such as how to make a Victorian gingerbread house and how to bake fail-proof Christmas cookies.

And don't forget all the other holidays and holy days throughout the year—New Year's, St. Patrick's Day, Halloween, Lent, Hanukkah. Use an unexpected, unique twist—"Give an Indoor July Fourth Barbecue," "Low-Calorie Passover Dishes," "Eire Fare" (maybe with a collection of green veggies for St. Patrick's Day).

Plan ahead for other types of seasonal food stories related to graduations, summer picnics, June weddings, birthdays, baby showers, harvest celebrations. You might want to narrow the field down with a query on what wines to take on a picnic; unusual ways to arrange foods or set tables, both indoors and out; making party favors and cleaning up efficiently. New wedding punch drinks, tips on storing leftovers, and ways to decorate cakes are always needed.

Plan ahead for special food "seasons," too—blueberry season, winter apples, zucchini time. The key is that seasonal food stories are published at the *beginning* of that food's "season," so target queries accordingly. Newspapers work two months ahead and longer on holiday food features. Magazines need at least a six-month lead. Think about your Fourth of July barbecue story around Christmas. Around Valentine's Day, mull over your "pumpkin recipes for Halloween."

How can a freelancer find out when each food has its season? ("We just *know* these things," one food editor told me.) Contact your state's Department of Agriculture, your local county agricultural agent, or the federal Department of Agriculture (while you're at it, obtain some of their good, basic recipes). Another wise move: Make friends with the owner of a good fruit/vegetable market in your area.

PINCH OF SALT

Pay attention to trends in eating habits, as reported in magazines and newspapers, and on the news. For example, because of the increased interest in their health, Americans are moving away from meat, potatoes and Mom's apple pie; we're favoring fish, soups, salad, vegetables and fresh fruit desserts. Interest in ethnic foods and regional fare has been renewed. Nutrition is especially important, too: *Bon Appetit*'s recipes now call for only minimum amounts of salt and butter.

While fast, easy food preparation is the rule for Monday through Friday meals, there is greater interest in the ritual of leisurely weekend gourmet cooking. Oh, and when we indulge in desserts, we still go for the gusto—with rich, high-calorie goodies.

Keep an eye out for all ethnic festivals and celebrations in your neck of the woods. Ask local chefs for tips and suggestions. Quiz cooking teachers about unusual classes or what students really want to know.

Whatever your topic, be certain that your ingredients are generally available nationally (unless you're doing a regional story). McIntosh apples are New England favorites, but are not necessarily readily available elsewhere. And while Vidalia onions are popular down South, they're virtually unknown in other areas.

Speaking of regional stories: Often, a region may take its own cuisine for granted. My query to Atlanta publications about church suppers didn't get a nod. But when I queried a national publication, it was a timely, interesting idea.

SECOND INGREDIENT: THE INTRODUCTION

Article length varies according to space requirements and format of the publications. A newspaper food story might run 800 to 2,000 words. *Family Circle* and *Woman's Day* use considerably less introductory copy, letting titles, full-color photography and recipes tell most of the story.

The "leads" on both my *Family Circle* food/recipe features averaged only about 125 words. My "No-Fuss, No-Fail" story included eight recipes; my Atlanta church supper story used sixteen (to give a fair representation to the various church denominations). Introductory copy tells readers why they'll enjoy trying these dishes, plus other background "sell copy," such as why the dishes are easy to prepare.

My church supper article began:

Although the tradition of church suppers began hundreds of years ago, it's something that congregations still look forward to—and with good reason! These affairs usually feature the best of local cooking (be it all-American or deliciously ethnic), and eating too much is almost guaranteed. In fact, at the yearly two-day festival of the Greek Orthodox Cathedral of the Annunciation in Atlanta, some 175,000 servings of food are dished up. Among the good things featured are Greek Salad, Stuffed Zucchini, Pecan Cookies and Honey-Dipped Pastry. Other recipes from this "city of churches" include Sour Cream Cake from Belvedere Methodist and nut candy from Temple Or Veshalom.

Woman's Day uses even less introductory copy. A recent feature, "Elegant Chicken for Thrifty Gourmets" has this lead:

Nothing beats chicken breasts for high-class dining without a high-class price tag, as these recipes prove.

Writing style varies according to the specific publication, so it's important to *read* and *understand* your market (although rules can always be broken for good ideas). While first-person, personal style is not often used by service and women's magazines (unless you're a famous chef or you're doing a story on your grandmother's Ukrainian food favorites), a number of the gourmet/leisure magazines use this style from time to time.

THIRD INGREDIENT: THE RECIPES

Chances are, you already have many recipes that you and your family have collected over the years. Some of my favorites came from local sources—cookbooks compiled by churches, synagogues or civic clubs. Friends are another great source.

Or, if you're doing a recipe roundup story, contact the individuals or groups you plan to feature and ask them to provide you with their recipes (a warning—some of the best cooks are the "pinch of this," "pinch of that" school, so beware of those recipes). Regional stories are easy to obtain because most people want recognition for their cooking. The churches I contacted in Atlanta for my church supper story were delighted to be featured nationally in *Family Circle*.

Do not, however, copy recipes word for word from magazines and newspapers. Food editors are pretty sharp cookies—they know right off if yours is a leftover idea. So, constantly read and seek out recipes to get an idea of what is different, what is hackneyed and what might be a trendsetter. And for true creativity, go into the kitchen and try your hand at inventing dishes.

The listing of ingredients in a recipe cannot be copyrighted. However, the presentation of the recipe, including directions for preparation, *can* be copyrighted. Thus, many authors may alter recipes in some way—by adding, changing or omitting one of the minor ingredients, and rewriting instructions to avoid word-for-word copying. Many experts believe that there's really no such thing as an "original recipe." Somebody, somewhere has probably made any particular dish before. Even Aunt Harriet's rhubarb cake might have been copied by her mother from a package or label.

You can sell single recipes but such a sale won't pay much. Suppose, however, you do have a marvelous family recipe for Aunt Harriet's rhubarb cake. You'd be better off entering the dish in one of those lucrative national cooking competitions—such as the Pillsbury Bake-off.

THE RECIPE RECIPE

Be as brief but as accurate as possible when writing recipes. List each ingredient in the order in which it will be used. Be specific about the size of pots and pans, the cooking time and any variations, the number of servings, and other pertinent information, such as whether the dish can be prepared ahead and frozen, and if it tastes better the next day. If you're not sure how to write your recipes, check the style of the publication you're considering. Some publications like a bare-as-bones style; others like a one-two-three preparation procedure; while *Gourmet,* for example, has a rather warm and chatty descriptive style.

To me, less is more. Instead of saying, "Drain a 17-oz. can of fruit cocktail," I'd word it: "One 17-oz. can fruit cocktail, drained."

Should you test recipes? While most magazines have their own test kitchens, newspapers' food editors, as a rule, do not. They must rely on their instincts and your accuracy. Do try and test recipes that you've collected. I like to combine business with pleasure by inviting family and friends over for a "taste-test" dinner. If one or two of the recipes are beyond your culinary talents, have a friend who's a good cook test the dishes.

Remember to carefully proofread ingredients and instructions.

When you're ready to submit your food recipe feature, send a query or outline, with either a brief description of your proposed recipes, or a couple of your best recipes. Tell how you obtained the recipes, and detail any "plus factors" (for example, they are especially high in nutrition, use no salt, taste better two days later, etc.).

And above all, when querying, whet the food editor's appetite with "drool copy"! This is the grabber that evokes an image of time and place, flavor and texture, whatever the story ideas. As an example, my "Atlanta's Heavenly Church

Suppers" query described long tables, covered with starched white tablecloths, an early summer evening, and the food:

> *. . . From the kitchens of the church's finest cooks comes a mouth-watering array of favorite specialties. Platters of crispy, golden-brown fried chicken; casseroles of Brunswick stew; hot, spicy chili; creamy potato salads; vegetables picked fresh that very morning from the garden and slow-simmered. . . .*

Another few lines told about the warm, flaky biscuits and rolls, and honey, fresh from honeycombs. Then on to desserts—"juicy peach cobblers, thick slabs of fresh-grated coconut cake."

FOURTH INGREDIENT: THE TITLE

Titles are important, too. "Send me a good coverline title," says an editor with *Family Circle*. A title can sell the entire idea. Even if the recipes aren't unique, an editor can still work closely with the writer to obtain other recipes if the concept works.

Come up with a grabber of a title suitable for the magazine's cover. Some examples: "Foods That Put You in the Mood" (*Cosmopolitan*); "Express-Line Dinners: Quick Shopping for Quick Meals" (*Family Circle*); "Chinese Cooking Made Easy" (*Bon Appetit*), "Valentine Dinners to Seduce the Heart and Appetite of Your Valentine" (*Gourmet*).

A title like "Elegant Entrees at Everyday Prices" (*Better Homes & Gardens*) sounds far more appealing than something like "Inexpensive Company Meals." "Cap It With Mushrooms" sounds more appealing than "Favorite Mushroom Dishes," doesn't it?

Romance your recipes with yummy, intriguing recipe names, too. Like "Northern Fried Chicken," "Apricot-Glazed Oriental Beef," "Luscious Lime Crunch." If you're stuck for a name in a recipe with no distinctive ingredients, give it a personal or regional name—"Miz Mary's Marvelous Marble Cake" or "Boston Blueberry Pudding."

OTHER TYPES OF FOOD-RELATED ARTICLES

Food is a subject that *sells*: And not, I assure you, only the food/recipe article, but the general food article, which I call the "food-related" feature. This is essentially a lifestyle, personality or nostalgia piece that always seems to find a home.

The market for this kind of story seems to be growing—in general interest publications, inflight magazines, outdoor magazines, regional publications, Sunday supplements, newspapers—you name it.

Without even realizing it, I've somehow frequently written about food-related themes. And these stories have been purchased by the *Atlanta Journal-Constitution, Christian Science Monitor, Atlanta Magazine*, and some others I'm keeping my fingers crossed about. These include a story about the struggles of a pioneering woman chef, a piece about a man who sells Girl Scout cookies, and the story of a lady who baked some wild, crazy, and X-rated cakes.

Such stories hold universal appeal. For instance, my story about Leonard Tchorz, the cook on a fishing boat, might seem of interest only regionally, because he sails out of New Bedford, Massachusetts. But his story has been sold and resold to the *Boston Globe, Providence Journal, New Bedford Standard-Times, National Fisherman* and *People on Parade*'s "Celebrity Chef."

And do you know why? My theory is that query letters are usually read somewhere before lunch time, when the editor or assistant is getting kind of hungry. And reading about fish chowder, doughnuts, or homemade candy is awfully appealing.

Food and/or recipes make good subjects for nostalgia, op-ed and think pieces, too. I sold a personal experience piece to *Rhode Islander* magazine on how I won six pounds of nuts in a contest (with deliberate mentions of filberts, pecans and such); and I once did a nostalgia story about Coca-Cola and Coke fountains for *Everywhere Magazine*.

What could *you* write about? Do you know of a family that likes to cook together? How about a nostalgia piece about making root beer in the cellar back in the good old days, or the fun of cooking the fish you've caught. If you know of a particularly good chef or cook, try celebrating his expertise in a local or regional publication.

Another suggestion: If you have a story that you can't sell, see if you can slant it to some aspect of food. Maybe your bachelor father piece didn't make it—but try revising it as a food article about "How Single Dads Cope in the Kitchen."

Restaurant features (profiles, not reviews) are popular with specialized food magazines. Maybe a roundup of appetizers from top restaurants across the country. Or an in-depth feature about a marvelous, out-of-the-way eatery whose cuisine or decor is unique. You should obtain at least one or two of the restaurant's best recipes (preferably scaled down to serve four to six people). Plus such other information as the history, decor, service, pricing and cooking techniques.

Here's an example of a delightful restaurant feature. Hawthorne Cottage in suburban Atlanta is a restaurant-cum-antique shop, once reviewed by Helen and John Friese in *Creative Loafing Magazine*. Wrote Helen, "If you don't like the food, you can always purchase the table." So intriguing was the story that the restaurant was overwhelmed by scores of new customers, and it completely ran out of food.

The magazine restaurant review, on the other hand, is frequently handled by staff or regular contributors since it requires a good knowledge of food and beverages. How might one become a reviewer? Consider starting by first querying your local newspaper or leisure publication and enclose some lively, provocative reviews of both well-known and not-so-well-known restaurants. Even the humblest byline can help. After Helen and John Friese started reviewing restaurants for *Creative Loafing,* Helen sent clips of her reviews to *Fine Dining,* which named her a contributing editor as the magazine's Atlanta correspondent.

You won't get rich, but the power is awesome. Your favorable review can cause a stampede in a restaurant. Remember, however, that the criteria for ratings are based on your audience. In my hometown, the emphasis is on value for the dollar. Reasonable price garners better ratings than gourmet fare.

JUST DESSERTS

One last point. It helps *not* to write on a full stomach! Be a little bit hungry—especially when you query—hungry enough to convey how much readers will lust after your "Luscious Ways With Leftover Lentils."

And, yes—there's a warning. Writing food/recipe articles *can* be hazardous to your waistline. So, after you sell your lentils story, do a follow-up that features two weeks of delicious low-calorie meals that are ethnic, natural, one-dish, simple and sexy, that can be prepared ahead, served to company, and frozen, and that cost only 29.5¢ per serving.

I guarantee that any food editor will eat it up!

BY ELAINE FANTLE SHIMBERG

Writing for the Women's Magazines

"Women's magazines are the greatest form of communication since women chatted as they washed their clothes on the rocks by the river." So says Sondra Forsyth Enos, an editor at *Ladies' Home Journal*. Her view is echoed by the millions of women who turn each month to one or more of the women's magazines to be educated, entertained, and assured that others share their problems.

"Women have complicated lives," says Enos. "We have health problems unlike those of men. We have less time for our friends. Women are at a time in their lives when they want help with concerns they would have shared with another woman. It's back-fence conversation, woman to woman. All the things that touch a woman's life. The women's magazine acts as the formal extension of our sisterly lines."

You don't have to have children to write for the women's market. You don't even have to be a woman. You need only an interest in women and their lives. You don't have to live in New York, either, where, as one writer told me, "Everyone knows editors by their first names and everything happens!" Don't worry about it. There's gold in Yankton, South Dakota, and Parrott, Georgia, too. In fact editors have said that writers not known to them are more likely to succeed if they offer something they can't get elsewhere—good personal experience or information about what's unique in their area. Editors may not have heard about a day-care center organized by elderly women in your hometown or your neighbor who has turned her pool exercises into a million-dollar business. It's up to you to bring stories like that to the editors' attention.

DEFINING THE WOMEN'S MARKET

Women today are like sparkling diamonds. They have many facets. The majority, close to 60 percent of them, according to the Bureau of Labor Statistics, work outside the home. They're interested in their families, their jobs, themselves, health issues, and the world around them. To find out more about these concerns, they turn to a wide variety of magazines. There are the "Seven Sisters," traditional women's magazines that include *McCall's, Good Housekeeping, Redbook, Ladies' Home Journal, Woman's Day, Family Circle*, and *Better Homes and Gardens*. There are the specialty magazines that focus directly on a woman's particular career area, such as *The Woman Engineer, Women in Business* and *Farm Woman*. The women's market also includes such specialized magazines as *Glamour, Savvy, Self, Ms., Working Woman* and *Parents*. It incorporates religious magazines like *Catholic Digest* and *Guideposts Magazine*; political, like *Po-*

litical Woman; and sports and fitness magazines, like *Tennis* or *Slimmer*. In short, you'll find magazines catering to women's interests in almost every possible category.

If you haven't read a woman's magazine in the last five years this may not be the market for you. As many cooks have discovered, yesterday's fare seldom sells. A *Ladies' Home Journal* columnist of 1950 wrote, "Marriage settles into a routine—the husband earns a living, the wife runs the house." His additional advice to the wife was, "Respect his privacy, build him up, take an interest in his appearance."

Even as recently as 1960, the *LHJ* columnist wrote concerning role acceptance, "No matter how career-oriented she may be, the happy wife is a woman who voluntarily and by preference makes her first objective being a good wife."

In defense, Sondra Forsyth Enos says that "the traditional women's magazines have always kept pace with the social climate of the day. *Ladies' Home Journal* has always responded to the women's needs. We couldn't have survived this long [over 100 years] if we *didn't* reflect the times."

In the '30s, during the Depression, *LHJ* published articles about "getting by" and "keeping your spirits up." In the '40s, stories and articles were slanted to "Rosie the Riveter" and the war effort. In the '50s, the magazine reflected a peaceful era. Today, *LHJ* editors look for hard-hitting, newsy stories they call "Ladies' Home Journalism." The articles are provocative, discussing finances, child-rearing, health and social issues, consumer advocacy, and ways to help women cope.

Some magazines attacked change head-on. Publications like *Working Woman, Savvy, New Woman* and *Self* began telling women how to merge new professional lives with former traditional ones and to compete in the business world. They stress caring for one's physical and emotional health, handling finances, believing in one's self, and coping in a society with few role models. Articles in *Savvy*, for instance, discuss the business lunch, investment tips, postponed motherhood, earning more than your mate, and how to gain power in one's professional life. Issues in *Working Woman* have dealt with outsmarting the (business) competition, relocation, volunteerism, and how to go after a new job.

Editors agree that women want more depth in their magazines. Today's women are better educated, more aware. Women's magazines have always offered more pragmatic information than men's. Although the man's role as husband, father and caregiver has grown and become more acceptable, men still tend to read more for escape and entertainment.

WHOPPER IDEAS, WHOPPER PRICES

To know what interests women, listen to what they talk about. Eavesdrop. Your mother may have told you it was impolite, but it's standard operating procedure for a writer.

Hearing friends talk about their children's bad experiences at camp gave me the idea for "How to Help Your Child Enjoy Camp," which I sold to *Lady's Circle*.

Overhearing women talking about giving a party without spending a great deal of money helped me reach into my personal experience and come up with a few low budget costume parties my husband and I had given. I wrote about them and sold "It's Easy to Give a Party" to two regional issues of *Woman's Day*. A friend and I were part of a group discussing whether a woman should "expand" her credentials when applying for a job. We developed our ideas and sold our article, "Little Whoppers to Big Lies," to *Glamour* for $1,000.

What do women talk about? Tune in. You'll hear them talking about coping with single parenthood; loneliness; getting old; getting by; caring for aging parents; exercising; being successful, happy, healthy and wise. Listen to what the kids and men say about the women in their lives, too. Write to these concerns.

Begin by examining your own life. Most of us have uniquely coped with some common problem. All of us have done something better, quicker, cheaper or more creatively than others. These daily experiences—often so trivial that we don't think twice about them—are possible material for an article.

I can't sew, and it occurred to me that similar lack of talent might be frustrating other women reading articles on "How to Knit Your Christmas Gifts," "Crochet for Christmas," and "Fifty Nifty Needlepoint Gifts." I came up with a list of gifts one could make with drawstring bags (i.e., cookie bags, button bags, etc.) and wrote an article, "Christmas Presents a Non-Sewer Can Make." It sold the first time out.

Rather than keeping a journal describing family vacations with our five children, I've turned the fiascos, fun, and knowledge gained into numerous articles as well as a book (*Coping with Kids and Vacation*) published by Ballantine.

When one of our children, as a toddler, ingested the contents of a bottle of baby aspirin, I added research and interviews to our experience and sold the article to *Essence* in the United States as well as to a women's magazine in England.

These and other articles triggered by personal experiences sold because other women could relate to them. My life was no different from theirs. We shared the same fears and joys.

You also can get ideas from what others have written. Most article writers read at least one newspaper daily. Take a general topic—like car safety. How could you slant it specifically for the women's market? What type of car should a teenager drive? What extras should a woman demand for her car?

A listing of classes offered by our local community college gave me an idea for an article. The course, "Car Care for Women," had been offered every term . . . and with good reason. It taught women to take an interest in what was under the hood of their cars. They learned to identify each part, how it was supposed to work, what type of repairs could and should be done, and whether it was a simple repair that could be done without going into the shop. The course was taught by an excellent mechanic, and the class had a long waiting list. I turned interviews with the instructor and his students into a salable article.

Don't forget to read the sports section, either. A report of a youngster being injured in a football game could conjure up ideas for you. What is the emergency procedure if there *is* an accident? What questions should a parent ask his/her child's coach?

A filler describing the average income of writers gave me the idea for an article on writing as a way to supplement one's income. I interviewed writers who also were military wives, added information I have picked up over my twenty years in the writing game, and sold "How to Earn Money as a Writer" to *Military Lifestyles*, a magazine for the wives of military personnel.

Seeing "Secretary's Week" on the calendar triggered another idea for me. I interviewed (by mail and telephone) numerous secretaries throughout the country, learned how they felt about their profession, and turned the information into "What Do Secretaries Want—And What Are They Getting?" for *Glamour* (for $1,200).

SHORT AND CRISP

Another good way to create ideas is to ask yourself "What if?" *What if* you weren't there when your first grader arrived home from school? What alternate plans should be established? *What if* your house catches fire at night? Have you held fire drills? Would your family know what to do? *What if* you lost your job? How would you look for another? Could you handle it emotionally? By thinking, "What if . . .," you can write articles that help prepare your readers for emergencies.

"How to" are magic words. Pick up any of the women's magazines and chances are good that the title of at least one of the stories begins that way. It may be worded, "Seven Ways to . . ." or "101 Ways to . . ." but the idea's the same. Readers always look for ways to do things better, faster or cheaper.

Think in terms of "cover lines," the one-liners on the front of the magazines that say, "Eleven Ways to Be a Better Mother," "Lose Weight on a Dessert Diet," "How to Become Computer Literate," "Could You Use More Time, Money, and Laughter in Your Life?" These cover lines catch the buyer's eye.

How you develop an idea depends upon the particular market you select. An idea on "How to Cope With Parents," for example, will be slanted differently for *Redbook* (where the average readers are in their 20s and 30s), than for *Ladies' Home Journal* (where the average reader is about ten years older and therefore likely to have older parents and a different set of problems).

Present your specific slant in a query letter. The query is your sales tool, a letter of introduction. Most editors prefer it over a completed manuscript. The query shows what you have in mind and how you write. It also gives the editor the chance to work with you on developing the article. Because the query represents you and your idea, take time to be certain it conveys your message clearly and in a positive manner.

As with any sales presentation, the query should do a complete selling job. Tell why your story is more important than any of the others piling up on the editor's desk. Describe what information you'll include, who you'll interview, a few of your findings so far, and why you are uniquely qualified to write this piece.

My query for "How to Avoid Mess Stress," which I sold to *Military Lifestyles*, began:

Much of the stress in our lives is caused by our possessions. We spend too much time cleaning, repairing, storing, and caring for them.

I would begin my article, "How to Avoid Mess Stress," with a brief description of stress, including the fact that the late Hans Selye, the first scientist to study the effects of stress on our health, found that unrelieved stress can create chemical changes that can upset digestion and sleep patterns, and cause high blood pressure and a myriad of other diseases.

I will include a quiz to determine the reader's "mess stress tolerance," discuss how we determine what is "clutter," and describe ways for clutter to be condensed and contained.

I have lectured on this subject, and have written about it in both my books.

The first paragraph was intended to attract the editor's attention.

The second paragraph showed that I had done some homework, knew something about the effects of stress, and would be able to quote from experts in the stress field.

The third paragraph showed what the article would include. A quiz usually interests readers. I also mentioned that I would include other information concerning mess/stress, and I detailed some steps readers could take to overcome the problem.

In my last paragraph, I told the editor why I was qualified to write about mess/stress. As I had done other work for *Military Lifestyles*, I did not include any of my other credits. With a new editor, I would have done so.

"Don't write a stuffy business letter," says Sondra Forsyth Enos of *Ladies' Home Journal*. "Prove that you're a writer. Keep your query short and crisp. One page is plenty." She suggests that experienced writers send clips. "We prefer to see what you've done. Don't worry if it's from a technical journal. Good writing is good writing."

Be sure the information is available *before* proposing an idea. Many writers get fantastic ideas and dash off a query without determining how they'll conduct their research. If you can't get the information (because it's in India or requires an audience with the Pope), narrow your scope. Be realistic.

If you've put thought into your idea and developed it specifically for the market you're querying, if you sound positive and well informed, chances are you'll get a go-ahead. If you do, *please* write the piece. The editor may have turned someone else down and expects you to come through. One editor told me that she is amazed by the writers who put together excellent query letters, get assignments, and then never are heard from again. Don't do that. If you get that far, take the next step. Write the article.

SPECIFICALLY SPEAKING

There is no "best" way nor "right" way to organize and write an article, only the way that works for you. But here are some guidelines.

First, it's not enough to write about a problem. You must also describe how the reader can solve it. It can be done as a straight article (i.e., "How to . . ."), an exposé, a profile of a person who has overcome the problem, a humorous tale or an inspirational story. Most writers develop their articles from outlines of one sort or another. Sherry Suib Cohen, author of articles for *Ladies' Home Journal, Mademoiselle* and *Playgirl*, says she writes "in pieces . . . nothing so grand as index cards. I write in chunks—dealing with medical information first (if there is any), interviews, commentaries, and conclusions, depending on what (and who) is available. Then, I spread the whole thing out on a large surface in a general and flowing order, make transitions and corrections and finally, edit."

If you have a computer, it's fairly easy to compose your first draft, then insert new information or quotes from interviews as they're received. Most likely, your software program handles "block moves," allowing you to shift paragraphs around easily, much as you did in the pre-computer "cut-and-paste" days.

The lead paragraph probably is the most important part of your article. It must compete for a busy woman's attention. Ask a question, tell a brief but moving anecdote, or give a shocking or amazing statistic. Study your notes and try to figure out what would grab the reader's attention. What aspect have *you* found most shocking, interesting or moving? Would a bit of dialogue (real or made up) be most successful? What about a quote that sums up what you're talking about? I had many good quotes for *this* article, and selected what I considered to be the strongest for my lead paragraph.

My lead for an article on eating disorders began:

> *Sixteen-year-old Peggy's daily diet consists of half a hard-boiled egg (the white only), two stalks of celery and, sometimes, a cup of tea. She isn't the victim of the Ethiopian drought; nor is she a child of the projects. She is the daughter of a successful professional man, part of an upper-middle-class family living within miles of you.*

On the other hand, I began a humorous article this way:

> *I found an Easter egg behind the couch last week. I think it reflects badly on my skills as a housekeeper.*

In both cases, the remainder of the article was true to the lead. The reader didn't discover halfway through that the "funny" story really was serious or vice versa.

Carefully balance significant quotes, only the most meaningful statistics, and the most poignant anecdotes. Strive for natural transitions.

Visualize your reader at all times. Use examples she can respond to. Just as a good actor plays to his audience, you must write to yours. Tell her what she wants, needs, or fears to know. The most important key on your typewriter is the "you." Don't tell the reader about "some people." Instead, say "*You* may find that . . .," or "*You* should watch for the following symptoms. . . ."

Remember that your readers are human. We're not Wonder Woman. Our bracelets are tarnished and we have runs in our tights. We like the woman we're reading about to occasionally forget to thaw something for dinner, to have a pimple on her nose and stubble on her legs so that we can still identify easily with her.

Also, it's important for you as a writer to care about your reader's feelings. When writing about accidental childhood poisoning for *Essence*, I wanted to avoid accusing readers of being careless. I began by describing how *I* had almost poisoned my child (by leaving the bottle of baby aspirin out on a dresser). My message was, "It happened to me. It could happen to you, too."

I have used personal experiences with our five children as the basis of many of my articles. My family complains that anything they do is likely to find its way into print. And they're right! I've written about handing out allowances, getting ears pierced, and helping your child adjust to camp. It's important, however, to respect your relationship. Never embarrass your children. Say, "One of our boys . . ." rather than mentioning one by name.

But it's seldom enough just to tell about your own personal experience. Your articles need the support of expert opinion, quotes, moving anecdotes, etc. These are important because they substantiate your ideas. They keep your article from seeming as though it were written off the top of your head. Quotes also help enliven an article. They are the "dialogue" in your nonfiction piece.

Finally, don't speak in general terms; be specific. If you're writing about teenage pregnancy, interview some of the girls and their boyfriends too. Talk to their parents. Tell their individual stories to explain the general. Make your statistics human. Rather than saying, "Last year, one out of every ten teenage girls in America became pregnant," zero in on that one girl. Find three in a typical gym class of thirty. Get to know them. Learn why they didn't use birth control, feel their fears, understand their helplessness and confusion, hear what they say. Let them touch you as one human to another; then write their story. As with fiction, it's better to show than to tell.

TO SUMMARIZE

Finally, give your reader a conclusion, the "fruit and cheese" at the end of a satisfying meal. Don't let your article just drift off as though you've run out of things to say. Propose action, summarize, or use a quote, anecdote or punch line. Let the reader know that your story's not continued on another page.

To conclude my article on eating disorders, I wrote:

> *It may take two or three months; it may take years. Some anorexics or bulimics never really are cured and go through life hating themselves when they gain even the slightest bit of weight.*
>
> *The Duchess of Windsor is credited with saying, "No one can be too rich or too thin." Obviously, she never had heard of today's eating disorders.*

My article, "I Lost as 'Housekeeper of the Year,' " ended with these words:

I'd rather have a glow in my children's cheeks than on the silver, play Monopoly than mop, and have laughter peeling throughout the house along with piling laundry.

What if you can write in the dust on my piano? Make it a love note.

I don't worry that the plants talk to me begging for water—or that there's something fuzzy and fluorescent growing out of the dish lost in the back of the refrigerator. Maybe I've discovered a new strain of penicillin.

Housework can wait. Living can't. How nice, one day, to rest eternally under a stone that reads:

Here lies Mom
Her day is done.
The housework waited
But we sure had fun.

For the writer, the women's market is exciting for the very reason it can be troublesome. It's fluid. It changes like the sand bar at the beach, shifting ever so slightly even as you watch it. Women's basic interests—self, family, husband/lover, work, and community—probably won't change all that much. But the world she moves in does change. Forecasting these changes, recording today and anticipating tomorrow is what makes the women's market fascinating. If you follow one magazine throughout a period of years, you'll find that it's a microcosm of women's history. With determination, dedication and discipline, you can be part of it.

BY LOIS DUNCAN

Writing the "As-Told-To" Article

Because the people who live through life's most dramatic events—events that are the stuff of compelling and salable articles—often lack the skills to set their stories to paper, a writer who can absorb other people's experiences and present them from the subject's own viewpoint has a grip on the trunk of a money tree.

I know, because I've been "collaborating" with nonwriters who have interesting stories for some years now, selling the results to such magazines as *Ladies' Home Journal* and *Good Housekeeping*. I write what is called the "as-told-to" article.

"As-told-to" pieces are similar to ghostwritten articles; in fact, both types of articles rely on the same general writing principles. The big difference is that a ghostwritten article leads the reader to believe that the *subject* of the story is actually the author. The "as-told-to" credits the true writer with a byline along the lines of "by John Jones [the subject], as told to Mary Smith [the writer]."

RETELLING IT LIKE IT IS

The as-told-to has more depth, intimacy and credibility, and is filled with more emotional detail, than a profile told in the third person with a journalistic approach. Several years ago, *Ladies' Home Journal* sent me to San Francisco to interview the mother of a little boy named Matthew Amos. Matthew was a "miracle baby," born three weeks after his supposedly sterile mother learned, to her amazement, that she was pregnant. The "baby who could not possibly have been conceived" was born four months prematurely, and, at birth, weighed 1½ pounds.

Since the editor had not assigned this story as an as-told-to, I wrote my first draft in third person. It was interesting enough, but it lacked the feeling of deep personal involvement that such an emotionally charged subject required. I experimented with writing the story in the first person as an as-told-to from the viewpoint of Matthew's mother, Donna.

Here is how the two versions differed:

First draft:

> Donna stared in horror at the tiny, wizened child lying in the incubator. She could not believe that a baby this premature could possibly survive. Would she, she wondered, be able ever to experience the same spontaneous love for

Matthew that mothers felt for healthy, beautiful, full-term babies? She prayed that she could, but found the prospect doubtful. Her lack of maternal feeling horrified her, and she was filled with a terrible rush of guilt.

Second draft:

I wish I could say that I was flooded with motherly love, but I wasn't. My main emotions were fear, revulsion and guilt for having brought this tiny broken creature into the world. His head was the color of a ripe plum, and his outstretched legs were like pencils. He looked as though he had been crushed by some great machine. My husband might fool himself that this half-developed embryo was going to live and grow, that the bruises would leave its body and the scrawny legs and arms would get pink and chubby. I knew better. This was a little robot with a tube for breathing, a tube for nourishment; it would never be able to survive apart from this machinery. The situation was hopeless—utterly hopeless!

Donna *did* soon learn to love her tiny son, and the story of her emotional growth, as well as Matthew's miraculous conception and survival, made this article meaningful and inspiring. I submitted both versions of the story to my editor; she selected the as-told-to version.

Dramatic real-life stories are in demand by almost every type of magazine, from *Reader's Digest* to juvenile publications. For the women's magazines, the subject of the article is often a woman who has steered her family through a major crisis or who has committed some heroic act for the benefit of others. For the men's magazines, the subject is usually a man who has had a dangerous adventure. Inspirational publications use stories about people who have overcome adversity with God's help and whose religious convictions have been strengthened in the process. Retirement magazines use nostalgic reminiscences, and teen publications seek first-person stories told from the viewpoints of their young readers.

AS I WAS TELLING YOU . . .

Your first source for potential as-told-to ideas is your local newspaper; human-interest tales abound in the feature sections. Look for the heroic ("Elderly Woman Battles Mountain Lion to Protect Grandson"); the inspiring ("High School Athlete Donates Kidney to Sick Sister"); the tragic with an upbeat ending ("Mother Reunited With Daughter Kidnapped Ten Years Ago"). The subjects of such stories, having tasted the fleeting glory of local recognition, are usually delighted by the thought of achieving a second round of fame by being written up for a national publication.

The best source for as-told-to material, however, is our everyday contact with the world around us. Almost everyone we meet has at least one good story to tell. One recent article of mine was the product of a comment dropped by a casual acquaintance at a cocktail party.

"This is the first glass of wine I've had in a year," she said. "I can't keep liquor in the house because of Bobby."

"Because of *Bobby*?" I exclaimed. Fifteen-year-old Bobby, a clean-cut youngster with an ingratiating grin, was my son's buddy.

"He's an alcoholic," Bobby's mother said. "For years, I lived in terror that he would kill me during one of his drunken rages. Finally, thank God, I was able to get him into an alcoholic rehabilitation program. I went through the same thing with his brother two years ago. Alcoholism runs in families, you know. The boys' father is an alcoholic, too. That's why I divorced him."

I hesitantly asked her how she would feel about having her story published.

"Would you really be willing to write it? How wonderful! If I could share what I've learned about teenage alcoholism with other parents, I'd feel that maybe something positive has come out of all this misery."

TELLING ALL

Conducting interviews for as-told-to pieces involves special challenges. You must first establish empathy for the person whose story you're telling: This can't be faked. You cannot regard your subject objectively; you must see him as he sees himself, follow his thought processes and experience his emotions. You must not only *understand* but *accept as valid* the "why" behind his words and actions. I've found this particularly difficult when writing "Can This Marriage Be Saved?" articles for *Ladies' Home Journal*, because three different viewpoints (the wife's, the husband's and the marriage counselor's) are involved, and two of these conflict with each other. When writing the wife's side of the story, I must view the situation through her eyes. When writing the husband's side, I must do a mental and emotional turnaround and see the same set of facts from a different vantage point.

You must also be a bit of a detective to write this type of article. Tiny, explicit details give a first-person story its intimacy, yet interview subjects usually consider such details too unimportant to volunteer. To dig out these tidbits, you must ask questions: "Did the children hear you tell Ed that you hated him? How did they react? Toby dropped his ice cream cone? What flavor? Chocolate? Boy, I bet that was a mess. What did it land on? Did he say anything? Oh, you must have felt awful when you heard that. Did he shout it or whisper it? How did you respond?"

Eventually, you obtain all the material necessary to create your scene, but such detail seldom pours forth, uncoaxed, from the subject's mouth.

Because of your need for details—and because of the emotional tension often involved in these interviews, tension that might distract you from proper note-taking—I recommend that you rely on a tape recorder. But be careful. My first "Can This Marriage Be Saved?" assignment involved a couple whose problems stemmed from the fact that the wife had been sleeping with her step-brother for five years. The interview took four hours, interrupted, as it was, by floods of tears. By the time the ordeal was over, the couple, the counselor and I were emotional wrecks.

In the cab on my way back to the airport, I decided to play back the interview on my tape recorder. To my horror, I discovered that I had neglected to press the "record" button down hard enough. The entire tape was blank. Although I did manage to reconstruct the interview from memory, I learned a valuable lesson. Ever since, I have made it a policy to back up taped interviews with hand-written notes.

Some writers disagree with this practice, believing that the recorder's presence freezes subjects. They also point out that transcribing an entire interview of taped material consumes time.

I, on the other hand, have found that few people are intimidated by the recorder. There may, at times, be a little initial stiffness, but before many minutes have passed, the subject becomes so engrossed in the details of his story that the instrument seems to fade away. And though transcribing the tapes can be a chore, I find it much easier to bring a subject's experiences to life if I can refer back to the phrasing and inflections of a voice—not just to jotted notes. When writing from another person's viewpoint, the closer you come to capturing the flavor of the personality through speech patterns and precise wording, the more credible your effort will be.

When working from an interview, you don't just transcribe the subject's words from the tape and submit them as they stand. If the subject's rendition of his story were publishable without alteration, there would be no need to have someone else write it. The transcript constitutes the raw material from which your final article will be formed. Often, in telling his story, your subject will give the climax first, since that is the most important event that occurred ("You can't believe the relief I felt when I looked up and saw that search plane and realized that after a week on that freezing mountain top, I'd finally been found!"). When you, as the writer, lay out the skeleton of the story, you will place this scene at the end, where it belongs. You will then line up events in chronological order to build toward the rescue. In this process, you are not *altering* facts, just rearranging them to build suspense and create a more satisfying presentation.

Authors of as-told-to pieces perform as much as editors as they do as writers. They must cut superfluous material, reword for clarity, trim, smooth, correct grammar and reshape what is all too often a rambling and disjointed monologue into a tight and polished story. Here, for example, is a section of an interview taped for a "Can This Marriage Be Saved?" article, contrasted with the corresponding paragraph of the article as it was printed:

Taped Interview:

Like I say, it's really hard to—you know—I can't remember how the conversation went and everything exactly. I told Ed something that made him real hurt—like he was a rotten bastard—that kind of thing—I was just so mad. He'd asked me how I felt. That was just asking for it, right? But I felt bad afterward for saying it anyway.

Article as Printed:

> *A couple of nights ago, my husband, Ed, asked me if I hated him. I told him,*
> *"Yes." He was shocked, of course, and I felt terrible because I'd hurt him.*
> *Worse still, though, was the realization that what I'd said was true.*

Also, the interview often isn't the only source of material you will use in an as-told-to piece. I have on my desk an interview with a middle-aged woman who was raped by a neighbor. She didn't report it. "I couldn't stand the thought of describing the humiliating experience to strangers," she told me. "Besides, I was afraid of my husband's reaction. What if he blamed *me* for what happened? What if he thought I'd led the man on?" Six weeks later her teenage daughter was raped by the same man. This woman wants to share her story to impress on other women that reporting sexual molestation is imperative.

To be meaningful, this article must be more than a horror story; it should be backed up by information and advice from experts. How prevalent is rape? How can a woman best protect herself against it? What should this particular woman have done under the circumstances? Gone to the police? To a doctor? To a rape crisis center? What would her chances have been of winning a case against this man had she pressed charges?

Such material might be injected into this article in two ways. One would be to create a scene in which a doctor, psychologist or social worker talks with the subject and presents her with this information. This scene would probably have to be fictional, and my subject would have to agree to its inclusion in the story. The other alternative would be to write the information from the experts in third person and run it adjacent to the first-person article as a sidebar.

I tend to favor the former method, but the final decision will be the subject's.

IN THE FINAL TELLING

In fact, the subject should have the final decision about the suitability of the entire article. I never allow the subject of a third-person profile to read and approve the manuscript before I submit it, but I always allow as-told-to subjects that right. The subject's name will appear in the byline, and he is the one who will be held responsible for the content. If he isn't happy with the story, he has a right to request specific changes, and he and the writer should attempt to compromise. Once the subject has read and approved the article, I ask him to sign a simple release form saying that he has reviewed the piece and is willing to have it published under our joint byline.

The writer of an as-told-to usually receives full payment. The magazine may sometimes make an additional payment to the subject, but this should not affect the amount paid to the author. In the case of "Can This Marriage Be Saved?" stories, payment is made not only to the husband, wife and counselor, but also to the counseling service that supplies the case history. *Guideposts*, a publication that buys a large number of as-told-to or ghostwritten stories per year, pays an honorarium to the subjects of its first-person articles. "We don't think of this as a 'payment' exactly," says *Guideposts* editor Van Varner. "It's simply our way of saying, 'Thank you for talking to our writer.' "

If the magazine you're working with doesn't offer additional payment, you and the subject must work out your own financial arrangement. (I know no guidelines to use for this; it's sticky and awkward. Personally, I'd rather forgo the story altogether than have to bicker about it. Put whatever terms you decide on into writing, and sign them—*before* you begin work on the story.)

Different rules apply when the subject employs a ghostwriter on a work-for-hire basis. In this case, the writer is paid by the subject, who then owns all rights to the work and can market it under his own name. Fees for ghostwriting vary. *Writer's Market* suggests fees of $15-$40 per hour or $5-$10 per page of completed manuscript.

Of course, I don't write these articles purely for the money. I also enjoy another reward: personal satisfaction. If you like people—a prerequisite for this sort of writing—your soul is regularly revitalized. I once wrote a story with a woman named Evelyn Walker, whose sixteen-year-old son, Tim, and his fifteen-year-old girlfriend were shot to death in the Walkers' front yard. Evelyn was also shot when she ran out to help. Although she was not expected to survive, she forced herself to recover by simple strength of will so she could testify against the murderer.

Although Evelyn and I live in the same town, I had never met her and I did not contact her about doing the article. *She* called *me.*

"I've heard you're a writer," she said. "Would you please consider writing my boy's story? I'm so obsessed with it, I can't get past it. I'm spilling my bitterness out on my friends and family. If I could just get the pain onto paper, maybe I could break free of it."

The result—"I Had to Live for Tim," bylined "by Evelyn Walker, as told to Lois Duncan"—was published in *Good Housekeeping.*

Several weeks later, I received this letter from Evelyn:

Dear Lois—

I want to thank you for helping me with Tim's story. I've felt such relief ever since I saw it in print. I will always remember what you did for me. Short as Tim's life was, it has now touched many people. Readers all over the country know how beautiful my son was and how much love he gave. Now, I've got to get on with my own life. I can finally close the door on this and move onward.

A Friend Always,
Evelyn

BY HELENE SCHELLENBERG BARNHART

When the Writer Teaches— Writing the How-to Article

The how-to is one of the most popular types of articles published in today's newspapers and magazines. If you can write articles telling others how you found an easier or faster way to build or make something, or how you found a new solution to an old problem (or a new one), you'll find a wide open market waiting for you.

In addition to the popularity of how-to-make and -do articles and problem-solving ones, there's a big market for the self-improvement type of how-tos, pieces in which you show how you learned new habits to replace bad ones; how you developed a new skill; or how you made yourself into a more attractive and lovable person.

Why are how-to articles so in demand? There are many answers to this question. Strangely enough, in our mechanized world where almost everything comes to us through the push of a button or the turn of a dial, where the only struggle in cooking is often the opening of the well-sealed frozen package, there is a great hunger felt by many people, the young included, to go back to basics and to the "old" way of doing things. People want to know how to start from scratch. The almost forgotten art of quilt making is once again popular. Many other almost lost skills such as knitting, tatting, weaving, macrame, furniture making, and a host of other *handwork* activities are now included in school curriculums and in adult education programs.

The upsurge in do-it-yourself projects is not only a reflection of an interest in the nostalgic past, however. It is a result of our change in lifestyle. More people are living longer in good health with more time to do the things they've always dreamed of doing. Freed from time-consuming tasks, thanks to modern conveniences, people of all ages have more time to take up hobbies and to learn new skills.

Not everyone can get to a class; those who can't, pick up newspapers and magazines to keep informed and to read over and over again *how to make, how to build, and how to be.*

Glance at the Table of Contents page of almost any magazine and you'll see the word *how-to.* You'll find it helpful in your study of the how-to article to keep a list of titles with the word *how-to* included. *How-to* is one of the most salable word signals in print today. You can capitalize on its salability by making a list of your own skills and accomplishments for use as material for your how-to articles.

SUCCESS STORIES

Many of my students made their first sales by writing various kinds of how-to articles. One student, Charles Floyd, missed a class because he was reroofing his house *himself*.

"Write an article about it, Charles," I told him. "Bring it to class next week."

The next week Charles returned with article in hand, a big smile lighting his face. He told the class how he'd put his wife up on the roof to photograph his roofing procedure step by step. Eventually the article sold to *Popular Mechanics*.

Charles sold a second how-to on a space-saver bookcase he built, and a third on how he invented a traveling light to put over his garage workbench. Each article was accompanied by black-and-white photographs showing exactly how he accomplished his goal. The second and third articles also sold to *Popular Mechanics*. Another beginning writer was on his way.

Gerry Fleming was another student who began her writing career with how-tos. Gerry's absorbing interest was in the American West and in treasure hunting. I couldn't begin to list her sales in the allowed space. I can only mention a few, such as her articles titled, "How to Buy a Metal Detector," "How to Treasure Hunt Safely in Off-the-Beaten-Path Places," and many other "camping" pieces.

Gerry hit the jackpot with her how-to technique when she finally wrote what she knew about keeping Cub Scouts busy. As a den mother, she was appalled to find that there was virtually nothing published to help den mothers plan craft and building projects to occupy their active Cub Scouts during meetings. Gerry wrote a book on the subject, "Scrapcrafts for Youth Groups."

Still another student, Diane Crawford, recently achieved publication with her articles on what she calls "Handy Hints," how-tos on sewing and various other handwork that she likes to do in her spare time. Her interest in charitable organizations led to a how-to sale, "The Box Project," to *Lady's Circle*.

"I've sold a total of twenty how-to articles," Diane told me at our last class meeting. "I sell to markets such as *Junior Trails, Woman's World, Grit, California Highway Patrolman, Family Circle, Touch, Byline*, and *Refunder's Magazine*."

Diane is a firm believer in the rule of *write what you know*. She took a good look at what she had to offer in the way of interesting skills and ideas, then started writing how-tos.

Bernice Curler, another successful writer in the how-to category, confesses she's a collector.

Every nook and cranny of my house proves it. One of my collections is made up of old cookbooks. The first how-to I ever sold was to a little magazine called The Nebraska Electric Farmer. *In the article, I told how to have fun brows-*

ing through old cookbooks. The article came out under the title, "Grandma was a Blue Ribbon Cook." Using different anecdotes and different recipes, I sold the same idea to Modern Maturity *with the title, "Treasure Hunting Through Old Cook Books."*

After these two article sales, I wrote and sold many more on anything that interested and excited me. I sold "Make a Mushroom Candle" to American Girl, *and "Five Cogs in the Wheel of Success," on how to stimulate self-drive, to* Success Unlimited. *This article was picked up as a reprint by the Amway Company for an article in their sales training manual.*

Bernice has this advice for beginners.

Know your market. If you know the readership, you can write several articles out of the same source material by changing the slant and using a different type of lead.

For instance, from my brother-in-law, an artist, I learned how to use imitation gold leaf to gild picture frames inexpensively. I sold a how-to article on this subject to Canadian Homes, *titled "The Midas Touch." By taking a different approach for different readerships directed to a middle-income, higher income, and home-interested reader, I used the same basic information for another article, titled "Secret of Framing," which sold to* House Beautiful.

Still another sale on the same subject of framing a picture sold to Lady's Circle, *a family-oriented magazine. My lead was: "A picture that's a first-place winner should be framed in gold." I went on to tell how I hunted for the proper but inexpensive frame and finally decided to make my own. The title on the published article in* Lady's Circle *was "How to Make an Elegant Imitation Gold Leaf Frame."*

There are several ways in which you can use the same how-to idea for several noncompetitive markets. For example, you can change the lead by using one type for one article and another type for a second, third, and so on.

Bernice's sales are a good example of how a writer can take one article idea and spin it off into several sales. The key to multiple sales from one idea is in Bernice's explanation that she changed the slant and used different leads for each article sale. She took "different approaches," one article slanted to middle-income readers, another to home-interested ones, and another to a higher income readership.

In spinning off your article ideas, make sure that you submit to noncompetitive markets. Bernice knew that *Canadian Homes* magazine drew a different readership from that of *House Beautiful* with its mostly American readership.

SECRETS OF SUCCESS

The students I told you about, students who are examples of how the beginner can get published through the how-to, all share common requisites for success:

1. Taking the time to learn the basic techniques for writing salable nonfiction.

2. Writing about what they can do well.

3. Getting excited about what they do and making this excitement shine through in their writing.

4. Making a list of possible markets, markets they had researched *before* they mailed.

5. Not giving up when they got rejections but continuing to submit material.

6. While heeding the requirements for a specific market, they were able to inject freshness and style into their writing.

TYPES OF HOW-TOS

There are many kinds of how-to articles you can write in addition to the *how to make and do* kind. The students' examples I've shown you I think of as the *physical* or concrete kind of how-to, inasmuch as they require two hands and some sort of material: wood, cloth, paint, nails, potting soil, seeds, etc.

Another type of how-to is one I tag *psychological*. There *can be* concrete material involved as in an article showing one how to improve one's taste in dress, or in a piece describing how the use of certain skin care products can lead to a better complexion and a more attractive makeup which in turn can lead to a better self-image. The main focus in this type of how-to, however, is on the *psychological* benefits rather than on the products used. The material objects involved are secondary—necessary, but not the primary interest. The primary interest is in attaining a psychological lift. We call this type of how-to, the *self-help* piece.

If you're interested in learning the required technique, it won't take you long to grasp the writing technique that goes into *all* how-to articles.

Keep in mind that you are not only a writer when you put together a how-to article; you're also a teacher. You don't have the advantage of a classroom situation, however. When a question arises, there are no hands going up to tell you that you didn't make some point quite clear. There's only the unseen reader somewhere staring down at the words you wrote, brow furrowed in a puzzled frown. You get only *one* chance to make yourself understood.

HOW-TO-DO HOW-TOS

In the first type of how-to, you show the reader how to make or create products, such as hand-knit garments, custom-designed jewelry, cuddly toys, or a more convenient workbench. You may tell how to convert wasted attic space into additional bedrooms or a playroom, or how to do it yourself in just about any area you can think of.

This type of article can also focus on how to *make do*. As an example of making do, my brother-in-law, Gordon, recently made a fine wood shed out of lumber taken from an old abandoned corn crib. The corn crib had fallen in, but the lumber was still good.

"That corn crib must have been almost a hundred years old," my brother-in-law told me, as I admired his latest project. "The shingles were pretty moldy, but I cleaned them off, turned them over and they made a good sound roof for the new shed."

I recognized a good possibility for a *make-do* how-to. Any time you can show someone how to take material he already has on hand to make something new, you've added a real plus to your do-it-yourself how-to article.

When writing how-to do articles, you must present your instructions in clear, easy-to-understand language. Check and double-check your measurements, the amount of material needed to complete the project, whether your article shows how to build a birdbath, make a quilt, knit a baby sweater, or convert a corn crib into a woodshed.

Here are several important guidelines to success in writing salable how-to articles.

1. Tell the reader where to get the material, how much to get, and the approximate cost.

Always tailor the cost of your do-it-yourself project to the reader's purse. There's no use in trying to sell a how-to article on building an expensive lanai on a beachfront home to a publication read by people struggling to make ends meet in a city apartment complex.

2. Be specific. It isn't enough to tell the reader that something doesn't cost much. Prices vary across the country, but you can estimate the cost in round figures, such as "under five or ten dollars"; "not more than fifty dollars," etc.

In addition to wanting to know the cost, readers want to know how long it takes to build or make something. Tell your readers how much time they should expect to invest in the project.

3. Keep your instructions as simple as possible. You achieve simplicity by using short sentences and paragraphs limited to one facet of instruction. Avoid giving too many ideas in a lump. Break your explanations down into easy-to-digest segments.

4. Step-by-step illustrations or photographs are a great help to the reader in visualizing your instructions. Show the crafting of a product from the ground up—first you do this, and then you do that, following through in easy-to-comprehend guidelines.

If you don't know much about photography, by all means take a course in the subject. Or you might have a friend who is a good photographer. He or she might be more than happy to give you instruction for free or for a nominal fee; or you might work out an agreement where your friend takes the pictures and you do the writing.

Your photographs must look professional—clear, sharp pictures that illustrate the procedure you use in a craft or construction article step-by-step.

Unless you are a professional artist with sales to your credit, don't try to sketch or draw your own illustrations. Again, find someone to work with you, someone whose work is of professional quality.

5. Finally, make sure you've included in your article the joy, the satisfaction, and the sense of accomplishment that comes to you through the making or building of your hand-crafted product.

What to Write About

Here are just a few ideas for how-to-make and -do articles:

Construction—*build your own doghouse, dollhouse, darkroom, workroom, woodshed, gameroom, bookcase, desk, model planes and ships, cabin, house, boat, furniture.*

Cooking—*everything from gingerbread men to a full-course menu.*

Domestic—*how to clean house properly. How to avoid and get rid of clutter. How to accident-proof your kitchen, bathroom, pool area. How to take care of your possessions, furniture, silver, rugs, linens.*

Gardening—*how to plant and grow every conceivable kind of vegetable, flower, and herb. How to get rid of insect pests.*

Handcraft—*knitting, quilting, sewing, needlepoint, crocheting, macramé, weaving, ceramics, batik, découpage.*

HELP YOURSELF TO SELF-HELP

The *self-help* how-to article focuses on how-to-*be*. In this kind of how-to, you work hard to motivate a change in attitude which in turn brings about a happier state of mind. These articles may deal with the same problems as those in inspirational articles, problems such as coping with loss of a loved one, loneliness, fear— any negative emotion brought on by a difficult situation. The difference between the how-to and the inspiration article is in the *solution to the problem.*

In the inspiration type of article, the solution to the problem comes about through faith in the power of *Divine Influence* to point the way at the critical hour. In self-help articles, the solution comes through recognizing one's own innate strength of character and allowing it to assert itself when needed most. The writer says, in effect, "You can overcome, cope, manage, survive—if you will follow my suggestions." The writer then offers concrete steps the reader must follow in order to change a negative attitude into a positive one. The phrase, *self-help* spells the premise of this kind of article. You get there, or you win, by *helping yourself.*

Self-help how-tos require a very special approach to a subject. You must have a wealth of solid information, backed up by careful research. Often you must document your methods and theories with the expertise and experiences of others involved with the subject you're writing about.

How Can I Help?

The structure of these articles is clear cut:

1. Start with the problem clearly stated.

2. Talk about possible causes of the problem.

3. Give five or six easy-to-follow suggestions for solving the problem.

Here's how we might structure the self-help article on retirement.

1. The lead. The problem clearly stated:

For thirty years you've had the house to yourself except for the children clattering through the kitchen. Suddenly, you're no longer Queen of all you survey. You've got a King on the throne—your husband has retired! He's underfoot twenty-four hours a day. Not only is he under your feet, he's constantly telling you how to do what you've been doing for more years than you wish to recall.

You feel as if you're in a cage.

2. Causes of problem—the motivation for problem.

You feel sorry for that man of yours wandering like a lost soul through your kitchen, living room, and yard. You realize retirement isn't the dream he visualized. It's turning into a nightmare because he didn't retire *to* something. He's got too many idle hours unfilled.

3. Five or six suggestions to cure problem.

Is there a solution? Of course there is. Start off by making your husband your partner instead of a hindrance. Let him share in a few of your activities. Don't lock him out.

Encourage him to talk about what he'd like to do and then give him the support he needs.

You can think of two or three other ways this problem could be solved. Write them down. Finish the article.

Brainstorming the Theme

Here are several self-help article ideas:

Alcoholism—How to treat it.
Drug Abuse—How to get help.
Health—How to lose or gain weight. How to deal with debilitating illness in yourself or a loved one. How to have healthier skin, hair, eyes, heart, lungs, etc.
Housing—How to buy and how to sell your home and other real estate. How to cope with the empty-nest blues. How to co-exist with grown children who return to the nest. How to survive a move.
Love—How to find it. How to keep it. How to survive losing it.

Money—How to get it. How to invest it. How to cope with losing it.
Career—How to get a job. How to keep a job. How to advance your career. How to survive when you lose your job.
Personal Development—How to overcome shyness, loneliness, fear, grief, poor self-image, insecurity.
Relationships—How to get along better with spouses, children, parents, friends, bosses, fellow employees.
Retirement—How to make the adjustment to having a spouse home all day. How to shift gears into other activities. How to choose the right retirement location.

INFORMATION PLEASE

The third kind of how-to article informs the reader on a particular subject or situation, rather than describing how to use a skill to build, to make, or to make do.

Subjects to write on under this category might be:

Shopping—*How to get the best bargains in anything. Clothes. Furniture. Produce. Meat. Canned goods. Automobiles. Homes. Loans. Travel Clubs.*

Services—*How to get a good doctor, lawyer, dentist, accountant, psychiatrist, teacher, class, home repair, loan, travel bureau.*

For information on a given subject, as in writing other types of how-tos and other types of articles, you can draw on your own experience. It is wise, however, to back up your own experience with information researched from experts in a particular field, as for instance, travel, services, and shopping. Writing off the top of your head isn't enough. Editors want *your* ideas, supported by the opinions and expertise of authorities.

Go to the professional source: your doctor, lawyer, dentist, accountant. Tell your physician you're doing an article on how to find a good doctor when you're a stranger in town—or any other topic you choose. You'll be surprised at how eager the experts are to share what they know with a writer. That old magic of seeing one's name in print is working for you. Your authority will be pleased and proud when he sees his advice published in your article.

WHICH HOW-TO SHOULD YOU WRITE?

Inventory your own skills, hobbies, experiences, and jot down the items that have a special interest or meaning in your life. What do you like to do best in your spare time? Would other people find the same enjoyment if they were to follow your lead? Is what you do inexpensive and are the materials readily available? Is it rewarding and fun?

If you've coped successfully in a difficult life situation, how did you do it?

Whatever type of how-to you write, be positive in your own attitude toward the project, the situation, or the condition. Let your enthusiasm and feeling of excitement breathe life into your article.

The lead for a how-to article is easy to write. Its purpose is to give instant reader identification with the subject of the how-to, whether it's something involving making, building, growing, or self-help.

As an illustration of the simplicity of a how-to lead, here are a few examples from magazines.

Title: "Tie One On!" in which the reader is told how to "Whip up witty Christmas aprons for kitchen helpers" (blurb).

Lead: "Dad's fireplace apron, Mom's candle apron, and the child's tree apron (all illustrated in color on the facing page) are take-offs on the butcher-block apron style."

See how simple that lead is? We know instantly we're going to learn to make aprons. (The article appeared in a December '84 issue of *Woman's World*, by Ruth Philips.)

The instructions follow the lead in an orderly fashion. "First you back all fabric pieces." A step-by-step procedure is given for each type of apron, as well as material needed and exact dimensions.

In the section titled "Medinews" in the *Ladies' Home Journal* (May '84) is a short (under 300 words) filler-type how-to titled, "Mastering Motion Sickness." The page is staff written by Beth Weinhouse.

The lead: "For many people, travel—whether by car, bus, train, plane or boat—means motion sickness. But NASA physician and engineer Dr. Bryant Crammer . . . has found that there are psychological factors that contribute to queasiness."

Again the instructions to avoid the psychological conditions that lead to motion sickness are given in a simple and straightforward manner, beginning with a suggestion that the reader try other methods before resorting to medication, methods such as breathing slowly and deeply with mouth open, and concentrating on tensing and relaxing the body.

In a self-help type of how-to titled "Put P.E.P. into Your Life," by Robert L. Gedaliah (*Reader's Digest* article condensed from *P.E.P.—The Productivity Effectiveness Program*, Holt, Rinehart and Winston), the lead is simple, a direct address type wherein the author starts off with:

It's 2 p.m., but you feel as though you've already put in a full day. Work is piling up on your desk. The phone is ringing, etc.

What reader wouldn't identify with that stressful state in today's world? The premise of the article follows the *you* lead: "The truth is, you're not really exhausted. But your inability to deal with stress has made you feel that way."

The author then tells us how to avoid this stressful feeling in seven easy-to-follow suggestions.

I repeat: Whatever kind of how-to you choose to write, remember to keep your lead simple and direct. Focus it on the specific subject.

If you've never written any type of how-to article before, it's a good idea to begin with *short* articles—these run from 500 words to approximately 1,500. Get started by making a collection of the kinds of articles you particularly like. Clip examples and enter the title, the author, the name of the publication, and the date of publication in your notebook or on index cards. Tag the article as to the specific type of how-to it is. Identify the kind of lead. Did the article begin with a quotation, an anecdote, a description, or with dialogue? How many step-by-step instructions were given, if the article was a build-it or make-it type? How many suggestions were given if the article was focused on changing attitudes in a self-help how-to?

How-to articles meet the same competition as other types of articles. You may think you're the only one building a doghouse with solar heating, but at the same time you get your inspiration, so do a lot of other people. It's always a good idea to query an editor before you submit.

You'll find many markets for your how-to articles in *Writer's Market* and *The Writer's Handbook,* as well as in various monthly issues of *The Writer* and *Writer's Digest.*

Readers' Guide to Periodical Literature is a library reference book that will tell you what other articles have been written on your subject. Knowing that, you have a better chance to give your piece a fresh slant or treatment.

CHECKLIST FOR YOUR HOW-TO ARTICLES

1. What specific how-to did you write?
   How to Make and Do
   Self-help—How to Cope
   Informational—How to Get the Best

2. If your article tells how to make or how to do, are your instructions easy to follow in a step-by-step sequence? If it's a self-help article, did you offer concrete suggestions for changing the negative to positive?

3. Did you double-check your facts and figures, your quotations, and your anecdotes? (Anecdotes must prove a point; tag each one as to the point it proves.)

4. Do you have plenty of backup from other people who have succeeded in making the product you're writing about, or who have successfully handled a similar self-help situation?

5. Have you put a shine to your article through expression of your own positive attitude, your enthusiasm, your excitement, and your strong conviction that the reader will experience the same emotions through following your instructions?

BY REBECCA MULLER

Selling the Seasonal Article Is No Piece of Cake

As a general rule, you can sell a story with a "time tag"—as long as it isn't poorly written—faster than kids can open Christmas packages.

The business of writing a piece with a time tag is a matter of marketing strategy. It can be very rewarding, and can produce sale opportunities that writers might otherwise overlook. It is a way for the new writer to approach editors and break into print and it has the potential for repeat sales of holiday or seasonal pieces. The benefits of this type of writing are so attractive that you can easily forget the problems involved.

ENTER THE PIECE-OF-CAKE MYTH

An idea rolls around the map of your mind, takes a charming, interesting, perhaps poignant back road, and *whammo!* you have a neat, timely little slant as welcome as extra money when the rent's due.

"That's going to be easy," you say to yourself. "I'll whip that out in a couple of hours and pick up a quick sale. It will be a Piece of Cake." You've got the taste of it by now: de holiday-sale delirium. Be wary of it.

Looking for the timely tag to increase an editor's interest in an article is an excellent, and often successful, idea. But it is wise to remember that most editors' idea of "timely" is usually some months before the actual event. Failure to notice a timely slant until the last minute not only stacks the odds against you, but also can result in certain odd commitments in blood to meet editorial deadlines and make the sale. (Which can also lead to a great deal of sweat and many tears.) Try not to put up your first-born child (unless he's very old and about to leave home anyway) in these high-stakes deadline deals. That little piece of cake you're betting your all on can backfire in the most surprising ways: *Nothing* is that easy to write!

Anniversary time tags (looking back the tenth or fifteenth or twentieth year after Woodstock or the Los Angeles earthquake . . . that sort of thing) can also be a real moneymaker—and a real culprit. They *always* look like easy money. Piece of cake.

The Piece-of-Cake problem is both syndrome and disease. It *does* go by these pseudonyms in some parts of the country—I see affirmative nods around Pennsylvania and Texas. However, to set the record straight, P.O.C. has only one proper name: *myth.*

EXIT THE PIECE-OF-CAKE MYTH

My first piece of cake was iced even before I realized I had baked myself into a three-tier literary trap; that is to say, I had blithe-spirited my way into a casual conversation with an editor who trusted my pen and received a pleasant, "That sounds good. About 1,000 words?"

I had the slant.

I had the assignment.

I also had approximately 4,000 words wadded up on the floor of my office after 20 hours of work.

The problems I encountered and the amount of energy and ink ultimately expended in producing the "quick" holiday sale yielded a good check, but also a neurotic tendency to pace and chant four-letter words at the cat.

Here's how it began . . .

Given: The Christmas season filled with bright lights, colorful decorations and festive music everywhere we go . . . from shopping malls and grocery stores to churches. *Slant*: What about the many among us who do not see or hear all these things; what is Christmas like for the blind or deaf? *Editor's reaction*: Fine, do it. *Writer's reaction*: A piece of cake.

However, after a couple of interviews and a couple of false starts (each of which went on for quite a few pages before I realized it wasn't going) I was deep in the inherent traps of the piece, and trying to find my way out . . . before deadline. It had backfired on me.

Trap #1: If you're going to talk about the variations in the way Christmas is experienced through *some* disabilities (I thought), you're going to have to consider other disabilities as well (I decided). What about those who cannot talk, for instance? Suddenly my slant had broadened considerably.

Trap #2: The words *blind, deaf* and *crippled* are *accurate* words, but not the *cheeriest* words in a Christmas vocabulary, I found as I placed them on paper. How in the world to find synonyms (if there were any) that did not have the opposite effect of being so cheery that they seemed to wholly discount these problems? The word *disabilities* is a place to start, but not a good enough place to stop, I felt. After three days I decided on the word *limitations*, and broadened my thought to encompass "all the limitations in the world" in an effort to be realistic, but not overly pessimistic.

I didn't think I could possibly be in for more problems. Until I started my next draft.

Trap #3: About 500 words into the article I realized that the piece sounded patronizing, dividing the *us* (who see and hear, etc.) from the *them* (who do not). It bordered on being maudlin, which was only about 180° from what I wanted the piece to be.

Finally, after much rewriting, "The Silent Night" was born. It ran in a weekly Sunday supplement magazine before Christmas a few years ago. This is how I ended the piece that *wasn't* a piece of cake:

At midnight, just as it turns Christmas morning, I shall step outside into the dark night of all our burdens and think softly and secretly: "He is arrived in Bethlehem. And so am I. My Christmas journey is complete."

We are all complete, exactly as we are. All the world's limitations fall away in the light emanating from the manger.

Breathe of the air on which the silent chorus of a multitude of angels is borne. Hear the traffic of their wings with the inner ear of love. Touch the silent night. Behold, the sight and silence of Christmas.

Holiday articles only gain freshness after you've completely wilted. Believe me.

BRIDGE FOR SALE

A second case history from this writer's muddled memoirs might be called "The Holiday That Got Away." In the euphoria of having met several difficult deadlines, with my typewriter feeling rather plump and satisfied, I decided to dash off a little piece of fluff on "The Week Between Two Years"—or some such—regarding the annual breathing space that exists between Christmas and New Year's. Unfortunately, I thought of it around Dec. 20, when even those nice weekly magazine supplements all over the country had already been on—and off—the press for about a month.

Yet another item drawn from my file came from the anniversary category, illustrating how you can build a timely lead as a supporting bridge to a sale . . . especially the short filler piece.

Given: Young man in town has a marvelous, comprehensive collection of authentic Civil War-period uniforms and boots, saddles, bridles and bits, rifles, etc. *Slant:* Local boy as serious collector and historian, with photos . . . and a tie-in to the U.S. Bicentennial. *Editor's reaction:* Sounds interesting, OK. *Writer's reaction:* P.O.C.!

Trap: Civil War collection, I said to myself as I put pen to yellow pad. Not *Revolutionary* War! Now I had to find a way to link the wrong war (as it were) to the right reflection.

After shooting off cannons in all the wrong directions I decided the "lead" was going to have to provide the link with America's 200th birthday, somehow. Solution was a middle-of-the-night flank attack which allowed me to skip about 100 years, somewhat inconspicuously. The lead to "Christiansen's Cavalry" read:

Talking face-to-face with a uniformed U.S. Cavalry officer, circa 1870, is a little unnerving—like Alice in Wonderland stepping through the Bicentennial looking-glass to find herself at Little Big Horn.

That one ran during the Bicentennial year.

The recipe of our last P.O.C. shows the value of keeping time tags (and old notes) in mind at all times: "A Conversation With Crume," a posthumous profile published a few years ago, was developed from interview notes *five years old* by using the anniversary-tag premise. It, too, held some surprise ingredients.

Given: Paul Crume had been a front-page columnist and undoubtedly the most popular writer in Dallas for almost a quarter of a century. In the spring of 1980, a book of many of his finest columns had been published (compiled and edited by his widow). November, 1980 marked the fifth anniversary of his death. I had what proved to be the last interview Crume ever gave. *Slant:* Because of the new book and the anniversary date, a reflection piece would now be very timely. *Editor's reaction:* Let's see what you can do with it. *Writer's reaction:* Simple. Just get out the notes and write it up. A piece of . . .

Wrong.

Because of the large population influx in Dallas within the last five years, I realized that a substantial percentage of local readers had not even lived here in 1975, and had probably never heard of my subject. How was I going to make a posthumous profile interesting or important to them? There was also the delicate problem of *tense*; use of past tense would smack of "yesterday's news." I decided the conversation *must* be written in the present tense; I must turn the clock back . . . to the present.

FINAL SOLUTION

The final solution seemed obvious—after about five yellow tablets. I would have to speak *personally* to the reader, in an introduction that would make it important to meet Paul Crume:

> *For twenty-four years his front-page column, Big D, in* The Dallas Morning News, *was our morning cup of coffee and our antidote to the garish headlines of daily life. Paul Crume tickled the ribs of Dallas and reported on the world at large.*
>
> *By late summer of 1975, when he had been a part of my world for over two decades, I unabashedly wrote requesting an interview with "the writer, the observer, the man whose shadow casts a giant 'D' on the city who loves him." That overripe plum of prose must have given him a chuckle; he consented. I had no way of knowing that it was one of the most private seasons in time for Paul Crume. His last.*
>
> *In his choice of written words, Crume always knew what to leave out. He knew what mattered and what didn't. His conversation was equally well-crafted. He said what he meant to say, thereby leaving out all the things he'd wish he hadn't said. Much of what he chose to say about the author of Big D showed that he respected the man. And accepted him as he found him.*
>
> *I'm not sure what I expected, but I've always been sure I found it.*

Using the subtitle "October 1975," I slipped the reader silently into the past tense, and into the presence of the man.

Finding that which is timely, or can be tagged to a timely event, is a matter of using your calendar as a *tool*. By studying it with an eye to the past, present and future, writers can uncover many items of editorial interest and potentially easy sales. *Easy*, however, is a relative word; the kind of word the Piece-of-Cake Myth feeds on.

You *can* have your cake and eat it too. But the recipe for an article sale is still hard work, good writing, marketing skill and meeting deadlines.

TIMELY AND SEASONAL

Remember these tips when trying to sell the timely tale:

• Editors like timely articles. And the holidays are a very timely subject indeed. Especially the Christmas holidays; editors everywhere start looking for a good, fresh slant on a Christmas piece the day after last Christmas. But like writers everywhere, I start looking for a good, fresh slant on a Christmas piece the day after October.

There are all kinds of holidays that can be held accountable for the euphoria which brings on a writer's attack of the Piece-of-Cake syndrome: Christmas, New Year's Day, Valentine's Day, April Fool's Day, Easter, Mother's Day, Father's Day, Independence Day, Labor Day, Halloween and Thanksgiving, just to name a few.

• Don't confuse the timely tie-in article with more journalistic terms such as *topical*, or *hot*, referring to the daily news beat. Most freelancers will not have the freedom of schedule or other resources (expense accounts, staff photographers, wire services, etc.) that are available to staff writers. If you try to beat them at their own game you will probably be second in line, writing on their coattails every time out. Editors don't need freelancers to be *reporters*.

Editors *do* need freelancers to be *writers*: to think, look ahead, look back, plan and offer them good, fresh slants with timely tie-ins on holidays, seasonal subjects, anniversary stories worth reading about in perspective, and even profiles or point-of-view pieces regarding current sports such as politics, Latin America and baseball.

• Research the *events, people* and *interests* of your locality—and the nation. What occurred a year ago? Five, ten or 100 years ago? Find something that offers you a good "anniversary-of" tag to do a follow-up article, or a reflective think piece.

An excellent source for valuable, timely tips is an almanac (such as the old *Reader's Digest* annuals). I buy old copies for 25-50¢ each at Goodwill Stores, dated five or ten years ago. (If you shop for one remember that the book will deal with coverage of the *previous* year; e.g., a 1981 almanac covers 1980, etc.).

• Circle these on your calendar: *July 4* and *the entire month of December!* Editors of both monthlies and weeklies say that the Independence holiday is a vast wasteland waiting to be cultivated by writers willing to plow *fresh* viewpoints into the red, white and blue field. And an editor recently shared this with me, regarding *December*: "Nothing hit my desk for four solid weeks! What happened to all the freelancers? Don't they realize that I need to be looking at manuscripts for early spring features *during December?*

    Freelance sales are a matter of *months* . . . not *moods.*

● To stay informed of possible timely slants in your city, write to the Chamber of Commerce requesting to be placed on their mailing list.

● After first publication, start looking for the most appropriate "second rights" (reprint) market for next season. In many cases that second sale might be a reprint in a national market, since a number of larger magazines like to use good "pick ups" from smaller publications. Your second sale could conceivably net you more money than your first!

BY LOUISE PURWIN ZOBEL

What to Notice for Your Travel Stories

Well equipped and well prepared, here you are—on the scene at last. You look around and wonder where to begin—there's so much to see, hear, smell, taste, touch, know, and enjoy.

Sometimes you start by looking for particular information, to flesh out specific ideas or to fit specific markets. Other times you approach the travel experience with an open mind, waiting for your story to find you.

In homes or palaces, temples or cemeteries, deserts or rain forests, the travel writer is always exploring, sampling the action, seeing for himself whether there's anything worth writing about.

You have to remain aware and alert, continually searching for ideas and information. Even "relaxed," on holiday, your mind is always working. One travel writer, who says 100 percent of his wanderings are related to writing and selling articles, admits that even short trips to attend weddings or visit his parents provide the basis for future travel pieces. That's because he's always on the lookout for the potential story.

When a story finds you, sometimes you immediately recognize its plus value. When we joined Japan's "Strangers into Friends" program, our visit to a Japanese home included a venerable grandmother who tore open her kimono to show us her gall bladder scar; a family argument about whether to buy a motor car, which the old lady vetoed as too dangerous; and a farewell with us standing in the doorway struggling into our shoes while the beautiful young daughter accompanied herself on her koto as she sang, "Oh, say can you see by the dawn's early light. . . ."

Other times the story seems elusive and you have to *create* the plus value. On the Mediterranean island of Malta we saw what seemed like a jumble of prehistoric temples, Roman ruins, reminders of the knights, beach resorts, British tourists, and bomb damage. It was hard to fuse them into an article. Then hospitable locals gave me a clue. Remembering that Saint Paul, shipwrecked on Malta, was also well treated by the native people, I emphasized Maltese hospitality over a period of thousands of years, which gave my story a focus.

LOOK FOR OTHER STORIES, TOO

Usually the best stories cover all the ordinary things as well as some special, unique angle. Search for that special angle while you're traveling. But don't neglect the "ordinary."

Search out the details of your story, but also remain on the lookout for additional stories. Often you'll see something more interesting than you expect.

I had intended, for instance, to include a paragraph or two about the museum of San Francisco's Presidio in an article about nearby Fort Point. Exploring the museum, however, I found there was much more than military history there. The diorama of the 1806 Presidio, with a Russian ship in the background and a Russian captain in the foreground, reminds viewers that the captain fell in love with "the prettiest girl in California," who waited many years for him, only to learn that he had died on his trip home seeking permission to marry her. The diorama of the San Francisco earthquake and fire is flanked by pictures of the city before the calamity, pictures of the city being rebuilt, of the 1915 Panama Pacific International Exposition, of the building of the bridges, and of Alcatraz and Angel Island. From an exhibit of Civil War clothing and antique medical equipment, to models of the early missions and a collection of John Wayne memorabilia, here was a fascinating museum, deserving a story of its own.

"Sometimes the best story ideas come from the little happenings that fall through the cracks in the itinerary floor," says Dee Henri. She tells of traveling to Nova Scotia in a forty-six person bus which stopped unexpectedly at a tiny roadside cafe. The single young waitress-cook was overwhelmed, simply unable to serve so many cold, hungry tourists; whereupon the passengers made themselves at home in the kitchen, opening cans of soup, brewing coffee, and serving each other. "The spirit of the lunch stop was more impressive than the sights we saw," says Henri.

ORIENTATION COMES FIRST

A brief sight-seeing tour is the best way to orient yourself to the important landmarks and obtain an overview of the topography. Sit or stand near the guide. Don't be bashful. Ask questions. If you're overflowing with questions—too many to ask—try to determine which answers you'll be able to find elsewhere—and ask the other ones. If the guide is a good one, write down his name and address, in case you have a question to ask later. (If you do write later, be sure to enclose a self-addressed, stamped envelope or, if he's in another country, an International Reply Coupon, purchased at the post office.) If the guide is a very good one, write a complimentary letter to his boss, to encourage excellence in tour guides.

Whether or not you take subsequent tours, do rely on public transportation for much of your sight-seeing. Procure a good map of the bus or subway system. If you're in a hurry in a big city, take the subway. But if you want to see the people and the neighborhoods, the kids walking home from school, the housewives pinching the fruit at the greengrocer's, the workers relaxing on front stoops, look for surface transportation. In addition to buses, trolley cars, and trams, consider the jitney, the shared taxi so popular in many areas; horse-drawn carriages; rickshaws. Bicycles and motorcycles give you still a different view, as you actually become part of the street scene. Riding a funicular or a cable railway or even on the top of a double-decker bus presents another perspective—farther removed, more telescopic.

Whenever you can, go by water. Practically all riverfront or lakefront areas offer waterborne transportation. From Westminster, for instance, you can take a water bus along the Thames, downstream as far as Greenwich, upstream as far as Hampton Court. Queen Elizabeth floats no more comfortably. The boat on Lake Geneva is a floating kaffeeklatsch. Mrs. A. embarks in Geneva, saving three seats for her friends; Mrs. B. comes aboard ten minutes later from the dock of a lakeside house; Mrs. C. boards at a small village five minutes away; then they order coffee and cakes, so they're all ready when Mrs. D. joins them at the next boat stop. The four chatter in rapid-fire French all the way to Montreux. The travel writer may not understand a word they say, but their appearance, their postures, their gestures, offer intimate insights that flesh out the story.

THE UNIVERSAL AND THE SPECIFIC

One of the world's biggest transportation bargains is a ride on a ferryboat. While on assignment in Turkey, we remained on deck as the ferry that leaves from Istanbul's Galata Bridge sailed past the elegant DolmaBaHçe Palace and the frowning fortifications of Rumeli Hisar and Anadolu Hisar. We zigzagged between European Turkey and Asiatic Turkey, letting off and taking on passengers and cargo at dozens of docks. Water traffic of all kinds crisscrossed the Bosporus around us. After debarking in Sariyer, where the restaurant sent a fisherman out front to catch our lunch, we took a bus back to Istanbul. The half-hour ride through fields, orchards, and peasant villages taught us much about rural Turkey. On-the-spot "research" aboard the bus and the ferry provided background for a number of stories.

It's not hard to find exotic transport. I've ridden a camel, an elephant, a mule, a donkey, and an ostrich, and I'm not very venturesome.

Camel rides across the Sahara or mule rides through the Alps can make for interesting articles focused on the method of transportation, but usually such episodes are just one sentence of a story. Exotic conveyances can help you get the feel of a place, but overall, the most satisfactory type of transportation for a travel writer is shoe leather. On your own two feet is the best way to catch the most intimate glimpses of everyday life, as well as close-ups of parades, fiestas, and wedding processions.

To really know what a place is like you have to see its most important landmarks several times, at different hours of the day. Some sights, like the Taj Mahal or Ayers Rock, are always surrounded by rapt tourists at special times—sunrise, sunset, the light of the full moon; but even the modest plaza in a Mexican village looks different and feels different at dawn, at noon, and at twilight.

Notice what they call their plazas and squares and how they name their streets. Is the town laid out with First Street and Second Street intersecting A and B and C? Or are the streets, the squares, the gates, the areas named for famous people? What kinds of famous people? Politicians? Generals? Writers? Artists? Musicians? Entertainers? Millionaires? Sometimes it's the date that's important—Mexico City's Avenida 16 de Septiembre (named for the Mexican Independence Day), Buenos Aires' Avenida 9 de Julio (a crucial day in Argentina's struggle for liberty), Leningrad's Decembrists Square (the month of an early, unsuccessful version of the Russian revolution).

The place names give you the flavor of the community. California's San Jose and La Jolla, New Orlean's Bienville Street, Chartres Street, and Beauregard Square, evoke the areas' origins. Be sure to note interesting names to use later in stories or titles. Or to write an article about the names themselves. A newspaper story, datelined Norway, Maine, explains how such a true-blue Yankee state happens to have place names ranging from Madrid, Moscow, and Mexico to Paris, Poland, and Peru. Other travel writers have studied the history or patterns of street names or town names in certain areas, and have come up with salable stories.

Other clues to what the people of an area consider important can be found in their parks. Often there'll be trees planted by well-known people, noteworthy political or military figures. Prime ministers and rear admirals are invited to plant trees in parks all over the world. In whose honor were the fountains, statues, or other monuments erected? Are there more playing fields or hothouses? Has the city attempted to provide green space for its citizens?

The travel writer needs to look for the universal as well as the specific. Never be a mere name dropper, enumerating the airports and train stations you've waited in during your trip. Instead, cultivate the essence of the place so you can interpret it for others.

MEET THE LOCAL PEOPLE

Visit a family at home if you possibly can. Practically every country has a program that encourages local families to extend hospitality to visitors with similar hobbies, professions, interests, or whatever.

Better still, take along the names of friends of friends, relatives of relatives, and even acquaintances of acquaintances. Any opportunity to see how local people live provides the traveling writer with invaluable background material for stories: It's within the family circle that you really grasp the people's relationships with each other, their relationship to their government, and their relationship to the rest of the world, whether they live in august mansions crumbling in shabby gentility or in overcrowded apartments with wall-to-wall sleeping bags. The food they serve you is important in more ways than your observation of the kind of food it is. *How* it's served is a clue to the people's lifestyle. So is *who* is eating. Do the women do the serving, but don't serve themselves? Is the oldest person present served first? Are the children at the table?

Do the people speak freely about their government's shortcomings or parrot "everything's perfect" slogans? Sometimes when you dig a little deeper, long-held images are shattered. At a Moscow apartment the college professor's wife complained about the difficulty of obtaining eyeglasses in the Soviet Union. Since she was obviously wearing glasses, the American visitors wondered how she had managed to procure them. "Oh, *glasses* you can get," she said. "But it's impossible to find any designer frames."

Play where the local people play. One of my favorite memories of Venice is a vaporetto ride to the Lido, where we bounced a beachball with a group of Italian children, and sipped red wine in paper cups with a visiting family from Naples. Of course, I wrote about it.

Eat where the locals eat. Sit and sip at a sidewalk cafe. Order the house specialty. Talk to the waiter. Don't rush. Observe. Eavesdrop. Stare.

Seek out old-timers to spin yarns about yesterday. You'll often find these people, who are, as John Wright says, "priceless" to the story, at the local mom-and-pop cafe. Search for a restaurant that's a "step above a greasy spoon, but a cut below fancy nonsense."

Picnic in the park. Let the sun caress your shoulders. Listen to the squeals of the children somersaulting on the grass. Watch the grandfathers pondering the next move in their eternal chess game. Taste the vanilla ice cream. Listen to the calls of the local birds. Throw back the errant ball that comes your way.

Go to the grocery store. Is it a supermarket, selling everything from laundry detergent to fresh fish, from shampoo to tennis shoes? Are the displays of canned goods veiled in layers of dust, their prices so high in relation to wages that the display is merely decorative?

Go to the outdoor markets, too. You have to start before dawn at Bangkok's Floating Market, where mangoes and bananas, coconuts and papayas are bargained for and bought from boat to boat, and you, drifting through the klongs and canals, are poled right into the center of the action. Start early, too, for Curacao's colorful Schooner Market, where dockside customers haggle with vendors in sailboats for fresh fish, exotic vegetables, and flashy fabrics. Go early, also, to Singapore's Chinatown, where customers dicker for snakes and lizards to brew into virility-producing broths; to North African suqs, where they sell spices and grape leaves and tiny cups of strong, sweet Turkish coffee; or to Pennsylvania Dutch markets selling pig stomachs, Amish pretzels and old-fashioned sweet bologna.

LOCAL COLOR

Stop in at the *boulangerie*, which lures you with the seductive smell of crusty bread and chocolate tarts, and the *charcuterie*, where the aging lamb is flanked by a pair of peacocks and a selection of wild hares.

You may be surprised at some of the places where food is sold. Ferryboats which cross international boundaries may cater to long lines of people who've taken the ride for the groceries. As soon as the boat's commissary opens, the passengers crowd around, eager to buy coffee, liquor, and whatever edibles and potables are scarce or expensive in their own country.

You will also get a realistic view of the people at the laundromat. Who's there?

Career singles from the roominghouses in the next block? Camping families with muddy duffle? Senior citizens? I remember a stormy day in Southern California when the first mate of a small ketch commandeered all the dryers for her life jackets, cushions, bedding, foul weather gear, and dock lines. On another day, halfway around the world, in Alice Springs, Australia, an aborigine woman lugged into the laundromat bag after bag of blankets, towels, and clothing—enough for every washing machine in the place—as five children marched behind her, licking dripping ice cream cones that were getting their shirts into condition for next month's wash. Puerto Vallarta's main "laundromat" is on the edge of town—rocks for scrubbing, riverbank for drying. Immediately behind the washing area, at the city-built playground, the children of the laundresses sing as they scramble down the slides or swing out over the sharp stones. You can learn a lot at the laundromat. (Someday I'm going to write an article about conversations overheard in a cruise ship laundromat!)

Check out the department stores. Do they feature more dress patterns and sewing notions than ready-mades? More work shoes than ski boots? Electric orange juicers; manually operated orange juicers; or no juicers at all? What does all this tell you about the people in this community? How about the local shoppers in the department store? Are they queued up for a special bargain or because some household item, heretofore in short supply, has just been received by the store? Are people carrying string bags or elaborately decorated shopping bags? Do they look well dressed? Fashionable? Are they swathed in furs or shivering through threadbare wraps on a cold day?

Are most of the items in the store manufactured locally? If not, where are they from? What other services does the store offer? One huge Tokyo department store not only presents kimono fashion shows and demonstrates the art of flower arranging, but also provides lessons in the use of knives and forks—for chopstick users who want to learn Western ways.

Don't stop with the department stores. Visit the specialty shops, the bazaars, the suqs, the flea markets. "Shopping" is more than a frivolous pastime when you're searching for your story.

Even beauty parlors and barbershops abound in clues to an area's reality. My first time in Cairo, sixteen different people worked on my simple shampoo and set, from the young girl who handed me a plastic-bagged comb, brush, and towel, to the man who, two hours later, wielded the hairspray can. How to tip? Egyptian and European ladies were going around dispensing the equivalent of one cent to the teenager who brought the coffee, five cents to the shampoo girl, two cents to the young boy who had removed the rollers, and ten cents to the maestro who set the hair, etc. That bit of local color found its way into one of my stories on Egypt.

JOIN THE CONGREGATION

While many of us are naturally reluctant to intrude upon the religious rites of others, I've often stumbled into a ceremony and been invited to stay: a prayer meeting in a Turkish mosque; a christening in a Greek church; a coming-of-age ceremony at Saint Peter's and another one, very different, at the Wailing Wall; a Buddhist funeral in Japan; a Presbyterian wedding in Brisbane. Religious ceremonies always provide special insights. Be sure to look up your own religious affiliates when you travel. You'll not only meet pleasant people, but you'll probably be invited to attend a coffee hour after the service, a congregational pot-luck supper, or the annual Sunday school picnic.

LOOK FOR LOCAL RECREATION

Do you feel you could never bear to see a bull fight? You might find it less gory and more interesting than you expect. And the real show is the people around you and how they act and react.

Ball games bore you? Don't be too sure. Whether it's sandlot or Super Bowl, with a little pregame explanation you'll understand enough of the action to understand the other spectators' enjoyment.

Too old for circuses? No, you're not. Applaud the elephant ballet and shiver in fear for the high-wire artists along with the rest of the audience.

The successful travel writer not only attends the event, he observes the crowd. Watching the people around you often leads to a story angle. My article about the Boxing Day race meeting in Auckland, New Zealand, focused on the women spectators' hats. In an era when women the world over practically never covered their heads, these stunningly dressed New Zealanders all wore their millinery proudly. I guessed there must be a reason, so I asked the woman in front of me in the buffet line. It's an annual contest, she explained, sponsored by Auckland's milliners, with a prize—a vacation in Australia for two—given for the most attractive hat at the meeting.

One of the most pleasant evenings I've ever spent was in Tampere, Finland, at the Pyynikki open-air revolving theater, where the audience is moved around to face the various changes of scene. We didn't need to understand a word of Finnish. The play was obviously the old story of the farmer's daughter and the traveling salesman. The audience laughed at all the right places. My readers enjoyed hearing about it, too.

The best part of participating in local entertainment is your opportunity to see the people of the area relaxed and having a good time. You learn from watching them, talking to them, joining them in joy, fear, amusement, grief, devotion, satisfaction, or anxiety.

Although *Sleeping Beauty* in Leningrad was one of the most beautiful ballets I've ever seen, what I wrote about was the young Russian girls in front of us who insisted, with gestures, that we share their chocolates, and the coat checkers who told us, in pantomime, that there was still another act, when we thought it was over.

Your readers will want to know how many people were present at any kind of public gathering—parade, concert, ballgame, political demonstration. This figure is not only important in gauging the popularity of the concert artist or the political candidate, but it lends meaning to the occasion. Are there a hundred people waiting in line for the art show to open—or only a dozen? Are there a hundred demonstrators waving signs—or a thousand? I've never forgotten my high school journalism instructor's directions to "count the house" first thing. For a quick estimate, if the crowd is seated, count the number of seats in a row, and multiply by the number of rows. If it's a restaurant, count the number of tables and the average number of seats at each table; then consider carefully the degree of fullness of the room. (If the number of seats is common knowledge, all you have to do is count those that are empty.)

Professor Herbert Jacobs of the University of California offered this formula for estimating standing crowds: First measure the length and width of the area in feet; then add the two figures together; if the people seem to be moving around fairly easily, multiply this sum by seven; if they're tightly packed, multiply by ten. Thus, an area 100 by 150 feet—a sum of 250 feet—contains approximately 1,750 freely moving people or 2,500 tightly packed people. Learn to "eyeball" an area measurement. Outdoors, is it bigger than a football field? Indoors, is it as long as three bathtubs or wider than two full-size beds?

WELCOME CHANCE MEETINGS

While you're traveling, encourage chance encounters. Speak to the person sitting next to you on the plane, train, or bus. That person may turn out to be a pleasant traveling companion; and he may be the very person you need to alert you to an important story breaking along your route. Or he may be from a distant country, with ideas and insights that introduce you to that country in a way that years of reading never could.

Getting lost may be one of the very best ways to see an area. Local people love to show you the route, and the experience often leads the travel writer down interesting bypaths. While struggling with his high school French in France, John Pollack remembered Ben Franklin's advice to let others do *you* a favor if you want them to like you. He went around asking strangers to photograph him with his camera. This led to interesting conversations, vast amounts of inside information—and a huge collection of dull pictures.

While he was able to practice *his* French, in many countries people like to practice *their* English. When an English-speaking person asks for directions they're delighted to help. Never hesitate to ask questions. All over the world, people young and old like to show off their surroundings, and will often take an unbelievable amount of trouble to lead you to something they think you should see. Often the "something" is more charming, less crowded, richer in beauty and meaning than the well-known sight nearby. A stranger's description and a nudge in the right direction led us to the Roman ruins under the city of Barcelona. Other strangers have sent us to exquisite secluded beaches, exciting but little-known galleries, and hole-in-the-wall restaurants with tasty regional menus. Always listen to local people's recommendations. Pay attention when somebody says, "Don't miss seeing. . . ." or "Be sure to stop at. . . ."

Make use of every person-to-person opportunity. Sometimes you'll need special help while pursuing your on-trip research. But finding the individual who can give you the exact information you need isn't as hard as it sounds. Your at-home research provides a starting point. "Then it's easy," says Caryl Hansen. "Ask each source to suggest other sources." Jo Combs likens it to "unraveling a ball of string—find a starting person, and he will direct you to others, who will help you find still others."

While your embassy or consulate might assist in arranging interviews with people you need to see overseas, usually they won't do it until you actually arrive in the country. They've found too many people change plans at the last moment. (Remember, if you need the services of a translator, the interview will take twice as long, so budget your time accordingly.)

The hotel concierge prides himself on being able to answer practically any question or solve any problem. Ask him for advice and printed information as soon as you arrive. Lois Kirchner forgot to do this at the Park Lane Hotel in London. Only as she was leaving did she discover she could have walked through nearby Green Park to Buckingham Palace and witnessed a leisurely and uncrowded Changing of the Guard.

LOCAL LIBRARY RESEARCH

Others can help you, too. Question the saleslady, the flower seller, the cobbler, the proverbial man in the street. The more people you talk to, the better feel you get for the place, the more you know about it, and the better story you'll write. The dining room maitre d' led one writer to a French organization that dates back to the Druids and gave her the name of a book on the legends of Brittany that was exactly what she needed.

Go into a bookstore and ask if they have anything on local history. Listen for folk tales and stories of local heroes. Jot down the names of people and places you'll be able to look up at home.

Be sure to buy local newspapers and magazines (many foreign countries publish English editions, also) to find out more about the local scene, as well as events of interest. Read the want ads. Listen to local radio and television programs.

Even though you've done your library research in advance, you may want to pursue some special interest while traveling, and you'll find librarians everywhere glad to help you when you show sincere purpose.

When Winifred Johnson spent four months in Jackson, a town in California's gold country, she visited the museum so often that the curator set aside a special room for her to work in. On days when the museum and the library were closed, docents took her on tours, showing her memorabilia the more casual observer doesn't get to see, some of it from the time of the gold rush itself. She did her research in 1850s newspapers, and in private homes, whose owners heard about her project and invited her to visit.

James Winchester also found more help than he expected. Trying to complete a *Reader's Digest* assignment about Russian trawlers off Newfoundland, he was ready to give up when he heard on his rental car radio that the Russian ocean-ography ship working with the trawlers had put into port with a sick seaman. He hurried to the pier, though he didn't really expect to be allowed on the ship. He was, however, welcomed aboard. Many of the crew spoke English. The captain himself took Winchester on a complete tour. Whenever they came to a locked door the captain sent a seaman for the key. While they were waiting—and there were many such waits—they had a glass of vodka, bottoms up. Winchester was happy to report that he upheld the dignity of American journalism by remaining on his feet all day.

While you may often deal with less glamorous opportunities for imbibing, you'll still have to work out your own rules about alcohol. Will your hosts be in-sulted if you refuse? Will you be too sleepy to get your story if you accept? Should you stick to Perrier? A refreshing beer? Wine with lunch? There aren't any "standard" answers.

Check into alcohol-related etiquette and establish a pattern that seems com-fortable to you. In general, I remind myself that *every day* is a working day for the travel writer, and a professional manner is imperative.

Knowing what to look for, what to listen for, what to think about, and how to use your other senses are the travel writer's "secret weapons." Take full advan-tage of your on-scene position as you gather material for the stories you've al-ready planned—and the stories you didn't plan because you didn't know ahead of time what terrific stories they could be.

BY STUART COHEN

How to Supplement Your Articles with Photos

A writer who can supply reproduction-quality photographs has a better chance of selling his or her work than one who can't. Busy editors in all but the top markets would rather buy writing and photos together than track down pictures to accompany manuscripts. In addition, an illustrated article will command a higher fee than would the writing by itself.

Photography, like writing, is a learnable skill. You can't simply borrow a camera once, bang off a few snapshots, and expect to come up with something a magazine will print. But you *can* take satisfactory photographs even with a minimum of experience, if you understand how photos convey information and stimulate emotions.

To develop your photographic skill, you must shift your thinking from the linear, verbal mode of transmitting information to the spatial, photographic mode. Photographers observe scenes differently than other people. They see forms, patterns and colors where others see information. You can begin to learn to see more photographically by looking at the world in a more naive way: See what's in front of you as it appears, rather than as what you know it to be.

For example, look at a shelf of books. In the verbal mode, you see a dictionary, a thesaurus and a couple of novels. But in the visual mode, you see a series of vertical forms of different thicknesses and colors. You can see two planes of the book nearest you, which gives it a sense of a third dimension. Notice how the light falls on the books, creating lighter and darker areas that we interpret as shape and depth.

Photographs transmit information by visual representation alone. With words, you can interpret data for the readers; in pictures, the viewers must do that themselves. As you choose subjects, camera angles and lighting, you will be looking for a three-dimensional situation that, when translated to two dimensions (and sometimes reduced to black and white), will convey your message effectively.

STALKING YOUR STORY: PURPOSE AND APPROACH

When planning photographs to accompany an article, ask yourself: "What is the purpose of the photograph? What does it need to communicate, and to whom?"

Are your pictures simply for illustration, presenting the visual equivalent of the information in the article? Or do you also need to catch the readers' eye to tantalize them and make them want to read your article? Perhaps you want your photographs to evoke an emotion that will begin to win the readers over to your point of view. Whatever your purpose, consider both your subject and your audience, so you can choose a suitable approach for your pictures.

For example, an article about roller coasters written for the general public might open with a photo of laughing riders whizzing by in an open car, hands waving in the air. The photo shows the fun of roller coasters. But the same subject written for engineering students would have to show how the structure that supports the track is built to withstand lateral forces involved when the car comes reeling off a high-speed turn. If you are writing for concerned parents about how dangerous these rides can be, you might show a worn and hazardous section of a local roller coaster track. And if your piece is a personal reminiscence about your childhood, a color photo of the sun setting behind the great white super-structure in an abandoned amusement park would set the tone perfectly.

Choosing an approach for your photographs is like choosing a voice for your writing—except deciding on an approach for your pictures is easier because the tone of the piece is already set: You know what you are saying before you pick up the camera.

PEOPLING YOUR PHOTOS

No matter what your article is about, remember that people are naturally interested in other people. In a selection of pictures depicting all but the most technical of subjects, you should include some pictures that show how human beings are involved with whatever you are writing about.

If you feel awkward or embarrassed photographing people, try to find a topic that both you and the subject are interested in and carry on a lively conversation during the session. Props and relevant activities give an uncomfortable subject something to do, and often add information value to the picture. If people appear stiff or posed while you're shooting, they will look that way in the finished photograph, so try to put them at ease.

Decide whether you want candid or posed pictures beforehand, and give your subjects specific and clear directions. Your confidence, or lack of it, sets the tone of the session, so be as well-prepared as possible when photographing people.

FRAMING YOUR SUBJECT

You want what matters in the frame and what doesn't matter out of it. Many inexperienced photographers make the mistake of putting the principal subject in the dead center of the frame surrounded by empty space. While that's better than cutting off someone's ear, it makes your subject look unimportant and weakens the image. A good practice to help you to see the whole frame is to run your eye around the edges of the viewfinder before you snap the picture. Chances are that seeing all that open space will make you move in closer or choose a longer focal length lens.

Fill the frame with the substance of your picture. When in doubt, frame it several different ways, from farther away and tighter in, vertically and horizontally. If you know that one picture is critical to your story, don't be afraid to shoot a whole roll of film, trying all the different possibilities.

HOW MANY PICTURES?

It helps to know approximately how many photos will actually end up in print. Determine how many you think are needed to do the subject justice, and check with the editor. If he can't give you a precise answer, look at recent copies of the magazine for articles similar to yours, and see how many photos appeared. It would be foolish to photograph all your interviewees if you knew that only a single lead picture will be used.

In our roller coaster example above, the reminiscence piece would do fine with one evocative picture. More than that would start to become a photo essay. The piece for engineering students, however, would need as many pictures as there are significant mechanical details that can be better shown than described. You would also include an overview of the roller coaster to put the subject in perspective, though an editor short on space might not run it. An article on "The Fun of Roller Coastering" could get by with a single shot of people having a good time, or it might be heavily illustrated with people pictures or shots of exotic or old roller coasters. In this case, the magazine's policy and style would determine the number of pictures you should take.

Shoot far more than you will actually need. Overshooting is a cardinal rule all professional photographers follow. You want the best possible photos, and while taking more pictures doesn't guarantee better pictures, it increases the odds.

Don't try to save money by being stingy with film: Film is the cheapest part of the job. If you're not sure exactly what to shoot, try a number of reasonable variations and a few unreasonable ones besides. If one aspect of your subject is particularly important, shoot it several ways, from different angles, or with different lenses. Better to have to request expense money from the magazine than end up with only a kill fee because your photographs were inadequate.

TAKING CARE OF BUSINESS

Be sure to check financial arrangements before you go out to shoot. Most magazines pay extra for photographs, but you'll want to be sure that you're getting enough to pay for your time and expense, especially if taking the photos involves travel.

Remember that photography takes time and energy. It will take you longer to both write and photograph than to do either alone. Don't overcommit (or undercharge) by offering to bang off a couple of shots in an hour, when actually doing the job will take you two hours of travel, three hours of scouting and getting permission, thirty minutes waiting for the sun to come out, and four twenty-minute trips to the processing lab.

If you are under time pressure and the writing isn't done, ask the magazine to provide, or at least pay for, a photographer. Many writers who are capable photographers themselves insist on freelancing out the pictures just to avoid the distraction. If you don't know any photographers, meet some. Writers and photographers are in two sides of the same business, and can often benefit from one another. It's just smart to have someone to call on for advice when you find yourself in a pinch.

Remember, too, that no matter how good a photographer you become, there will be times when the wise choice is to have a professional take the photographs.

Some of these times are obvious, such as when you need a lot of light to illuminate a subject and you don't have the equipment. Other times you'll simply want to collaborate with another creative source. Here are a few types of photos that are harder than they look, and need the experience of a seasoned photographer.

● Formal portraits: Casual or environmental portraits present few problems, but formal ones require a knowledge of portrait lighting. A portrait photographer may use as many as five lights at once to make the lighting look "natural."

● Room interiors: Light intensity must be fairly even. Lamps and windows usually can't do the job. You need a tremendous amount of light to balance the daylight coming through a single window.

● Food: Even fresh-looking food may look unappetizing in a photograph. Tricks of the trade include spraying the food with water or glycerine. Except for raw fruit and vegetables, most food looks terrible in black and white.

● Most commercial products that require a studio-type setup: Glass and jewelry are especially difficult because of reflections.

YOUR BEST FRIEND: YOUR LAB

You want to develop a healthy working relationship with a commercial-grade photo processing lab. Such labs are listed in the Yellow Pages under "Photofinishing," though you'll be better off choosing one based on the recommendation from an established photographer. The lab will process your film and make contact sheets for you, and eventually print the pictures that will appear with your article.

Print quality is the bottom line in choosing a lab. Lively prints make an editor happy and an art director proud. Because the readers' initial impression of your article may come from the photo that accompanies it, you can't afford to start with anything but the best. Also, image quality is always degraded by reproduction. The photo on the printed page will never look as crisp as the one you submitted. Seek out a lab that prides itself on its print quality.

It is worth your while to cultivate the relationship with your lab. Not only will the people you work with be more willing to try to save your pictures if you've exposed the film badly, but also they can provide a lot of advice. Most lab technicians are photographers whose expertise runs to the technical side. Once you have established a relationship, they'll probably be only too glad to share their knowledge with you.

You can, of course, learn to process your own black-and-white film and some color slides. For a few hundred dollars you can set up a darkroom and learn to print your negatives. But it takes many months to become a decent printer, and the darkroom novice has all too much opportunity to destroy a roll of film while attempting to process it. Basic photography courses abound in most cities, and you should avail yourself of one if it interests you. But until you are completely confident of your abilities in the darkroom, leave the lab work to a professional.

Special warning: Don't discuss photography with your nephew in the junior high camera club. He'll want to develop your film for you and "save you money." You wouldn't let him write your lead, would you?

GETTING TECHNICAL

Three areas of photographic technique deserve your attention if you plan to take your photography seriously:

Exposure

If the film isn't exposed properly, the picture comes out either too light or too dark. Severe under- or overexposure cannot be remedied once the film is developed; the pictures are worthless.

Insure yourself against such problems by making certain that your equipment is working properly and by always "bracketing" your exposures. Bracketing means taking each shot at the indicated exposure and at one (or more) f-stops over *and* under. For example, if your meter indicates f8 at 1/250th of a second, try shooting at f5.6 and f11 as well. This will triple your film consumption; it may also save your neck. Experienced photographers frequently bracket *two* f-stops in both directions at half-stop intervals (that's nine exposures for each picture).

An automatic-exposure camera will take care of the exposure for you, but if your automatic camera has a manual override system, you can still bracket. Be especially careful if the average brightness in the viewfinder (the whole frame, not just one part of it) is particularly light or dark.

Contrast

Our eyes adjust readily to large variations in contrast, but film does not. A picture with too much contrast between adjacent areas is hard to read and will likely be rejected by an art director. Don't photograph anyone with half of his or her face in the sun and the other half in shadow; the contrast is too great for the film to record legibly. Even worse are photos of people under direct overhead lights, where noses pick up extra brightness and eye sockets become black holes.

The safest light to photograph under is broad-source light, such as from an overcast sky or a light bounced off a ceiling. Professional photographers often fill in dark areas with illumination from a lower-intensity light bulb or reflected off a large white card placed next to the subject just outside the viewfinder.

In direct, hard-edged light from the sun or an artificial source, watch out that the shadow line doesn't fall across an important part of your subject.

Sharpness

A sharp picture is both in focus and shot at a fast enough shutter speed to freeze all the action. As long as your subject is not moving toward or away from the camera, focus is relatively simple. But you still have to look carefully, because approximate focus isn't good enough for print-reproduction. Usually a distinct vertical or horizontal line somewhere in the picture is easiest to focus on. Make sure it is the same distance from the camera as your principal subject.

Depth of sharp focus, also called depth of field, is determined by the aperture (f-number) of the lens during the exposure. A wide-open aperture, indicated by a low f-number such as f2.8 or f4, yields the narrowest depth of field, while a small aperture, such as f16, produces greater depth. You'll rarely have a depth problem on bright days outdoors. But even with an automatic-exposure camera, you must focus carefully and keep your subjects within the same plane (approximately the same distance from the camera) when the light is low. The relationship between lens aperture and depth is analogous to squinting to see more clearly.

The average recommended shutter speed is 1/125th of a second, fast enough to freeze stationary subjects. Slower than 1/60th of a second, you are likely to see blur from normal kinds of movements. At 1/30 of a second or less, it is almost impossible to hold the camera completely steady: Use a tripod if you must shoot that slow. Shutter speed and aperture have an inverse relationship: Consecutive click stops of each exactly double or halve the amount of light reaching the film. With a manual camera, determine your higher priority (depth or a fast shutter speed) and set the other accordingly.

THE FINISHED PRODUCT

The standard black-and-white print is 8x10 with a glossy finish. Though it will probably be reproduced much smaller, 8x10 is the size you should submit unless instructed otherwise. RC (resin-coated) papers are easier to work with and therefore more common than traditional fiberbased papers. If you prefer fiber paper, use the doubleweight glossy (called F surface) which dries to a semi-gloss finish. Prints need to be spotted (that is, dust spots filled in) and fiber paper flattened before turning them in. A commercial lab will take care of all this for you as a matter of course. Don't send negatives unless specifically requested.

Slides should be placed in plastic see-through pages, not boxes. Plastic pages show off twenty slides at once and protect them from dust and fingerprints. Send only the slides you would be willing to see end up in print, and put your favorites at the top of the page. Unmounted slides should be placed in special plastic sheaths and cut in strips of five or six.

Caption slides by writing directly on the slide mount. If you don't have enough room, number each slide and write the captions on a separate sheet. Captions for black and whites should be typed on a small strip of paper and the strip taped to the print so that it hangs off the bottom. Caption writing is your job. Unless you are submitting a simple portrait of the subject of a profile, don't leave captioning to the art director.

Don't forget your own name. It should appear on every slide mount and on the back of every print.

DELIVERING THE GOODS

When mailing photographs, place prints or slide sheets between two pieces of corrugated cardboard. The boards should be larger than the prints sandwiched between to protect the photos' corners. Tape the package together on four sides and use a heavy manila envelope or a padded mailing envelope. Write "Photographs: Do Not Bend" on both sides of the envelope. A red marking pen speaks loudest.

Certified mail is adequate for sending pictures. Register them only if they are of determinable value. Insuring photographs for a lot of money makes no sense unless you can prove that they are worth that much. The money you might have been paid if somebody ever decided to buy them is not recoverable in an insurance claim.

Find out to whose attention you should send the pictures. You might be better off sending them to someone on the art staff rather than to the articles editor. You are entitled to a photo credit in the publication, and to receive all your pictures, used and unused, back afterward. A note requesting these in your cover letter will remind the art director.

THE GLORY

Few satisfactions of accomplishment rival the kick of seeing your photographs in print. You turn the page not merely to columns of words, however articulate, next to your name, but to an image. There it is, your work, for all the world to see.

During the late '70s, I was photographing regularly for several magazines in the Boston area. At virtually any time during a span of a couple of years I could see my photos in print at any newsstand in town. I've done better work since then and made more money, but that period stands out as the time when my successes were most evident, and in a sense most encouraging.

If you can learn to take photographs to accompany your articles, you will enhance the scope with which you cover your subjects and increase your marketability as a writer. Shooting pictures will increase your income, too, sometimes by a lot more than you'd get for a thousand words.

BY GARY PROVOST

How to Test Your Articles for The 8 Essentials of Nonfiction

One terrifying aspect of being a writer is that objectively viewing what you have written is impossible. Sure, the article looks well-written, but you know that your file cabinet is stuffed with atrocious manuscripts that you thought were fabulous when you wrote them. So how can you tell if this particular article should be mailed or flushed? Can you apply some objective guidelines that will tell you for sure either that your article is swell or that it's swill? Don't be silly. Of course you can't.

At least not with certainty. Too many aspects of an article defy exact measurement. Nobody has invented a style meter to gauge precisely the quality of your writing style. There's no perfect tuning fork to tell you when your writing has changed tone; you know it when you hear it, but what if you don't hear it? And what about fairness? If your article presents two sides to an issue, who is going to tell you if it does so fairly? There is no Solomon for writers.

Until your article gets to an editor, nothing can guarantee you that it's good enough.

But don't despair. There are a few solid things you can grab on to in this cloud of confusion. Some components of good article writing do have weight and size and you can measure them and say, "Yup, that's big enough."

There are tests you can run, and nothing is ambiguous about their results. If you score high on the tests, chances are that your article in in excellent shape.

1. TESTING THE LEAD

The lead is the beginning of your article. It can be the first sentence, or the first several paragraphs. You have just finished reading the lead of this article, and since you are still reading, the lead worked. It got your attention. The lead to this article, and the lead to any article you write, makes a promise, usually implicitly. The promise of my lead was, "This article will give you some ways to test your articles." When I have finished writing, I will look this over to make sure I have kept the promise I made in my lead.

That's the test you must run on your article. Look at the lead. What is the implied promise to readers? Have you kept that promise?

Let's say your lead is:

Before we settle down to wait for spring, let's brew some magic memories—Bill Rohr, 1967, the no-hitter that wasn't, and the impossible dream that came true.

Now read your article with that lead in mind. Were the memories you wrote about worthy of the adjective, *magic*? Did you explain "the no-hitter that wasn't"? And did that dream really come true against odds that made it seem impossible? If all the answers are yes, your lead has passed the test.

Be careful that you don't overstate in the lead just to grab the reader. Remember, the more you promise, the more you must deliver.

If you discover that you haven't kept your promise, write material that keeps the promise, or rewrite the lead so that it promises only what you've delivered. I once wrote an instructional article about glass-staining and I began, "Glass art is so simple that even a klutz like me can create works of art on his lunch hour." It sounded good but the implicit promise was that the reader could create a stained-glass artwork in sixty minutes or less. As I tested the article, I saw that my instructions added up to almost two hours. I was breaking my promise. So I rewrote the lead: "Glass art is so simple that even a klutz like me can create works of art while watching a football game on Sunday afternoon."

2. TESTING THE SLANT

You can never write *everything* about a subject, so instead you write *some* things about it. The idea that holds those things together is your slant. You can't write an article about blood. That's unslanted. So you write an article about the blood shortage. Every article you write has a slant, and everything in that article should relate to that slant. But when you begin to write, you can easily lose sight of the slant and drift into other areas, because you've learned some interesting things and you want to share them.

So let's say you've written an article about the blood shortage. To test it, re-read it with your slant in mind.

You wrote about the reduction in blood donations because people are afraid of getting AIDS; about the trend of people storing their own blood in anticipation of surgery; about the fact that hospitals are experiencing many shortages these days, in equipment, personnel and certain medicines; about a new invention that can help with the blood shortage because it can return the patient's blood to him during surgery.

With each paragraph, don't ask only "Is it a good paragraph?" Also ask "Is it a good paragraph relating to my particular slant?" You'll see that you wrote a paragraph or two about the shortage of personnel, equipment and medicines. That material belongs in an article about hospital shortages, not in your article about the blood shortage. It doesn't pass the test. Take it out.

If you find that a lot of your paragraphs don't pass the slant test, maybe you should leave them in and broaden your slant. For example, if you wrote an article about handicapped skiers but discover, when you test it, that several of your paragraphs refer to handicapped bowlers, marathon runners and ice skaters, maybe you should broaden your slant and write an article about handicapped athletes.

3. TESTING FOR TOPIC SENTENCES

Every paragraph you write should include one sentence that's supported by everything else in that paragraph. That is the topic sentence. It can be the first sentence, the last sentence, the sixth sentence, or even a sentence that exists only in your mind. When testing your article for topic sentences, you should be able to look at each paragraph and say what the topic sentence is. Having said it, look at all the other sentences in the paragraph and test them to make sure they support it. Here's an example:

Facing them were more than 600 passengers of the liner and enough cameras to start a movie studio. Obviously, this was a special wedding. In fact, all America will be invited, as it was filmed for Real People, *the series Purcell has co-hosted for the last five years. Five years is a kind of magic figure to television producers, because after five years a show is considered an appropriate candidate for syndication. The wedding segment will air this Wednesday, Nov. 2.*

The topic sentence in that paragraph is "Obviously, this was a special wedding." The sentences about 600 passengers on a luxury liner, filming the wedding for television, all support the idea of it being special. They pass the test. The sentence that does not pass the test is the one about syndication. That has nothing to do with the wedding being special. Get rid of it.

If you find that you have come up with the same topic sentence more than once, you have two paragraphs doing the same work. Cut one of them out.

If you find a paragraph that has several sentences that don't support the topic sentence, see if all the outlaw sentences support some other topic sentence and turn the one paragraph into two.

4. TESTING FOR QUOTES

"The most common mistake I see among writers of nonfiction is that they don't use quotes," an editor once told me. "Without quotes, the writing moves too slowly. If I don't see several quotes in an article I will reject it."

Of course, many lively published articles have no quotes in them, but usually they are short, or they have some other kind of change of pace, such as the writing examples in *this* article. But most articles written without quotes are as slow as sludge and the only thing fast about them is the speed with which they are rejected by editors. If you can quote the man or woman on the street, the expert on your subject, or the person you are writing about, you will usually make your article livelier, faster-paced, and more salable.

Nobody can tell you the exact number of quotes you should have in an article, any more than they can tell you the exact amount of butter to put on your ear of corn. It's a judgment call. But a pound is too much and a pinch is too little. Look for a balance that pleases the eye and the ear.

I have in front of me an article called "Meet a James Garner You'll Hardly Recognize," by Mary Murphy (*TV Guide*). Let's see, paragraph by paragraph, how Mary balanced her quoted and not-quoted material. Keep in mind that a profile like this would normally have a lot more quotes than, say, an article about "The Dancing Frogs of Ecuador."

1: No quotes. 2: No quotes. 3: Half quotes. 4: All quotes. 5: All quotes. 6: All quotes. 7: No quotes. 8: No quotes. 9: Half quotes. 10: About two-thirds quotes. 11: No quotes. 12: Half quotes. 13: No quotes. 14: Half quotes. 15: No quotes. 16: About 10 percent quotes. 17: No quotes. 18: No quotes. 19: All quotes. 20: No quotes.

There are fifteen more paragraphs, but you get the idea. Notice that Murphy never writes more than three paragraphs of quotes in a row, and never writes more than two paragraphs in a row without quotes. Exactly half of her paragraphs here contain quotes. I'm not saying you should adopt that particular formula, but this breakdown gives you an example of a balance that creates a pleasing pace.

To test your article, count the number of paragraphs that contain quotes. If fewer than 20 percent of them do, look at the other paragraphs and see if a few of them can be rewritten in the form of quotes. If more than 80 percent of your paragraphs contain quotes, consider replacing them with your own words.

5. TESTING FOR ANECDOTES

A woman in one of my writing classes handed in a story I liked, but on one page she had used the word *ironic* too many times. I told her to replace it with a synonym in a few places. "But I don't know any other word for it," she said. "Look in your thesaurus," I told her. There was a pause. She looked at me strangely. And then she said, "But isn't that cheating?"

I've just told you an anecdote: a little story, usually one paragraph, that illuminates a point you are trying to make in your article. Readers love anecdotes, because even when reading nonfiction they like the storyteller's touch, the presence of characters and even dialogue. Editors love anecdotes because readers love them. Anecdotes improve any article; many editors say they want at least three anecdotes in every article.

To test your article for anecdotes, just count the number of anecdotes in it. Three is a nice number in an average-sized article, but that number isn't mandatory. The important thing about the anecdote test is to discover whether or not you use anecdotes. If your article has none, ask yourself why. Many writers just never have developed the habit of writing anecdotes, and that could be costing them sales. If you haven't written any anecdotes in your article, look for an opportunity to use one.

For example, let's say you have written an article about photographers. At one point you wrote, "Though the good photographer knows exactly what he will get when the film is developed, the profession itself is not so predictable. Photographers have to deal with unusual, and sometimes risky, situations."

This is the kind of statement that could be brought to life by an anecdote. Go back through your research material and see if you have something. If not, call one of the photographers you interviewed. Don't ask him if he has any amusing anecdotes. People get stage fright when they are required to be amusing or clever. Ask him something specific, such as, "Have you ever been in danger while working?" You might come up with a paragraph like this:

> One of Dayton's clients makes harnesses for attack dogs and he wanted Dayton to photograph a dog wearing the harness. Dayton was a nervous wreck as he set up his equipment. "What about the flash?" he asked the dog handler. "I hope he won't think it's a gunshot or anything."
> "I don't know," the handler told him. "We never tried this before."

Your anecdotes don't have to come from the research you did for the story. They can come from anywhere, as long as they fit into the story.

6. TESTING FOR SERVICE VALUE

If you are going to spend your career writing opinion essays or profiles of Nick Nolte, skip this section. Those are not service articles. But if you intend to generate any serious income from your writing, you will be writing mostly service articles, and they must have service value.

A service article is one that serves the readers with some useful information. That is, after they read the article they can do something. "How to Bake a Cake" is a service article because readers learn to bake a cake. "The Nutritional Value of Cakes" is also a service article because readers can choose which cake to buy, based on your information. But an article like "The History of Cakes" is not a service article.

To test your article for service value, first ask yourself what readers should be able to do after reading it. Some examples:

● "How to See Europe for the Price of America": Readers should be able to go to Europe and spend no more money than they would have spent on a domestic trip of the same length.
● "How to Test Your Articles for the 8 Essentials of Nonfiction That Sells": Readers should be able to test the effectiveness of their articles eight ways.

Seems simple enough, doesn't it? But many writers leave out the vital service-value information, either because they don't have it, or because it seems too ordinary.

Once you know what your readers should be able to do, test your article by listing the information they would need and then making sure each item on the list is there.

If your service article were "Bed and Breakfast Weekends in Worcester County," your service-value checklist might look like this:

● *Price.* Did I give readers the weekend price? Did I give them the prices of nearby attractions that I mentioned? Did I tell them that children are half price?
● *Addresses, phone numbers.* Did I tell them whom to write to or call?
● *Directions.* Did I tell them what roads the recommended spots are on? Did I tell them the fastest routes?
● *Schedules.* Did I tell them when that museum is open? Did I tell them how long it would take to drive from key cities?
● *Tips.* Did I tell them how they could save money by skiing on Friday and saving the museum for Saturday?

Go through the getaway weekend (or the cake-baking or whatever) in your mind and note the questions that arise. If your article answers all the questions, it has passed the test.

7. TESTING FOR GRAMMAR, PUNCTUATION AND SPELLING

There is very little that is ambiguous about grammar, punctuation and spelling. Either they're right or they're not. Go back through your article, checking for all three. If you have doubts about anything, look it up. You can get help from *The Writer's Hotline Handbook*, by Michael Montgomery and John Stratton (New American Library), and *Pinckert's Practical Grammar*, by Robert C. Pinckert (Writer's Digest Books).

8. TESTING FOR ATTRACTIVENESS

After you are convinced that the content of your article passes all the tests, check your manuscript for form. It must look like the work of a fastidious person. A sloppy manuscript will flunk out with most editors.

Did you use a good, dark typewriter or printer ribbon? (Use a letter-quality printer, not a dot-matrix.) Did you use good-quality bond white paper? (Never use onion-skin paper.) Did you leave plenty of white space, and type on one side of the paper only? If you made pencil corrections, are they neat and is their meaning clear? (If you made four changes on one page, retype the page unless you have already established a relationship with the editor.) Did you use a common and easy-to-read typeface? (No script, please.)

If your manuscript fails any part of the attractiveness test, retype it.

GRADING YOURSELF

You don't have to score 100 percent on these tests. Articles are published without quotes or anecdotes, for example. And there are probably editors somewhere who don't take off marks for sloppiness. (Very few of them.) But if you put every article you write through these tests, and at least aim for 100 percent, you will sell a lot more of your work, and you will develop good professional writing habits. Speaking of good writing habits, I want to meet my deadline, so I have to put this manuscript in the mail (after I run a few tests).

BY DUANE NEWCOMB

Selling the Same Article Many Times

Can you actually *sell* the same article over and over? Of course you can. It's like everything else in the writing business; however, you can do it only under certain conditions and in certain specialized markets. You cannot sell the same piece to ten or fifteen different women's magazines, to all of the big three outdoor magazines, nor to any other magazines that compete with each other for readers. The one thing an editor hates most is to pick up a copy of a competing magazine and find an article there that he just ran. When this happens, you can be sure the writer of the article will never sell to either of those magazines again.

There are some publications, however, that don't mind buying articles that have appeared elsewhere. The reason is that these magazines serve specific groups of readers. They have no objection if you sell the same article to a publication that their readers will never see. These are called "non-competing" publications because they don't compete with each other for readers.

What you are reselling here is the exact same article. This is quite different from reslanting (target slanting) the material for different markets.

In most cases it is possible to photocopy these articles many times and simply send them out. The primary exception is articles sold to trade journals and non-competing general publications. In some cases, these are changed slightly to take into account particular readerships. I'll explain how later. This is still considered reselling the same article, not reslanting or target slanting.

You can often sell the same article a number of times within six groups of publications. They include newspapers, regional magazines, non-competing general magazines, juvenile religious magazines, global magazines, and trade journals.

NEWSPAPERS

Newspapers buy literally thousands of features every year on a wide variety of subjects from British gardens to whale watching. You can tell which newspaper features have been provided by freelancers by a notation just under the author's name that says, "Special to the *Chicago Tribune*," "Special to the *LA Times*," or whichever newspaper it happens to be.

Because I have students who specialize in selling newspaper features, I frequently clip articles from several of them each week just to keep track of what's being purchased. Believe me, the variety of subjects is mind-boggling.

A Collection of Subjects

I recently found the following titles in my files: "Sprucing Up Your Car with a

Used-Car Dealer's Finesse," "Biking Norman Rockwell Country," "Antique Tools—Growing Interest in a Young Field," "Family Papers—Proper Conservation Saves Treasures," "Ballooning: Thrilling, Invigorating, and Elemental," and "Ancient Teeth Yield Clue to Origin of Oldest Inhabitants of America."

Can articles like these be sold to a number of different newspapers? The answer is yes. After all, newspapers have only a limited circulation area. Some newspapers cover all or most of a state; others may serve a region or a single county; still others have a readership limited to one city and its outlying population area.

Most newspapers are perfectly willing to let you resell an article outside their circulation area. This means you can sell the same feature to the *Seattle Times*, the *San Francisco Chronicle*, the *Salt Lake Tribune*, the *Kansas City Star*, and other newspapers.

Several years ago, a friend of mine wrote a 1,200-word article on the many uses of computers. The first year he sent his computer article to about two hundred major, daily, noncompeting newspapers across the US. This resulted in sales to the *Denver Post* and a number of others. Payment, however, was extremely uneven and ranged from as low as $30 to a high of $120. The total for the first year was about $900.

The second year he sent the same article out to about two hundred smaller newspapers across the country, including the Bangor *Daily News*, the Jackson *Daily News*, the Montana *Standard*, and others. This time around, he picked up about $600.

The third year he mailed to weekly newspapers. This round netted only $300. The fourth year he started all over again with the state-wide newspapers.

Another writer, George Beinhorn, has had extremely good luck with an article on poison oak and poison ivy. The first year, George figured, he took in about $900. He then decided to get extremely scientific about it. From *Bacon's Publicity Checker* he put together a list of about 1,200 newspapers.

These he divided into state-wide papers, regional or metro papers, local papers, and lower levels of non-overlapping circulation. He entered this list on a computer disk. His object was to use a mailmerge program to automatically address both his cover letter and his mailing labels. This, he hoped, would allow him to mail out a number of articles quickly. As far as I know, he hasn't gone any further with this, but his approach sounds like the best one I've heard.

In class I have had inconsistent results in trying to make multi-sales to newspapers. Some students do well, others send out as many as eighty articles and make no sales.

Working the Newspaper Markets

From these experiences, I have put together a few rules that seem to work well.

1. *Study the newspapers to see what kinds of articles they are taking and how they want these articles put together.* Keep in mind that these features must appeal to a

very general audience. Clip out a few features as models and construct yours the same way. Keep the length to about 1,100 words or less.

2. *Make up your own newspaper list from either* Editor and Publisher International Year Book, Bacon's Publicity Checker *or* Standard Rate and Data. All are available in most libraries.

3. *Divide this list as George Beinhorn did so that you have separate listings for the statewide, regional, and smaller newspapers.*

4. *Mail to about thirty to thirty-five statewide newspapers the first year for each article.* The second year mail to all the regionals and so forth.

So far we haven't decided whether it's best to address these articles to "feature editor" at each newspaper or to address each individual feature editor by name. I personally feel you can make more sales by going directly to an individual editor. I have had students do well, however, by simply using the generic "feature editor." You will need to experiment to find which works best for you.

This again is the same article, simply resold "as is" without reslanting. We print up a hundred or so of any one article at a quick print service for about thirty-five dollars and mail them out without return postage. (We don't care whether the article is returned by the newspaper or not.) If we need more, we just have them printed.

Write "Exclusive to your circulation area" in the right-hand corner. In the upper left-hand corner put the word and symbol "copyright ©," your name, and "one time rights." By the way, the minute you write something, you then own common-law copyright. You do not need to register your work with the copyright office to have legal copyright on your own work.

JUVENILE RELIGIOUS MAGAZINES

This group represents a good market for articles on subjects like hobbies, handicraft, nature, outdoor activities, science, crafts, sports, bike riding, pets, and personal experiences. The reason they are willing to buy second (reprint) rights is that the readers of Presbyterian magazines don't read Methodist magazines, the readers of Methodist magazines don't read Catholic magazines, and so forth.

Some of the magazines that will take simultaneous and previously published submissions are *Action, Counselor, Crusader Magazine, Dash, Nature Friend Magazine, Our Little Friend, Primary Treasure, Story Friends, Touch,* and *The Young Crusader*. The markets here are low paying, sometimes in the two- to three-cents-a-word range, but you can usually sell each article several times.

Over the years, my classes have sold a number of articles in this field. Several years ago one of my students gathered up her own and several neighbor children and drove up to Lick Observatory near San Jose, California, where they were given a guided tour. My student took pictures of the kids looking through one of the telescopes, being shown pictures of the stars, walking up the outside steps, and other details. She also took some establishing shots of the interior and exterior of the observatory. When she returned home she wrote a very simple 800-word story entitled "Visit to an Observatory." The result: eight sales for a total of about $300.

Juvenile religious magazines are listed in *Writer's Market*, and the *Religious Writer's Marketplace*.

Multisubmission Basics

If you want to try writing for this field, always send for sample copies of all the magazines listed. Study each magazine carefully; then decide what topic you know about that several publications might be interested in.

Again, you will be reselling the same article to each magazine. You will, however, need two to five pictures for each article. The same pictures are sent to each magazine.

It has been my experience in over twenty years of full-time freelancing that at least 80 percent of all juvenile freelance articles require either photographs or illustrations. I suggest you send the manuscript, without querying, to all possible markets, and tell the editor that photographs or illustrations are available. This way you will avoid the expense of printing twenty to forty photos or the effort of putting together a number of drawings, without knowing whether or not you will make the sale.

Set up the first page of the manuscript here exactly as we did for newspaper features. But in the right-hand corner, instead of writing "exclusive to your circulation area," say "simultaneous submission."

Rule of Thumb

If you look in the juvenile listings in *Writer's Market*, you will find that many of these publications say that simultaneous submission is okay. With many of the five areas under discussion, however, the magazine's listing will not indicate that they take articles sold to other magazines. The only way you can find out is to try.

What I do as a rule of thumb is look for magazines that do not compete with each other, and clearly state on the manuscript what I am doing. After that the editor can decide whether he wants to accept multisubmission or not. In practice, I find that doing things this way is quite acceptable.

CITY AND REGIONAL MAGAZINES

City and regional magazines are probably one of the fastest growing of all magazine categories. A few years ago only about fifteen of these publications existed. Today there are about 150 and the end of the growth spurt doesn't appear to be in sight.

Titles in this category include *San Diego, Los Angeles, Texas Monthly, Wash-*

ington, Utah Holiday, Palm Beach Life, Twin Cities, and more. Some focus on city life, others specialize in business, home, garden, and sports.

"The city magazine," says Ed Prizer, publisher of *Orlando*, "is, in effect, a magazine for newcomers. It is the new, young, mobile blood that is coming into the community for whom the city magazines serve a definite service role. The great success of city magazines is in communities in which there is a heavy immigration of upscale persons."

As a result, many of these magazines offer an editorial mix of restaurant reviews, guides to local night life, lifestyle and service features, plus a wide range of articles slanted toward an upscale reader.

Regional Slant

Here are some samples of articles from selected issues of *Los Angeles*, and *Utah Holiday*: "A Train Lover's Tour Through Downtown Los Angeles," "Jazz Legends That Live in Los Angeles," "Joe Sam Chronicles the Life and Times of the Black Cowboy," and "Utah's Strange Case of Parental Kidnapping."

A few of these magazines also run a number of investigative articles. Ron Javers, editor of *Philadelphia*, believes that investigative journalism should be a crucial part of a magazine's editorial mix. As a result, *Philadelphia* has reported on topics as varied as organized crime and the search for fugitive financier Robert Vesco. *Milwaukee* reported on the politics of cable TV franchising and the manipulation of tax money by their city hall. Others have handled similar hard-hitting stories.

What to Submit

For the most part, city and regional magazines run fairly sophisticated articles with a local angle. If this is true, how can a writer hope to sell a story to more than one of these publications at a time? The answer lies in the fact that these publications cater to an upscale audience intensely interested in a full, rich life.

As a result, many run, in addition to their regular features, general articles on gardening, food, taxes, jobs, organizing your closets, updating your wardrobe, shopping, managing your time, divorce, marriage, and personal relationships. Some also feature quizzes such as "Rate Your Sex Drive," and "What is Your Creativity Quotient?"

It is true that these general articles represent only a small percentage of each magazine's total editorial content, but collectively they offer a significant market for multiple sales of the same article.

You will find the most complete listing of these magazines in the *Standard Rate and Data, Consumer Edition*, available in most libraries. Begin by sending for copies of as many of these magazines as possible.

Make a List

I suggest that you make a complete list of all the general articles you find. This will give you a good idea of what you can do. You can query each publication if you like. But most general articles are fairly short. Simply make as many copies of your article as you need and send them to every possible market.

NONCOMPETITIVE PUBLICATIONS

Sometimes when you sell an article to one magazine, you can turn around and sell the same article (second rights) to magazines that are noncompetitive with the original publication. Many times you must reslant it to make additional sales.

But some articles such as a short piece on "How Creative Are You?" "Are You Compatible With Your Mate?" and similar general features can be submitted to several different fields at once without change.

I suggest you go back through *Writer's Market*, and see how many additional possibilities you can find. Make up a number of copies at a quick-print shop, and send out a copy, without query, to any possible market. This again is the same article, not a reslant. What you want to sell here is "second serial rights." I simply mark this "second rights" after my name and address and copyright in the left hand corner.

Besides this, keep looking for new markets or markets you might have missed. To find these, I regularly go through the market announcements in *Writer's Digest* to see if I can turn up any new publications that look promising. I also thumb through the magazines on the newsstands to look for possibilities. I even go through magazines at the dentist's office. Be diligent and keep searching; you'll be surprised how many additional sales you will make.

THE GLOBAL MARKET

Worldwide, there are some 70,000 magazines published in forty nations where you can sell the same article ten to forty times for a total price of between $2,000 and $20,000. This creates a far different article marketplace than just the United States alone. In the future, the main market for freelancers may well be the entire globe and not one particular nation.

What Kind of Magazines

Worldwide you will find magazines published in virtually the same categories as they are in the United States; general magazines, women's, men's, science, automotive, trade/business, Sunday newspaper publishers, corporate, and organization/association magazines. These are listed in Ulrich's *International Periodicals Directory,* and *Europa Yearbook. Ulrich's* is essential for freelancers, and you will find it in most libraries.

What Is a Global Article? In simplest terms, a global article is one that will interest readers worldwide. An article about an American businesswoman who started a successful novelty pillow business in her garage probably would not be of interest around the world because few of the world's readers would relate to this. But an article on genetic engineering and how it is changing the world's crops, along with the impact this may make on the world's food supply, probably is.

James Joseph of southern California has sold numerous articles throughout the world. Here are some of the titles he finds to be of worldwide interest.

"Only Robots Will Apply: How Robots Will Soon Steal Your Job." With robots appearing in factories worldwide, you can see why this would be of interest to the world's workers who wonder what's going to happen to their jobs when robots take over.

"Man-Powering the Channel: The Flight of Gossamer Albatross" (the bicycle-powered airplane). How it was built and what went into the cross-channel bicycle-powered airplane flight. This was an extremely popular article that appeared in many magazines worldwide.

"Bass Madness: Who Will Catch the U.S. $1 Million Bass?" There is bass fishing only in the United States, but the fact that it is the most popular type of fishing here and that there is a $1 million prize makes it a global piece.

"Get Away Now: Everybody's Passport to Space." This article tells how to get aboard a future shuttle flight.

Querying the Global Market

A global query is simply a standard query that (1) hooks the editor, (2) explains what the article will be about, (3) details what you are offering: the article, color photos, maps or graphics, and special sidebars, and (4) asks for the order. The query is sent out to as many markets as you feel might be interested.

Writing the Global Article

All articles are written in English and will be translated by the magazine. Since the translation won't be in your style, keep your writing extremely simple and the sentences fairly short. In addition, you need to remove anything which would Americanize the piece, or a slang term popular only in America.

Global articles can often be slanted to fit a number of markets by including one or more sidebars. An article about how genetic engineering is changing the world crops may be made suitable for the women's market by using a sidebar on a woman scientist who is a leading pioneer in the field. It might be turned into a business article with a sidebar on the business opportunities opening up because of the genetically altered crops.

Articles can be sold to magazines in each country by offering the exclusive rights for that particular country. If there are several languages in a country, as there are, for instance, in India, you can offer the exclusive rights to a particular language in that country.

The Total Package

When you receive a go-ahead, the total package you send should include the manuscript, six to twelve transparencies, sidebars, perhaps art, cover letter, an envelope, and coupons or a check for return postage. The standard way of including return postage is to purchase international mailing coupons at the post office.

TRADE JOURNALS

Trade journals are magazines published for readers in a wide variety of industries. In general, you'll find trade journals for manufacturers, wholesalers, and retailers. A number are also published for individual professions, such as medicine, law and education.

Approximately 4,500 trade journals are listed in the *Standard Rate and Data* business edition, available in most libraries. The listings contain the name of the magazine; the address and phone number; and the names of the editor, publisher, advertising sales manager, and others.

Usually, the listing contains a statement of the policy, which includes who the magazine is published for and the editorial content: news, product information, merchandising, and so forth.

Creating an Inventory

Because I owned a retail store, I have expertise in advertising and merchandising. For years I wrote dealer articles. That is, articles about how one retailer did something especially well.

One of these stories told how a paint retailer established a rental art gallery within the store to attract foot traffic. Another explained how a feed and farm store did an exceptionally good job with on-shelf merchandising. All in all, I probably wrote two thousand or more of these articles over a ten-year period.

I became so efficient at this that I could start at one end of a shopping center, visit every store in the center, take pictures, interview the owners or managers, and come out at the other end with ten or fifteen articles and picture shorts that some magazine would buy. I would then put these pieces on tape while driving, drop them off at my typist on the way home, and send them off to the magazines the next day.

I dropped out of this field for several years to write books. Then about four years ago, I decided that there might be a good opportunity here to write in-depth merchandising pieces that dealt with contemporary problems facing retailers.

As a result, I made up a list of two hundred retail-oriented magazines that will take either merchandising or advertising articles. These include such publications as *Yarn Market News, Jobber Topics, National Jeweler*, and *Fishing Tackle Trade News*. I am able to sell the same article here a number of times because the readers of jewelry magazines usually don't read toy magazines and these readers generally don't read retail photography magazines.

I then created what I call my inventory, a list of well-researched merchandising, advertising, and demographic articles. The titles on my first list included the following:

"Merchandising for Today's Great Decade of Change." This article details the tremendous changes taking place today that affect retailing: couples marrying later, working women, two-income families, more people working at home, the overall changing demographic picture, and several dozen other major changes. It also explains how the retailers can use these changes to keep their business up with and ahead of the times.

"The Advertising Workshop." This article explains why retailers waste at least a portion of their advertising with ineffective ads placed in the wrong media. It also helps retailers plan and execute each stage of their ad campaigns in newspapers, television, radio, and the Yellow Pages.

"Sharpen Sales Skills with Communication Sales Training." This article details a sales program developed by behavioral scientist Thomas Knutson, Ph.D., and shows how to approach retail sales in five basic steps (1) the approach, (2) the search for customers' needs, (3) the presentation of merchandise, (4) the request for action, and (5) the response to customer resistance.

Other titles in this series include "Creating a Selling Image for Your Business," "Tapping the Moving Market," "Target Marketing for the Retailer," and "Creative Outdoor Advertising."

The Making of an Article

For most of these articles, I rely on a combination of research reports, interviews with industry leaders, and anything else I can find. Many take three or four months to put together. These trade journal articles don't bring much individually, only $225 each, but if I can sell $1,500 to $4,000 worth of articles on any one subject, I can justify the extensive research.

One of my most popular "self-syndicated" articles has been "Merchandising to the Working Woman." I started this piece by reading a number of magazines and clipping anything that related to the working woman. I found a great deal on this subject in *U.S. News and World Report, Ad Age*, and the *Los Angeles Times*. Using this as a starting place, I sent for all of the reports and studies these and other magazines mentioned. The U.S. Labor Department had compiled statistics on the subject. Pollster Louis Harris issued a poll on working women, and *American Demographics* ran a number of articles on the subject that were loaded with statistics. There were also many others.

I then started calling about twenty authorities mentioned in these sources to do interviews; these included marketing consultants, advertising executives, and several university professors.

One of my most interesting interviews was with Dorothy Pollock, President of Vassarette (a major intimate apparel firm). She returned my call on a Saturday a few hours after returning from a fashion trip to Europe. I told her what I wanted and the next two hours she talked about the needs of the working woman. She also mailed me a fascinating study by *Glamour* magazine called the "Psychology of Fashion," which detailed women's shopping motivation and the changes in their spending patterns. When I finished this research, I had enough to write a book on the subject. So far, the finished article has earned about $4,000.

Merchandising the Syndicated Trade Article

I have two ways of merchandising these articles. I print what I call a "Business Editor's Article Hot List." This is a two-sided, 8½-by-11-inch page listing all of my available articles. I give a title and a one- or two-sentence description of each article. My first year's offerings featured eleven articles. Currently I offer forty-four articles a year printed on an eleven-by-seventeen-inch sheet.

I mail the "Hot List" to about 250 retail trade journal editors in February of each year. Along with this "Hot List," I include a cover letter and an order form. The cover letter states the price of the article, $225. For $100 more I will interview five to ten retailers in the magazine's field and work this back into the article. Eventually, I intend to also offer a graphics option for another $100.

The order form has a place for the editor to list the article number, the name of the article, and the date they need the piece. I now have editors who order four to six articles at a time. From the entire "Hot List" last year I received forty-seven orders for articles.

In addition to this, I make up a multiple query that lists two or sometimes three articles. I mail these every other month to my entire mailing list, which is handled by computer. Every letter has an individualized heading for each editor. This bimonthly mailing usually adds another seven to twenty assignments per mailing.

WRITING THE ARTICLE

When I write my original article, I make up a data base on a computer disk. That is, I write the article in a general way, referring to the reader as "retailer." I also indicate six or seven places where this particular article could be changed to tailor it to a certain readership. This is not reslanting.

The article itself basically remains the same. I simply insert material which makes it of greater interest to say, photo retailers, toy dealers, bicycle dealers, or whatever audience I'm writing for.

When I receive an order from a particular magazine like *Professional Furniture Retailer*, I copy the general article (called a "model") to another file to write the final article.

I then make the changes I need to tailor the piece to the *Professional Furniture Retailer*. There is a place in the working woman's article, for instance, where I list some women's shopping preferences in furniture for style, color, and upholstery fabric, plus some other general information. Here is the insert:

"Working women are extremely fashion oriented and are at home with contemporary styles and colors. They also are fabric conscious, preferring velvet, jacquard/textured/woven, nylon and cotton in that order (this refers to furniture upholstery).

"The Congress Office of Technology Assessment shows that more working couples are finding their entertainment at home. This means greater opportunity for entertainment and wall furniture. For working women, the master bedroom also is rapidly becoming a place to relax after the work day. As a result, many women are adding upholstered chairs, occasional tables, recliners, desks and electronic wall units to the bedroom furnishings."

When I'm finished, the article fits the magazine well. And it's even better if I insert retailer interviews. The market for these articles, I find, is getting stronger all the time. While I use a computer to tailor the articles, they can be written on a typewriter using the "cut and paste" system. That is, you simply type up the inserts on a separate sheet of paper, cut them apart and paste them in where you need them. When you finish, don't retype; simply photocopy the article with the inserts in place.

Is it possible to sell one article many times? Of course it is. I suggest you go back through your files and look for article ideas that can be sold to newspapers, the juvenile market, regional magazines, secondary magazines, or the global market. You may be surprised to find that you have already written articles you can resell for an additional $200 to $4,000. Trade journal pieces, of course, need to be written as originals, then resold to a number of magazines. The overall market, for all fields, is a big one that every writer should tap for as many additional sales as possible.

BY LAURIE HENRY

Manuscript Mechanics: How to Submit Your Magazine Article

You've finished an article, and you're ready to send it to an editor or agent. Before you run your paper through the typewriter or printer one last time, remember to review the sometimes irksome, but always necessary, business of properly preparing your work for submission.

Unfortunately, a well typed and efficiently submitted manuscript still won't guarantee your work's quick acceptance. If it did, the best published writers might be professional typists and postal workers. But the truth is, a sloppily presented manuscript will start its life with unnecessary strikes against it, which might keep it from ever being read at all.

Here are some points you should check before sending out your work.

TYPE OF PAPER

The paper on which you type your work *must* be white and measure $8\frac{1}{2} \times 11$. You might be able to find 100 sheets of paper for under a dollar at a grocery store, and this type of paper is fine—for rough drafts. A hundred pages of 25 percent cotton-fiber content paper at an office-supply store, on the other hand, can cost as much as $5. Not surprisingly, editors strongly prefer this more expensive, heavy-weight (16 lb.—or better still—20 lb.) paper, which feels good to the touch, shows type neatly, and holds up under occasional whiteouts or erasures. It's cheapest to buy a ream of 500, and you can use the box later for sending out long manuscripts.

Almost all editors discourage the use of erasable bond paper for manuscripts, as it tends to smear when handled and is hard to write on with a pen or pencil. And never use onionskin, or paper with notebook holes or a red line down the left margin.

YOUR TYPEWRITER OR PRINTER

Both pica (ten characters per inch) and elite (twelve characters per inch) are acceptable to editors, although many find pica easier to read. Editors *do* object to hard-to-read or unusual typefaces such as script, Old English, italics or all-capital letters.

If you are using a dot-matrix printer without a "near letter quality" setting, you may find that many editors object. If a cheap dot-matrix printer is your only source of type, you may want to consider hiring a typist or, if you do a lot of typing, buying another printer.

Always use a good black ribbon; the one-time, non-reusable kind, although more expensive, makes a crisper impression than multi-use ribbon. Never submit work with a grayish ribbon that should have been thrown out long ago.

If the spaces in the letters a, b, e and o, etc., on your typewriter get inked in, it's time to clean your keys. Inexpensive kits are available at office-supply stores. Occasional retyping over erasures or use of white-out is acceptable, but strikeovers give the manuscript a sloppy, careless appearance. Sloppy typing is viewed by many editors, rightly or wrongly, as indicative of sloppy work habits—and of careless writing and thinking habits as well. Strive for a clean, professional-looking manuscript that reflects your justifiable pride in your work.

FILE COPIES

Always make a carbon or photocopy of your manuscript before you send it out. You might want to make several photocopies while the original manuscript is still fresh and crisp-looking—especially if you've decided to submit the manuscript to different editors at the same time. Some writers keep their original typescript as the file copy and submit a good-quality photocopy to an editor. If your original manuscript contains a lot of corrections, it's an especially good idea to send a photocopy instead of the original, unless, of course, the editor has indicated that photocopied submissions will not be accepted.

If you have unlimited access to a photocopier, you might tell the editor simply to discard your manuscript if it is not accepted, and to notify you with a stamped, business-sized envelope (which you have enclosed). This saves on postage and is a particularly good idea if you are submitting an article to a foreign publication.

PAGE FORMAT

In the upper left corner of the first page, type your name, address and phone number on four single-spaced lines. In the upper right corner, on three single-spaced lines, indicate the approximate word count of the manuscript, the rights you are offering for sale and your copyright notice.

Now center the title of your article in capital letters about a third of the way down the page. Next, center your name a double space below the title. Then triple-space again, indent, and start typing. Remember to leave a 1¼″ margin on all sides of your pages. On every page after the first, type a slugline and the page number in the upper right-hand corner.

ESTIMATING WORD COUNT

A fairly quick and accurate way to estimate the word count of your article is to count the exact number of words on three full pages of your manuscript, divide the total by three, and multiply the result by the number of pages. For example, if you have a twelve-page manuscript with three page-number totals of 265, 316 and 289 words, divide your total of 870 by three to get 290. Now multiply 290 by twelve pages to get 3,480. On manuscripts over twenty-five pages, count five pages instead of three, then follow the same process but divide by five, to get the average number of words per page. Remember of course that your first and last pages are likely to be less than full, and adjust your count accordingly. And round your number to the nearest ten, since it is, after all, only an estimate.

COVER LETTERS

In most cases a brief (one page at most) cover letter is helpful in personalizing an unsolicited submission. Nothing you say about your article will ensure its acceptance, but the editor will be interested in hearing what you have to say about yourself, your publishing history, and any particular qualifications you have for writing the article you are submitting. If you have already queried the editor about writing the article, a brief reminder—"Here is the article we discussed last week. I look forward to hearing from you at your earliest convenience"—is enough.

If you are writing to a particular magazine editor for the first time, make sure you are using the editor's correct name and title. Don't bother sending a cover letter merely to "Editors." This kind of impersonal submission will probably result in your manuscript being read by an underpaid reader with no real authority to accept a manuscript—but plenty of authority to reject it.

PHOTOGRAPHS AND SLIDES

The availability of good quality photos can be the deciding factor when an editor is considering an article manuscript. Some publications also offer additional pay for photos accepted with the manuscript. When submitting black-and-white prints, send 8 × 10 glossies, unless the editor indicates another preference. The universally accepted format for color transparencies is 35mm; few buyers will look at color prints.

On all photos and slides, you should stamp or print your copyright notice and "Return to" followed by your name, address and phone number. Rubber stamps are preferred for labeling photos as they are less likely to cause damage: You can order them from many stationery or office-supply stores. If using a pen on photos, be careful not to damage them by pressing too hard or allowing ink to bleed through the paper.

Captions should be typed on a sheet of paper and taped to the bottom of the back of the prints. The caption should fold over the front of the photo so the buyer can fold the paper back for easy reading.

Submit prints rather than negatives, and consider having duplicates made of your slides. Don't risk having your original negative or slide lost or damaged. Look for a photography lab that can make a high quality copy.

MAILING YOUR MANUSCRIPT

Except when working on a specific assignment from a magazine, *always* enclose a self-addressed, stamped envelope (SASE) when you send out your manuscript. Manuscript pages should never be stapled together, and do not use a binder or folder when submitting an article unless an editor requests it.

To submit work to foreign publications, including Canadian markets, enclose one or more International Reply Coupons (IRCs), available at larger post offices. The weight of the manuscript will decide how many IRCs you need. Editors in Canada and other countries generally accept IRCs, but not U.S. checks or money orders. It's a good idea to send a manuscript to Europe, South America or Asia via airmail; a manuscript sent by seamail could take months to reach the country to which you have sent it.

Most editors won't object if manuscripts under five pages are folded in thirds or mailed in a business-size envelope. However, there is a preference for flat mailing for manuscripts over four pages. Your manuscript will look best if you mail it in the smallest envelope into which it will fit without being folded, so it won't move around inside the envelope while in transit—check an office supply store for odd sizes like $9\frac{1}{2} \times 12\frac{1}{2}$. Fold the return envelope in half, address it to yourself, stamp it, and put it into the outgoing package.

Mark both of your envelopes *FIRST CLASS MAIL* or *SPECIAL FOURTH CLASS MANUSCRIPT RATE*, as desired. First class mail costs more but assures better handling and faster delivery. Special fourth class is handled the same as parcel post (third class), but is less expensive than both first and third class. You can only use special fourth class rate for manuscripts mailed in and to the U.S., and for manuscripts weighing over one pound. If your manuscript weighs less than a pound it's better to send it first class. Send it first class also if it's a topical piece that is not likely to be published at all if it's not published soon. If you plan to submit a lot of work, you might want to invest in a postal scale and stock up on stamps, to save trips to the post office.

Note that if you use an office or personal postage meter, it's important not to indicate a date on the return envelope; this can cause trouble with postal authorities.

First class mail is forwarded or returned automatically if you should move while a manuscript is out, but special fourth class is not. To make sure you get your fourth class submission back if it proves undeliverable, print "Return postage guaranteed" below your return address.

You may enclose a cover letter with your manuscript sent at the fourth class rate, but legally you must also add enough first class postage to cover the letter and write "first class letter enclosed" on the outside of your package.

Postal insurance is payable only on the tangible value of what is in the package (i.e., typing paper), so your best insurance is to keep a copy of what you submit at home. Editors do not appreciate receiving unsolicited manuscripts marked Certified, Registered or Insured—especially editors of small publications, who might have to make a special trip to the post office to get them.

ELECTRONIC SUBMISSIONS

It's important to query before sending a story via disk or modem, even if an editor has indicated a willingness to consider such material. In any case, be sure to follow the editor's directions regarding electronic submissions very carefully. Some editors appreciate having articles they have already accepted re-sent electronically but will not look at unsolicited submissions on the computer.

THE WAITING GAME

The writer who sends off a manuscript to an editor should turn immediately to other ideas and try not to think too much about the submission. Unless you are under contract to do an article, or have worked closely with the editor or another staff member on the article you are submitting—in which case a phone call to your editor saying the manuscript is in the mail is quite appropriate—it's best to use your time on other writing projects and let the submission take care of itself.

If an editor has been holding on to a manuscript for longer than you feel is justified, however, it is time to inquire further. This is especially important with a time-specific article, of course. Don't feel timid about making an inquiry; an editor would probably think it odd if you *didn't* worry about the status of a manuscript that had been held an unusual length of time.

Write a brief letter to the editor asking if your manuscript (give the title, a one-or-two-sentence description and the date you mailed it) has in fact reached the publisher's offices, and if so, if it is still under consideration. Don't give the impression of being impatient with the editor, who may be swamped with work or short-handed or about to give your article another reading. An impatient or angry attitude from you could alienate the editor from you for a long time. Be polite and professional. Enclose another SASE to expedite a response. This is usually enough to stir a decision if matters are lagging in an editorial office.

If you hear nothing from a publisher one month after your follow-up letter, send the editor another short note asking if your previous follow-up was received. If after another month you have still heard nothing, send a polite letter saying you are withdrawing the manuscript from consideration (include the title, date of submission, and dates of follow-up correspondence), and ask that the manuscript be returned immediately in the SASE you sent with it. You are now free to market the manuscript elsewhere.

Even if your manuscript is rejected or lost and you have lost months of marketing time, be cool and professional as you set about the business of finding another publisher. Move on to the next name on your list, submitting your manuscript with a personal cover letter and the same methods outlined above. In the meantime, continue working on your next writing project.

BY GEORGE H. SCITHERS AND SANFORD MESCHKOW

Under Cover

Most writers we've dealt with believe that they should not mail manuscripts to an editor cold, that they should introduce the story with what is known as a "cover letter."

A cover letter is a business document, not a friendly letter. It is a letter of transmittal, stating for the record who sent what to whom on what date and under what circumstances. "Dear Editor: Enclosed is a 3,000-word manuscript entitled . . ."

Yet, despite what most writers believe, a manuscript submission does not *require* a cover letter. *If* an author is using the proper manuscript format, all the information the editor would reasonably expect to find in a standard cover letter should already be on the first page of the manuscript. This includes the title, the word count, the way the author or authors want their names listed (including pen names), and the actual names and addresses of all the authors (so that the publisher can mail them their checks). Therefore, you should devote your time, effort and paper to making the first page or two of your manuscript as irresistible as possible.

COVERING THE BASES

There are times when a cover letter is essential to selling the manuscript, whether fiction or nonfiction, prose or poetry. A properly written cover letter can help an author smooth the way to a positive author-editor relationship, in these situations:

1. *If the manuscript was written in response to a query letter:* "The enclosed manuscript, 'Darkroom Deluxe,' is in reply to your letter of Oct. 12 stating that you could use a do-it-yourself article on designing and building a home darkroom."

2. *If the editor has seen the manuscript before and sent it back with comments and suggestions for revisions:* "Enclosed is the revised manuscript of my sonnet cycle, 'Alexander in Troy.' As you suggested in your letter of March 6, I have transliterated the Attic Greek phrases from the Greek to the Latin alphabet and provided a short glossary for the benefit of modern readers 'with little Latin and less Greek,' as the saying goes."

3. *If you have previously corresponded with the editor and a summation would save the editor a search through the files:* "You commented in your letter of July 9 that you were overstocked on fantasy but were looking for short science fiction.

Enclosed is my 4,000-word story, 'Never Twist an Earthman's Tail.' " (Notice that in this case the word count is mentioned because the editor is looking for *short* fiction.)

4. *If you can sum up your special qualifications for having written the manuscript:* "Enclosed is my article 'Arms Control in the 1990s: A Progress Report.' I teach an honors seminar in arms control at Harvard and I am the author of *Arms Control in the 1980s* and *Progress Towards Arms Control in the 1960s.*" (Obviously, if your qualifications look weak on paper, keep quiet and let the content of your manuscript speak for itself.)

5. *If there is anything odd about the rights or timing of the publication of the manuscript:* "This article, 'Applications of Powder Metallurgy in the Apollo Space Program,' is taken from Chapter 9 of my book, *The History of Powder Metallurgy*, to be published by Doorstop Press in August 1990." Besides telling the editor that at least one other editor considers the material of publishable quality, it also warns that the manuscript must be accepted, processed and published before the book version is published. Editors want and need to know exactly what they are buying. An editor who finds out by chance that your article or story that they are printing next month is part of a book that came out *last* month will be hopping mad. (This isn't always the fault of a careless or devious author. Sometimes book publishers change their schedules and publish a book earlier than planned. When this happens, the author should inform the editor about the change as soon as possible.)

6. *If there are any special business arrangements the editor should know about.* For example, if two or more authors have collaborated on the manuscript, one of them might be designated to handle all correspondence with the publication. Of course, if two of the authors are a husband-and-wife team, one of the two might be authorized to receive the payment due both of them. Editors will honor such reasonable requests, especially if they also make life easier for the business office of the publication.

Letters 1, 2, 3 and 4 help sell your manuscript. Letters 5 and 6 make life easier for the editor and the author, respectively, once the manuscript is sold. How you handle these and similar situations in a cover letter can help build the impression in the editor's mind that you are a professional who understands at least some of the ins and outs of publishing and the author-editor relationship.

COVERING UP

Many authors shoot themselves in the foot by saying things in their cover letters that sound tactless or naive, or are otherwise better left unsaid. Here are some examples of mistakes to avoid:

1. *"Dear Sir or Madam:"* This starts off like a standard, generic cover letter you stuff in the envelope with anything to send to anybody. "Dear Editor" is better.

"Dear Ms. Kaiser," or whomever, is best. If you haven't read a recent issue of the magazine to be sure of the current editor's name, you will signal that you might not know your market well enough.

2. *"Enclosed is the fascinating tale of how . . ."* Avoid self-evaluation. Informing an editor that he or she is about to read an epic poem, a humorous essay, or a tale of quiet horror is acceptable. But let the editor decide if your manuscript is "riveting," "pulse-pounding," or even publishable at all.

3. *"I'm sending this article to your fine magazine, unquestionably the most respected in its field . . ."* Don't expect flattery to do anything for your manuscript but get it rejected.

4. *". . . in the hopes that you will buy it."* Don't waste an editor's time with the obvious. Would you have sent the manuscript if you *didn't* hope the editor would buy it?

5. *"I don't know too much about cooking, so I hope these recipes aren't too bad."* Never apologize about any aspect of your manuscript. Let editors find the deficiencies and make the criticisms. That's what they get paid for.

6. *"So, please let me know what you think of this story and please send me a copy of your writer's guidelines."* If a publication has a set of writer's guidelines, you are supposed to have read them *before* submitting a manuscript. If you haven't read the guidelines, don't say so in your cover letter!

7. *"Please buy this article. I really need a sale to keep my car from being repossessed."* Begging is tacky. Besides, telling an editor your troubles can put him or her in a bad mood and distract attention from your manuscript.

8. *". . . Magazine rejected this article, but I'm sure you will like it."* Editors know very well that manuscripts make the rounds from market to market, but you don't have to rub their noses in the fact that your manuscript was seen by a competing or inferior publication first. Just who rejected your manuscript last is nobody's business. Each manuscript should always get a fresh start from each editor who sees it.

9. *"I've shown this article to Dr. Jones and he suggested I submit it to your publication."* This is acceptable if Dr. Jones is a well-known editor, author, or expert in the field you are writing about. But if he is your creative writing teacher or your dentist, your manuscript is in trouble.

10. *"If you don't buy my interview article, I will send it to your competitor."* Now you've really done it. If you are an author of no great reputation or influence, an editor will read your threat, chuckle, write you off as a pugnacious fathead, and reject your manuscript. If you are an author of some reputation and influence, editors will be calling you up asking for your submissions and you won't have to threaten any of them. But if you did, the editor would read your threat, bellow with rage, tell everyone in the publishing field that you are a pugnacious fathead, and reject your manuscript out of principle.

11. *"I'll be watching your publication to see that nobody steals my story and I will sue you if they do."* This time your manuscript may get rejected so fast it might beat you back from the post office! Editors hate getting involved in a fight and certainly don't want to waste time with a lawsuit. So your manuscript gets rejected unread, just in case. Too bad you mentioned it. The world of publishing is just too small and the number of sharp eyes and sharp minds too great for an editor to risk stealing manuscripts. The reputation of an editor is too valuable to gamble with to make the crime worth being caught. If you are not an established author, your manuscript isn't worth stealing. And if you are an established author, your style is probably too easy to recognize and you are too dangerous to steal from.

12. *"By the way, I have not heard about the last story I sent you last month. Also, I moved last year and sent a change of address form, but your magazine still keeps coming to the old address. Who should I write to in the subscription department?"* Never muddle things by referring to anything in the cover letter but the enclosed manuscript. All queries about other submissions, complaints about the last issue, subscription problems, requests for writer's guidelines—whatever—should be in other letters. Each request should be in its own short letter.

UNDER COVER

While you may never have made any of these mistakes, you've probably made others if you've indulged yourself in long, chatty cover letters. We're not talking about letters to editors who are long-term business associates and also friends; we're talking about cover letters for fresh submissions to editors who may never have heard of you before. Nobody is going to buy the contents of your cover letters.

So, remember that most manuscripts really don't need a cover letter or can get by with the barest standard cover letter. When you don't have to write a cover letter, you probably shouldn't. Use a cover letter in those special situations where you *must* remind an editor of what has gone before, or *must* establish your credentials, or *must* make life less complicated for you or the editor. A well-written cover letter can help bridge the gap between the author and editor and increase the chances of selling your manuscript. But, a tactlessly written cover letter can distract the editor from the manuscript and might lead to a rejection slip.

Always remember: *the manuscript*, not the cover letter, is the star.

ABOUT THE AUTHORS

Robert L. Baker has been the editor and publisher of *Impact*, a newsletter for communicators.

Helene Schellenberg Barnhart is the author of *Writing Romance for Love and Money* and *How to Write and Sell the 8 Easiest Article Types*. She has also published five romance novels and many short stories, plus numerous articles on writing. Barnhart has conducted writing-to-sell workshops at a number of West Coast colleges. In 1988 she completed the text for a new Writer's Digest novel course.

Stan Bicknell has been a fulltime freelance writer for more than ten years. A writer on a variety of topics, Bicknell has had articles appear in *The New York Times, Boston Globe, Christian Science Monitor, Science Digest, Writer's Digest* and many other national and local publications.

John Brady, the former editor of *Writer's Digest* and *Boston Magazine*, has contributed to *The New York Times, Esquire, Penthouse, Cincinnati Magazine* and other publications. He is also the author of *The Craft of Interviewing* and *The Craft of the Screenwriter*. A popular speaker at seminars and workshops, Brady teaches magazine writing at Emerson College and is a partner in Brady & Paul Communications, a consulting firm for the publishing industry.

Michael J. Bugeja has published journalism handbooks, edited a volume of essays and is a nationally recognized writer in four genres. His essays, articles, poems and fiction have appeared in a variety of magazines. A former state editor for UPI, Bugeja is currently the editor of *Poet's Market*. His latest book is called *Culture's Sleeping Beauty*.

Stuart Cohen is an editorial and stock photographer who shoots primarily for school books and travel-related material. He is the author of *Lenses for 35mm Cameras*, one of the Kodak Workshop Series books, and the co-author of *The Joy of Photographing People*. He writes occasionally on photography and other subjects for various magazines.

Marshall J. Cook is an associate professor of journalism at the University of Wisconsin in Madison, where he develops a variety of writing and publishing workshops. Cook has published in *Wisconsin Trails, Madison Magazine, The Yacht, Writer's Digest, The Writer, Advertising Age* and *Editor and Publisher*; his fiction has appeared in a number of literary magazines. Cook is also the author of *Freeing Your Creativity*.

Lisa Collier Cool is the author of *How to Give Good Phone, How to Write Irresistible Query Letters,* and *How to Sell Every Magazine Article You Write*. Cool is currently a contributing editor to *Cosmopolitan* magazine, and has sold articles to *Family Circle, Glamour, Harper's Magazine, Lear's, McCall's, Penthouse, Publishers Weekly* and others.

Lois Duncan is the author of over 500 articles for such magazines as *Good Housekeeping, Redbook,* and *Ladies' Home Journal*, and she is a contributing editor to *Woman's Day*. She is also the author of thirty-five books, including *How to Write and Sell Your Personal Experiences* and the cassette tape *Selling Personal Experiences to Magazines*. She is a former Grand Prize Winner of the Writer's Digest Creative Writing Contest.

Lorene Hanley Duquin is a professional writer whose work has appeared in major national publications, including *McCall's, Redbook, Ladies' Home Journal, Family Circle* and *Woman's Day.*

Laurie Henry writes poetry and fiction. Her work has appeared in *The Missouri Review, The Antioch Review, POETRY, The American Poetry Review, Kansas Quarterly* and other magazines.

Dennis E. Hensley, Ph.D., is the author of twenty books, including *The Freelance Writer's Handbook* and *The Gift.* His 2,000 plus articles have appeared in *Reader's Digest, Modern Bride, Success!, The American Bar Association Journal* and other diverse publications. Under his pen name of Leslie Holden, he has written a series of mystery and romance novels.

Lois Horowitz, a former librarian, writes a weekly column for the *San Diego Tribune.* Her other credits include articles for *Family Health, Nutshell, Writer's Digest, 18 Almanac* and other San Diego publications plus her three books, *Knowing Where to Look, A Writer's Guide to Research,* and *A Bibliography of Military Name Lists from Pre-1675 to 1900.*

Nancy Kelton teaches writing at New York University and the New School. Her articles have appeared in numerous magazines and newspapers including *Parents, The New York Times, New Woman, Redbook* and *McCall's.* She recently completed her first novel.

Charles V. Main teaches creative writing and business communication at College of the Redwoods Community College in Eureka, California. He has published more than 100 magazine articles in more than thirty publications including *American Way, PSA, Kiwanis, Home Life, Entrepreneur,* and *Victorian Homes.*

Don McKinney has been the assistant managing editor at *True, The Man's Magazine,* the articles editor at *Saturday Evening Post* and for seventeen years, the managing editor of *McCall's.* McKinney has published recent articles in *McCall's, Writer's Digest* and book reviews in *The State* newspaper in Columbia, South Carolina. He has taught at and run numerous magazine writing conferences, and is currently teaching magazine writing and editing at the University of South Carolina.

Sanford Meschkow has edited three technical magazines and written two popular government publications on solar energy. He has also contributed to *Cities & Scenes From the Ancient World* and *Discovering Stephen King.*

Larry Miller has written for *Cosmopolitan, New York, Travel & Leisure, Manhattan Inc., Good Food, Food & Wine* and other publications. Before becoming a freelancer, Miller worked for *The New York Times* and was a rewrite man for the Dow Jones News Service.

James Morgan has spent most of his professional life editing the work of others, many of the finest writers in the country today. His editing jobs have been with Hallmark Cards, *Kansas City Magazine, TWA Ambassador* (editor), *Playboy* (articles editor), and presently he is the editorial director of *Southern* magazine. Morgan has also written for *Travel & Leisure, Playboy, Writer's Digest* and other magazines.

Rebecca Muller has been a freelance writer and contributor to *Scene Magazine* in the *Dallas Morning News.* She has also been an editorial consultant for *American English Today* and taught writing workshops and seminars at Brookhaven College.

Duane Newcomb is the author of more than 5,000 articles and twenty-three books, including *A Complete Guide to Marketing Magazine Articles* and *Sell and Re-Sell Your Writing.* He has contributed to most major magazines including *Family Circle, Better Homes and Gardens, American Home, Mademoiselle, Field and Stream* and many others. Newcomb is a partner in Newcomb and Newcomb, Literary Consulting and Marketing Services, located in Grass Valley, California.

Philip Barry Osborne joined the staff at *Reader's Digest* and is presently assistant managing editor. Previously he wrote and/or edited at *Business Week, Time* and CBS.

Gary Provost is a longtime prolific and versatile freelancer who has authored, co-authored and ghost-written more than a dozen novels, children's books, and over a thousand articles and short stories and columns. His latest books include *Good If It Goes* (written with his wife Gail), *Make Your Words Work, How to Write & Sell True Crime,* and *Finder,* written with Marilyn Greene. In 1987 Provost was one of seven national finalists in the Ann Landers Replacement Contest in Chicago.

Barbara Bisantz Raymond specializes in human interest and personal experience stories and has found her particular niche with women's magazines. Her articles have appeared in *Working Mother, Parents, Family Circle, McCall's, Redbook, Ladies' Home Journal, USA Today* and many other publications.

Candy Schulman, a New York correspondent for *Writer's Digest,* has written for *The New York Times, New York Magazine, Travel & Leisure, Family Circle, Glamour,* and other publications. She teaches writing at The New School for Social Research.

George H. Scithers was editor of *Isaac Asimov's Science Fiction Magazine* and *Amazing Stories* before he became editor of *Weird Tales.* Presently he is an agent for Owlswick Literary Agency.

Elaine Fantle Shimberg has written for *Glamour, Essence, Seventeen, Lady's Circle* and many other magazines. Her books include *How to Be a Successful Housewife/Writer, Teenage Drinking and Driving: A Deadly Duo, Coping With Kids and Vacation, Teenage Pregnancy: Explaining the Facts,* and most recently, *Relief From Irritable Bowel Syndrome.*

Art Spikol is the author of more than 200 magazine articles and columns, *Magazine Writing: The Inside Angle* and most recently a first novel, *The Physalia Incident.* The nonfiction columnist for *Writer's Digest* since 1976, Spikol is also a popular speaker at writers' conferences and seminars. Formerly the editor of *Philadelphia Magazine,* he currently is president of his own editorial and advertising consultancy.

Jay Stuller, a San Francisco-based journalist, has published articles in *Reader's Digest, Playboy, Smithsonian, Audubon, Success, Islands, Inside Sports, Ladies' Home Journal, Sport,* and many other magazines. His latest project is a book for Dodd Mead & Company on the business of the American wine industry.

L. Perry Wilbur has written and sold more than 5,000 articles to magazines and newspapers in the U.S. and overseas. An advertising consultant with an M.A. in Communications, Wilbur is the author of *How to Write Songs That Sell, Money in Your Mailbox, How to Write Books That Sell* and *How to Write Articles That Sell.*

Rona S. Zable has written hundreds of nonfiction articles for newspapers and magazines, including *Family Circle, Boston Globe, Christian Science Monitor, Providence Journal, McCall's* and other publications. Presently she is a writer/editor and writes a column ("Recipe Roundup") for a regional magazine for senior citizens.

Louise Purwin Zobel, a travel writing expert, has published a number of travel articles in magazines and newspapers, in addition to *The Travel Writer's Handbook.* A frequent keynote speaker and lecturer at national and regional writing conferences and workshops at sea, she has taught travel writing on 25 California college campuses and written and narrated 90-minute nationally distributed tapes on travel.

General Writing Books

Beginning Writer's Answer Book, Editors of *Writer's Digest* magazine $16.95
Dare to Be a Great Writer, by Leonard Bishop (paper) $14.95
Discovering the Writer Within, by Bruce Ballenger & Barry Lane $18.95
Essential Software for Writers: A Complete Guide for Everyone Who Writes with a PC, by Hy Bender (paper) $24.95
Freeing Your Creativity, by Marshall Cook $17.95
Getting the Words Right: How to Rewrite, Edit and Revise, by Theodore A. Rees Cheney (paper) $12.95
How to Write a Book Proposal, by Michael Larsen (paper) $11.95
How to Write Fast While Writing Well, by David Fryxell $17.95
How to Write with the Skill of a Master and the Genius of a Child, by Marshall J. Cook $18.95
Just Open a Vein, edited by William Brohaugh $6.99
Knowing Where to Look: The Ultimate Guide to Research, by Lois Horowitz (paper) $19.95
Make Your Words Work, by Gary Provost (paper) $14.95
On Being a Writer, edited by Bill Strickland (paper) $16.95
Pinckert's Practical Grammar, by Robert C. Pinckert (paper) $3.99
Research & Writing: A Complete Guide and Handbook, by Shah Malmoud (paper) $18.95
Shift Your Writing Career into High Gear, by Gene Perret $16.95
The 30-Minute Writer: How to Write and Sell Short Pieces, by Connie Emerson $17.95
30 Steps to Becoming a Writer, by Scott Edelstein $16.95
The 28 Biggest Writing Blunders, by William Noble $12.95
The 29 Most Common Writing Mistakes & How to Avoid Them, by Judy Delton (paper) $9.95
The Wordwatcher's Guide to Good Writing & Grammar, by Morton S. Freeman (paper) $15.95
The Writer's Book of Checklists, by Scott Edelstein $16.95
The Writer's Digest Guide to Good Writing, Editors of *Writer's Digest* magazine $18.95
The Writer's Digest Guide to Manuscript Formats, by Buchman & Groves $18.95
The Writer's Essential Desk Reference, edited by Glenda Neff $19.95
Write Tight: How to Keep Your Prose Sharp, Focused and Concise, by William Brohaugh $16.95
Writing as a Road to Self-Discovery, by Barry Lane $16.95

Nonfiction Writing

The Complete Guide to Writing Biographies, by Ted Schwarz $6.99
How to Do Leaflets, Newsletters, & Newspapers, by Nancy Brigham (paper) $14.95
How to Write Irresistible Query Letters, by Lisa Collier Cool (paper) $10.95
The Complete Guide to Magazine Article Writing, by John M. Wilson $17.95
The Writer's Complete Guide to Conducting Interviews, by Michael Schumacher $14.95
Writing Articles From the Heart: How to Write & Sell Your Life Experiences, by Marjorie Holmes $16.95

Fiction Writing

Beginnings, Middles and Ends, by Nancy Kress $13.95
Best Stories from New Writers, edited by Linda Sanders $5.99
Characters & Viewpoint, by Orson Scott Card $14.95
The Complete Guide to Writing Fiction, by Barnaby Conrad $18.95
Conflict, Action & Suspense, William Noble $14.95
Creating Short Fiction, by Damon Knight (paper) $11.95
Dialogue, by Lewis Turco $13.95
The Fiction Writer's Silent Partner, by Martin Roth $19.95
Get That Novel Started! (And Keep Going 'Til You Finish), by Donna Levin $17.95
Handbook of Short Story Writing: Vol. I, by Dickson and Smythe (paper) $12.95
Handbook of Short Story Writing: Vol. II, edited by Jean Fredette (paper) $12.95

How to Write & Sell Your First Novel, by Collier & Leighton (paper) $13.95
Manuscript Submission, by Scott Edelstein $13.95
Plot, by Ansen Dibell $14.95
Practical Tips for Writing Popular Fiction, by Robyn Carr $17.95
Scene and Structure by Jack Bickham $14.95
Setting, Jack M. Bickham $14.95
Theme & Strategy, by Ronald B. Tobias $14.95
The 38 Most Common Fiction Writing Mistakes, by Jack M. Bickham $12.95
20 Master Plots (And How to Build Them), by Ronald B. Tobias $16.95
The Writer's Digest Character Naming Sourcebook, Sherrilyn Kenyon with Hal Blythe & Charlie Sweet $18.95
Writer's Digest Handbook of Novel Writing, $18.95
Writing the Blockbuster Novel, Albert Zuckerman, with Introduction by Ken Follett $17.95
Writing the Novel: From Plot to Print, by Lawrence Block (paper) $11.95

Special Interest Writing Books
Armed & Dangerous: A Writer's Guide to Weapons, by Michael Newton (paper) $14.95
Cause of Death: A Writer's Guide to Death, Murder & Forensic Medicine, by Keith D. Wilson, M.D. $15.95
Children's Writer's Word Book, by Alijandra Mogliner $19.95
Comedy Writing Secrets, by Mel Helitzer (paper) $15.95
The Complete Book of Feature Writing, by Leonard Witt $18.95
The Craft of Writing Science Fiction That Sells, Ben Bova $16.95
Deadly Doses: A Writer's Guide to Poisons, by Serita Deborah Stevens with Anne Klarner (paper) $16.95
Editing Your Newsletter, by Mark Beach (paper) $18.95
Families Writing, by Peter Stillman (paper) $12.95
A Guide to Travel Writing & Photography, by Ann & Carl Purcell (paper) $22.95
How to Pitch & Sell Your TV Script, by David Silver $6.99
How to Write & Sell Greeting Cards, Bumper Stickers, T-Shirts and Other Fun Stuff, by Molly Wigand (paper) 15.95
How to Write & Sell True Crime, by Gary Provost $5.99
How to Write Mysteries, by Shannon OCork $14.95
How to Write Romances, by Phyllis Taylor Pianka $15.95
How to Write Science Fiction & Fantasy, by Orson Scott Card $13.95
How to Write Tales of Horror, Fantasy & Science Fiction, edited by J.N. Williamson (paper) $12.95
How to Write Western Novels, by Matt Braun $1.00
Police Procedural: A Writer's Guide to the Police and How They Work, by Russell Bintliff (paper) $16.95
Private Eyes: A Writer's Guide to Private Investigators, by H. Blythe, C. Sweet, & J. Landreth (paper) $15.95
Scene of the Crime: A Writer's Guide to Crime-Scene Investigation, by Anne Wingate, Ph.D. $15.95
Successful Scriptwriting, by Jurgen Wolff & Kerry Cox (paper) $14.95
The Writer's Complete Crime Reference, by Martin Roth $19.95
The Writer's Guide to Conquering the Magazine Market, by Connie Emerson $17.95
The Writer's Guide to Creating a Science Fiction Universe, by George Ochoa & Jeff Osier $18.95
The Writer's Guide to Everyday Life in the 1800s, by Marc McCutcheon $18.95
Writing for Children & Teenagers, 3rd Edition, by L. Wyndham & Arnold Madison (paper) $12.95
Writing Mysteries: A Handbook by the Mystery Writers of America, Edited by Sue Grafton, $18.95
Writing the Modern Mystery, by Barbara Norville (paper) $12.95

The Writing Business
Business & Legal Forms for Authors & Self-Publishers, by Tad Crawford (paper) $4.99
How You Can Make $25,000 a Year Writing, by Nancy Edmonds Hanson (paper) $14.95
This Business of Writing, by Gregg Levoy $19.95

To order directly from the publisher, include $3.00 postage and handling for 1 book and $1.00 for each additional book. Allow 30 days for delivery.

Writer's Digest Books
1507 Dana Avenue, Cincinnati, Ohio 45207
Credit card orders call TOLL-FREE
1-800-289-0963
Stock is limited on some titles; prices subject to change without notice.

Write to this same address for information on *Writer's Digest* magazine, *Story* magazine, Writer's Digest Book Club, Writer's Digest School, and Writer's Digest Criticism Service.